The Queen's
HOUSES

The Queen's HOUSES

ROYAL BRITAIN AT HOME

Alan Titchmarsh

BBC
BOOKS

Contents

The Houses of Windsor

'Glad to be in this dear place again after six
years, and to see all our nice people again.'

George V on Balmoral, 1919

We know them now as tourist attractions: iconic symbols of a state still governed, in name at least, by a monarchy. They are, in a way, architectural manifestations of a country's pride in its history. But royal palaces in the past were even more the physical representations of the power and prestige of the monarch, and the political and administrative centres of the kingdom. The grander and more sumptuous they were, supposedly the grander and more powerful the monarch. They were the centres of diplomacy, as ambassadors shuttled backwards and forwards, reporting back to their masters on the latest developments in the shifting political allegiances of kingdoms. They were the centres of patronage – in return for support, titles and riches might flow your way. And they were the centres from which everyday life was influenced and directed, in political thought, religious belief (being burned at the stake if you stepped out of line), in scholarship and in culture. Ideas in architecture, gardens, painting and sculpture, in what you wore and how you spoke, all flowed outwards from the royal courts. And the monarch had to be seen, so the court moved from place to place. By the time of his death, Henry VIII, fuelled by the great wealth that came his way on the dissolution of the monasteries, owned over 60 great houses and palaces and during his lifetime over 1000 people thronged his courts.

Today the great houses and palaces are no longer the power-bases of old – political power has passed to elected governments. But The Queen still has to represent the prestige of the country as head of state. Ambassadors and high commissioners from the nearly 200 foreign missions in London continue to present their credentials to her in a time-honoured ritual: they and their entourage and family are collected by state carriages from the Royal Mews, escorted by the Marshal of the Diplomatic Corps in his splendid uniform complete with ostrich-plumed hat. On arrival the Marshal presents them to The Queen and then walks backwards from her presence (today only the Marshal and Her Majesty's equerry have to walk backwards; for everyone else the ancient practice was abolished on health and safety grounds in 2009). The 20-minute audience with The Queen usually takes place in one of Buckingham Palace's state rooms, the blue and gold splendour of the 1844 Room, before the carriages return. No doubt the ambassadors will then report back, suitably impressed, on the pomp and grandeur of the occasion.

The first ambassador to present his credentials to The Queen in March 1952, during the first year of her reign, was the Ambassador of Mexico (fittingly, in 2012, The Queen's Diamond Jubilee year, his great-grand nephew held the same position). Since then The Queen has received over 3000 diplomatic missions and each is accorded the same ceremony, no matter how large or small the country. It's all a far cry from the practice in seventeenth-century France where how many steps down the special ambassadors'

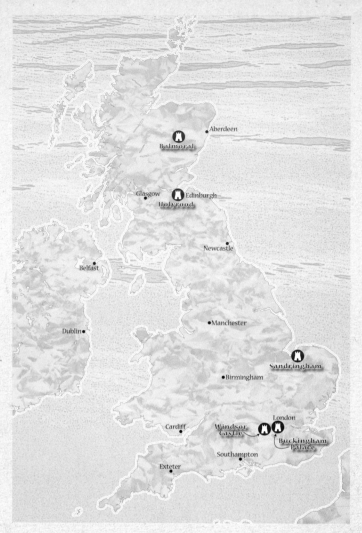

staircase at Versailles The King chose to descend to greet a new ambassador was an indicator of his view of the status of that country. The French Ambassador in 1952 remarked on 'the British genius of linking the past, the present and the future in one great pattern of continuity'. The royal houses play a key part in this 'great pattern of continuity', both publicly and privately.

The Queen and Prince Philip use five different houses throughout the year – Buckingham Palace, Windsor Castle, the Palace of Holyroodhouse, Balmoral Castle and Sandringham House. Of these only Balmoral and Sandringham are privately owned and maintained, and passed by will through the generations, although King George VI had to buy out his elder brother Edward VIII on the latter's abdication in 1936. The first two are the official London residence and the official country residence of the monarch, and the Palace of Holyroodhouse is the official residence of the monarch in Scotland. Other palaces and houses – St James's Palace (still the 'senior' palace, the Court of St James's, the official name for the British court, is administered from there), Clarence House, Marlborough House Mews, Kensington Palace, the Royal Mews and Paddocks at Hampton Court and buildings in the Home and Great Parks at Windsor, are used by members of the royal family as houses and as offices for the Royal Household. The residential and office areas of these various buildings, together with the official residences in England, are all maintained by annual funding provided by the government to the Royal Household. The government in turn receives any revenues from this 'Estate', which comprises a staggering 360 individual buildings spread over 160,000 square metres (1.7 million square feet), plus a further 280 properties used mainly as residential quarters for staff and pensioners.

The official residences are also known as the 'Occupied Royal Palaces', or the 'Estate' for short, to distinguish them from the palaces that are no longer official residences –

the Palaces of Westminster and Whitehall (all that remains is the Banqueting House where King Charles I was executed in 1649), Hampton Court and Her Majesty's Royal Palace and Fortress, more commonly known as the Tower of London. The official residences are held in trust for the nation by The Queen as sovereign and are used by her in fulfilling the role and functions of head of state – and that less definable but vitally important description 'head of the nation' that describes the emotional power of the monarchy – and by other members of the royal family in a support role. To ensure the Royal Household is run flawlessly and the vast Estate is kept in good order, over 1000 people work in the occupied palaces.

The Queen's role as head of state over more than 60 years has been epic in scale. Every year she invites the current crop of ambassadors and high commissioners, together with senior diplomats and their spouses or partners – around a thousand people – to the largest event held indoors in her yearly calendar, The Queen's Diplomatic Reception at Buckingham Palace. Drinks are served in the Picture Gallery followed by a buffet supper in the Ballroom and then dancing in the Ball Supper Room.

The Queen also hosts two 'Inward State Visits' a year when guests are invited to stay at Windsor Castle or Buckingham Palace, which is also the venue for other mass receptions, most of the annual investiture ceremonies and at least three great garden parties whose vast numbers dwarf any of the other receptions. Each year, 2500 people are granted honours and The Queen has held over 600 investitures, usually in Buckingham Palace ballroom but now also at Windsor Castle. Each of the garden parties is attended by 8000 people – millions have attended over the course of her reign. The annual garden party at Holyroodhouse at the end of June during her week-long stay at the palace is even larger – up to 10,000 guests throng the lawns.

The Queen moves between her different houses in a set routine. Every week while in London she leaves Buckingham Palace on Friday afternoon for Windsor and returns from Windsor Castle after lunch on Monday. To avoid a terrorist attack (alas always something to worry about), her route varies and a tracking device is fitted to her car. This is monitored by the police post at Buckingham Palace for any deviation from the planned route.

The annual routine starts around 20 December when, after a lunch party for her extended family (around 50 of them), The Queen takes over a first-class compartment on a morning train from King's Cross to King's Lynn. The famous Royal Station at Wolferton was closed in 1969, so a car now meets The Queen at King's Lynn station and takes her on the short drive to Sandringham. There she stays for six weeks, presiding over a large family gathering plus house guests. The latter are treated to legendary hospitality, down to the provision of 'wellies' of the correct size for each

guest. Accession Day, the anniversary of the death of The Queen's father, King George VI, and her own accession to the throne, is 6 February, which usually marks her last day at Sandringham before the return to London and the beginning of a new round of investitures, audiences, a full diary of other engagements and a lot more handshaking.

For four weeks of the year, around Easter, The Queen moves full-time with her staff to Windsor Castle, known as 'Easter Court'. During this period, in a tradition begun by Queen Victoria, distinguished guests are invited to 'Dine and Sleep' at the castle. The 'sleep' part is no more, but guests still dine with the sovereign. On Easter Sunday The Queen always attends the morning service at St George's Chapel. At Windsor, she also celebrates her birthday on 21 April, privately (her 'official birthday' is celebrated around the middle of June, a tradition begun in 1908 by King Edward VII whose November birthday parade was inevitably beset by bad weather).

The State Opening of Parliament, which formerly occurred in November, has since 2010 and the innovation of fixed-term parliaments, taken place in May. Escorted from Buckingham Palace by the Household Cavalry The Queen dons the 18-foot-long Robe of State and the Imperial State Crown and is preceded by a gentleman usher carrying the Great Sword of State, all symbols of royal authority. This is the only regular occasion when the three constituent parts of Parliament, the sovereign, the House of Lords and the House of Commons, meet on the site of the old Whitehall Palace to mark the formal start of the new parliamentary year.

The Queen is in residence again at Windsor in June, which coincides with the Royal Ascot racehorse meeting – which she has attended every year since 1945 – and the Garter Day ceremonies when the recipients of the Order of the Garter gather to lunch in the Waterloo Chamber and process in their robes to St George's Chapel.

Holyrood Week takes place at the end of June or beginning of July when The Queen is in official residence at the Palace of Holyroodhouse and presides over the investiture ceremony and the great garden party. The Queen also attends a wide range of other engagements in Scotland including the service for the holders of the Order of the Thistle at St Giles' Cathedral. Her arrival at the palace is always marked by the Ceremony of the Keys when the Lord Provost of Edinburgh hands her the keys to the city and bids her welcome to 'your ancient and hereditary kingdom of Scotland'. One hopes that this will continue. At the end of July she and her household, and the few remaining corgis, are again in Scotland, at Balmoral Castle, where she spends the whole of August and September before returning to Buckingham Palace, with weekends at Windsor Castle.

There are those who have little time for the institution of monarchy, seeing it as outdated, hidebound and irrelevant in the modern world. It will become clear from these pages that I am not of their number. It is not simply that I am dazzled by its pageantry, its power and its exalted position; neither is it simply because the history of the British monarchy is *our* history, though that is certainly a part of it. There are two main reasons for my continued belief in its worth. The first is the profound commitment to the country and its people that I have witnessed at first hand in those members of the royal family I have been privileged to meet and to know just a little. That commitment is genuine, heartfelt and tireless in the face of criticism. It also involves much hard work and a capacity to undertake an endless round of activities that others would find at best wearying and at worst plain dull. The second reason is that compared with other forms of government the British monarchy has – barring the occasional hiatus (and there have been several) – proved its worth over the last century in both practical and spiritual terms. Today, more than ever, the key members of the royal family are deeply conscious of their responsibility to both the country and its people. Their loyalty is without question.

The description of the role of sovereign on The Queen's official website explains that she 'acts as a focus for national identity, unity and pride; gives a sense of stability and continuity; officially recognises success and excellence'.

Few would argue that Queen Elizabeth II has not lived up to that description. It is also clear to see that the sense of national identity, stability and continuity are assisted by and embodied in the great official palaces and private residences that have been for so long the backdrop to the affairs of state and refuges from the 'press and pestilence' of London life. They remain a sanctuary to the sovereign and a symbol of a country's standing in the world, especially in the increasing turbulent and unpredictable years of the twenty-first century.

Alan Titchmarsh

Windsor Castle

The Queen, Prince Charles and young Prince Edward in the grounds of Windsor Castle, April 1969

'Windsor, a spot favoured by nature with the richest and most variegated scenery, diversified with hill and dale, beautiful parks, a luxuriant forest, and verdant meadows, animated by the windings of a noble river, selected for the residence of the Sovereigns of England, and enjoying for centuries the presence and support of an illustrious and elegant Court ...'

Royal Windsor Guide, c.1880

Windsor Castle is most people's idea of what a castle should look like: solid, imposing, battlemented and seemingly impregnable. The outline of its Round Tower, standing proud on an eminence high above the River Thames, is one of the most iconic images of royal Britain. Although Buckingham Palace, with its daily changing of the Guard, may be more famous to the tourists who flock there, it is Windsor Castle that was the true centre of power for nearly a thousand years. It is justly celebrated as the largest inhabited castle in the world and the longest occupied of any royal palace in Europe – 40 monarchs have played out their lives within its walls.

Windsor Castle was originally built under the orders of William the Conqueror soon after the Norman invasion of Britain in 1066. The site was previously occupied by monks who were offered alternative estates and relocated to Essex. The fortification was the first of a chain of nine simple wooden forts around London, designed to help bring to heel the indigenous population, to consolidate territorial gains and in due course defend William's men from repeated rebellions. Initially William used forced labour on a very large scale, construction often continuing at night by the light of torches and through bitterly cold winters.

The typical form of a Norman castle was a wooden tower built on a circular raised mound known as a motte, either man-made – again, usually by forced labour – or using existing topographical features. Around this would be constructed a bailey, or flat area defended by a ditch, and a wooden palisade. At Windsor there was clearly a double bailey, still defined by the footprint of the present castle, roughly corresponding to what are now know as the Upper and Lower Wards, with the motte standing between the two. The castle's setting close to the river and beside extensive forests, ideal for hunting, and its proximity to London meant that before long its purely defensive role would be subsumed by its function as a royal palace.

Today, Windsor is where The Queen and The Duke of Edinburgh go to relax on most weekends of the year, leaving on Friday afternoon and returning to the bustle and protocol of the office – Buckingham Palace – on a Monday. But the very stones of this weekend retreat are steeped in history, and act as reminders of the strong personalities who have stalked its towers and battlements and the dramatic events that have played out within its walls.

It was William the Conqueror's fourth son, Henry I, described by biographer Judith Green as 'in many respects highly unpleasant', who first established Windsor as a royal residence in the twelfth century. He enlarged the castle, built a chapel and in 1110, on the feast of Whitsuntide (Pentecost – the seventh Sunday after Easter), he invited the 'nobles of the realm' to attend him there.

This was the first court to be held at the new palace and also the occasion for the betrothal by proxy of his five-year-old daughter Matilda to Henry V, King of Germany and Emperor of Rome, then in his forties. Henry I held court at Windsor again in 1114, and in 1121 he was also married there to Adeliza of Louvain as his second wife, in an

Henry I

Henry II

attempt to provide for his succession following the death by drowning of his only legitimate son William the previous year. The couple were childless and after Henry's death in 1135, reportedly from a surfeit of lampreys (a type of eel), his succession was disputed, plunging England into nearly 20 years of what is known to history as the Anarchy.

Henry's grandson Henry II inherited the kingdom of England in 1154 at the age of 21 and within 20 years had expanded what became known as the Angevin Empire to include England, a large part of Wales, half of Ireland and half of France (he married Eleanor of Aquitaine as her third husband). Henry II was an inveterate builder of castles and royal residences throughout his empire, spending prodigious sums (it was the largest single item of royal expenditure) and he rebuilt and enlarged his grandfather's work at Windsor to convert it into a palace. The old timber walls surrounding the Upper Ward were gradually replaced with stone, as was the Round Tower on top of the motte. Two sets of royal apartments were created, along with a Great Hall where his large retinue could be entertained in suitably lavish style, as befitted a powerful king.

The rise of Windsor

Henry's son Richard the Lionheart spent most of his ten-year reign from 1189 out of England, either in his possessions in France, on crusade or in prison. His expenditure on castle building was considerable – but mostly spent on the vast Chateau Gaillard in Normandy. His younger brother John succeeded him and it was during his reign that the Angevin Empire created by his father Henry II collapsed. In order to raise the large sums needed to reclaim his lost territories John imposed a wide variety of taxes, penalties and fines.

In a long-running dispute with William de Braose, once a court favourite and one of his most powerful barons, John captured William's wife Matilda and their eldest son and, in 1210, imprisoned them in the vaults of Windsor Castle where they were starved to death. John's final defeat in his war with the French precipitated a revolt among the barons of England, weary of John's failures in battle and his despotic rule. Having taken several large cities, as well as London, the successes of the rebel

KSHIRE
CRIBED

PART OF OXFORD

Ewelme
Benington
Wallingford
Crannesue
Newneham
Busingwell
Ipsden
South Stoke
Mapledorham
Goring
Whitchurch
Mapledorham
Pangborne
Sutham
Thele
Bradfeld
Inglefelde
HUNDR.
Silham
Yston
Padworth
Aldermerston
Stretfeld
Mortimere
HUNDR.
Silchster
Aldermaston

PART OF BUCKINGHAM SHIRE

Little Merlowe
Great Merlow
Grenland
Medneham
Hedsore
Thames flud
Purley
Bysham
Opley
BRAYE
Remnacham
BERNERSH HUNDRED
HUND
Madenhead
Colbrok
Henley
Horspenden
Dorney
Eaton
Upton
Datchet
Shiplake
WARGROVE
Braye
Withwaltham
Windsor
Waisbury
Warigrave
Twiford
Lawrence
Waltham
Ruscombe
Shatsbrok
Chewerth
RIPPLESMORE
Oldwin
Stanes
Sunyng
Winsor forest
Winsor parke
Egham
Thames flud
Caversham
Hurst
Billmagsbere HUND
Winkfeld
SONNINGE
Loddon Bridge
Binfeld
Warfeld
Sunnyghill
Redding
READING
Loddon flud
COOKHAM
PART
Witley park
CHARL:
TON
Arberfelde
Shinsfelde
Part of Rip. HUNDR.
ples
OF
Barkham
Okingham
Swallofelde
Easthamsted more Hud.
Bagshot
WILT SHIR
Part of WILT SHIR
Finchamsted HUNDRED
Sandhest
Stretfeld
Mortimere
PART OF WILT SHIR
Yateley
Blackwater
Heksfelde
Surges
Euersley
F HAM SHIRE
SURREY

PART OF MID: DLE SEX

A map of Berkshire
in 1610, by renowned
seventeenth-century
cartographer John Speed

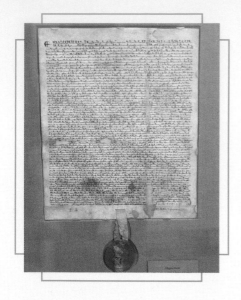

barons compelled John to sue for peace. The momentous meeting on 15 June 1215 at Runnymede, close by Windsor Castle, resulted in what came to be known as Magna Carta, an attempt by the barons to limit the power of The King. Nevertheless, war ensued and the future King Louis VIII of France invaded England and reached London in 1216, where he was proclaimed King in St Paul's Cathedral by the rebel barons. During the ensuing months Louis' supporters took many of the great strongholds between London and the coast. The rebels besieged Windsor for two months, causing great damage to the curtain walls of the Lower Ward, but the castle withstood.

In the midst of this war, in 1216, John died and his son Prince Henry, at the age of nine, inherited an uncertain crown. However, many of the rebel barons switched sides and in September 1217 Louis relinquished his claim to be King of England. In due course Henry III was to transform Windsor into one of the greatest palaces of the realm.

After Henry attained full power in 1227 he constantly shuttled between ten different palaces, castles, abbeys or priories, favouring Westminster (the seat of government and the usual venue for the fledgling parliament) and then Windsor above all others.

At Windsor Henry could escape from constant scrutiny, the hosts of petitioners and the daily pressure of business, yet remain close to the corridors of power. Consequently he pioneered the use of Windsor as a retreat for himself, his household and the immediate court, much as the royal family does today. It is a tradition, then, that dates back almost 800 years.

Windsor was also the base for Henry III's Queen, Eleanor of Provence, and their children, who were born between 1239 and 1253. After repairing the considerable damage caused by the siege engines and building the stone curtain wall and the three great towers that still today form the west end of the castle, Henry then set about refashioning the royal apartments to make them ever more comfortable. He left the Great Hall at a modest size since it was not designed to host great public events, but the rest of Henry's new interiors were lavishly decorated with copious use of stained glass, carved stonework, glazed tiles and painted walls. As a result of his work at Windsor a contemporary chronicler writing at the Abbey

Edward III

of Pershore in the *Flores Historiarum* described it as 'that most flourishing castle, of which at that time there was not another more splendid within the bounds of Europe'.

With considerable unrest, shifting allegiances, several uprisings and even deposition during the latter part of his reign, it was vital for Henry III to keep the most important bishops and barons on side. His hospitality at Windsor was lavish, impressing those he entertained with a display of regal wealth and power. The household rolls that have survived from that time are a mine of information. For example, the average *daily* fare for a week at Windsor in the late summer of 1260 was £13 (approx. £11,000 today), at a time when to pass muster as a knight required an *annual* income of £15 or more. Henry III was equally generous to the poor. When staying at Windsor it was his practice to feed 150 paupers a day.

Over 34 years, to the end of his reign in 1272, Henry had spent over £21,000 (approx. £14 million today) on the castle, a vast sum of money in the thirteenth century, and more than he had spent on any other of his myriad building projects, apart from the rebuilding of Westminster Abbey. During the nineteenth-century rebuilding of the Upper Ward, architectural fragments from the thirteenth century were uncovered – alas, they are all that remains of Henry's palatial building.

The Knights of the Round Table

Forty years after Henry III's death, in November 1312, Henry's great-grandson, the future Edward III, was born at Windsor Castle, son of Edward II and Isabella of France. Between the 1350s and 1370s, he was to become one of the castle's greatest benefactors. Edward III ruled for 50 years and is best remembered for his exploits as a soldier, subjugating the Welsh and Scots and initiating the Hundred Years War against the French in pursuit of his claim to the throne of France.

Fascinated by the legends of King Arthur, supposedly the very embodiment of chivalry, and with his knights of the Round Table, it was during a joust held at Windsor in 1344 that Edward announced the formation of a new chivalric order, the Order of the Round Table. Work commenced on a vast circular, arcaded structure within the Upper Ward of the castle to house the enormous table required to seat 300 knights and as a focus for feasting and chivalric ceremony. Royal clerk Adam Murimith described the occasion:

'the king gave a great feast at which he announced the foundation of his Round Table, and took the oaths of certain lords, barons and knights who wished to become members of the said Round Table ... he afterwards commanded that a most noble building should be built, in which to hold the Round Table ... and instructed masons, carpenters and other workmen to carry out the work, providing both wood and stone, and not sparing either labour or expense'.

Detailed building accounts survive, revealing that nearly 200 workmen were on site throughout the year 1344 and 52 oaks were taken from the woods of the Prior of Merton near Reading for The King's works. An archaeological dig by the television programme *Time Team* in 2006 discovered the foundations of the building and measured it at 60 metres (200 feet) in diameter.

Contemporary chronicles mention that as soon as he heard of Edward III's intentions. the French King, Philip VI, instituted his own Round Table to tempt the knights of Germany and Italy 'in case they set out for the table of the King of England'. But before Edward's impressive structure could be roofed it was pulled down. Times had changed. Instituted as an aid to recruiting knights for the wars in France, the purpose of the order became redundant once it was discovered, after the campaign of 1346 and the victory at Crécy, that service in France could be very profitable.

The scourge of the Black Death

In 1348 the Black Death reached England and over the next two years killed approximately one half of all those living in the country. In the close-packed city of London with its narrow, sewage-sodden streets it was far worse, with recent estimates by archaeologists suggesting that two-thirds of the city's population of 60,000 were killed by the disease. Edward III did not escape the calamity – his daughter Joan and two of his sons, Thomas and William, died of the plague. At Windsor, its population possibly doubled by the influx of craftsmen and labourers working on the castle – which was the largest secular building project in England during the Middle Ages – it is estimated up to one-third of the population perished.

ALMOST ALL THE
MASONS AND
CARPENTERS
THROUGHOUT THE
WHOLE OF ENGLAND
WERE BROUGHT TO
WINDSOR

Edward III's work at Windsor Castle took over 20 years to complete and as each stage of the work reached completion craftsmen ('diggers and hewers of stone' and 'glaziers' are specifically mentioned) from all over England were 'pressed' for service to complete the next phase, particularly after the Black Death had dramatically reduced the available pool of trained and experienced craftsmen. Writs were issued to the sheriffs of the various counties and men were forcibly brought to Windsor to work for The King and, under penalty of £100 (approx. £70,000 today), were not to depart without a licence.

The chronicler Raphael Holinshed relates in 1359 that The King 'set workmen in hand to take down much old buildings belonging to the castle, and caused divers other fine and sumptuous works to be set up in and about the same castle, so that almost all the masons and carpenters that were of any account in the land were sent for and employed about the same works'. Another wrote, 'almost all the masons and carpenters throughout the whole of England were brought to that building [Windsor Castle], so that hardly anyone could have any good mason or carpenter except in secret'. One group of recalcitrant masons on their way to Windsor from Yorkshire were made to wear distinctive red clothing 'lest they should escape from the custody of the conductor'.

The man who oversaw this extraordinary traffic in men and materials was the brilliant administrator William of Wykeham, appointed in October 1356 first as Justice of Labourers and finally as Surveyor of the Works at Windsor Castle and Park. His rise in The King's service from humble beginnings was meteoric. In 1361 he was ordained, five years later he was Bishop of Winchester and the next year he was appointed Lord Chancellor of England. He went on to oversee the building of two famous foundations of his own, Winchester College and New College, Oxford. He died in his eighties, one of the richest men in England.

Edward's alterations and rebuilding in the Lower Ward were a direct result of the requirements of his newly formed Order of the Garter and the clergy and officers required to service it. He placed his new private apartments close to the state apartments in one large palace complex that included his magnificent St George's Hall. This was obliterated in the rebuilding of the seventeenth century but is known to us from an engraving by Wenceslaus Hollar of the Garter Feast on St George's Day in 1672. This shows an impressive space, with a vast and elaborately

A Knight of the Garter

Above: Windsor Castle from the South, by Wenceslaus Hollar, 1666

Below: The emblem of the Order of the Garter

timbered roof above two rows of windows. The old chapel was entirely rebuilt but by 1390, scarcely 40 years later, it was described as ruinous and the celebrated poet Geoffrey Chaucer was appointed clerk of works to the chapel to oversee its repair.

The Knights of the Most Noble Order of the Garter

In 1348, the same year as the Black Death was decimating the population of England, Edward founded a new college dedicated to St George at Windsor, and with it a group of knights who were to be called the Knights of the Most Noble Order of the Garter. This order, with its 25 knights with the sovereign at their head, was initially divided into two 'teams' for the purposes of the jousts, Edward as captain of one, and The Prince of Wales – Edward, the Black Prince – the other. It is amongst the earliest of the chivalric orders founded at the major courts of Europe during the Middle Ages, and the longest-surviving, still inducting new knights as vacancies occur.

In October 1361 the Black Prince celebrated his marriage at Windsor to his cousin Joan, Countess of Kent, the 'Fair Maid of Kent' whom the French chronicler Jean Froissart called 'the most beautiful woman in all the realm of England, and the most loving'. She was the daughter of Edmund of Woodstock, son of King Edward I and Margaret of France. Four years later Edward III's eldest daughter Isabella married at Windsor and in 1369 Edward's much-mourned Queen, Philippa of Hainault, died aged 45 at the castle.

A Knight of the Garter

Edward III died after a stroke, aged 65, in 1377, the year in which he admitted his grandsons, ten-year-old Richard, son of Edward, the Black Prince who had died the previous year, and Richard's cousin Henry, son of John of Gaunt, to the order of the Garter.

The Black Prince

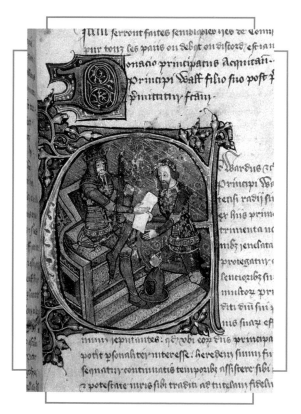

The castle that Edward III built at Windsor, at once a defensive stronghold and a magnificent palace, the centre of his court and government, cost him £50,000 (approx. £36 million today). Despite acquiring men and materials at reduced prices (until the depredations of the plague on the labour market resulted in higher wages) this sum was the largest ever expended on any building by any monarch throughout the whole of the Middle Ages. His castle provided the basic structure that survived for 400 years until the rebuilding undertaken in the eighteenth century refaced or encased much of his work.

The College of St George and the Order of the Garter

The insignia of the Order of the Garter

Henry III's chapel of St Edward, built at Windsor over a hundred years before, was refitted by Edward III from 1350 as the collegiate chapel of his newly founded Order of the Garter and rededicated to St George (it was still also dedicated to Edward the Confessor and the Virgin Mary). The same year, he gave his new foundation the Cross of Gneth – claimed to be a piece of the true cross – which became the chapel's most famous relic, and in the days when important relics meant a steady income from pilgrims, its most important asset. To Henry's chapel he added a new entrance porch in 1353–4 with exquisite tracery vaulting, and rebuilt the adjoining cloister and chambers to accommodate the Dean, 12 canons and 13 priest-vicars of the new foundation.

The Garter knights, established in 1348, were limited to The King and his eldest son as Prince of Wales (the first incumbent was the Black Prince), each with 12 Companion Knights drawn from those tested in battle, as in a tournament. Membership was a reward for loyalty to the sovereign and for military merit. Each knight was assigned a stall in the choir of the chapel (the choir stalls in use today were completed by 1484) from which a banner showing their coat of arms was hung and underneath which a helm – or helmet – was crowned with a carved and painted representation of the knight's crown or crest. A metal stall plate with the knight's arms was originally fixed to his stall on his death as a memorial but by the time of Henry VIII they came to be fixed during the lifetime of the incumbent; 800 stall plates survive, crowding the back of each stall in a jumble of heraldic history, the earliest dating from around 1390.

Archaeological fragments uncovered from the chapel of Edward III show it to have been built in the decorated English Gothic style and colourfully painted. The effect must have been dazzling, with colourful knights' banners and light streaming through the stained-glass windows. Edward III's state sword, as Founder of the Order, was brought from the old chapel to the new, and still hangs behind the altar.

In 1358, on the feast of St George ten years after the order was established, Edward held a great tournament at Windsor at which King John II of France, who had been captured by the Black Prince at Poitiers two years earlier and was being held prisoner at Windsor, was a guest of honour. He took part in the tournament 'on a horse richly caparisoned' together with several noblemen of his court who were also prisoners but who, due to the courtesies of chivalry, were allowed to take part. John's ransom agreement, signed in 1360, ceded one-third of western France to the English and required a payment of an enormous three million crowns – a king's ransom. Earlier, in 1349, King David of Scotland and several French noblemen including the Constable of France, to whom the prize of the day was given for his prowess, had also taken part in the Garter tournament, despite being captives of the English Crown.

Henry VII

When the Lancastrian Henry VII came to the throne after defeating the Yorkist Richard III at Bosworth Field in 1485, he married Elizabeth of York, the eldest daughter of Edward IV and niece of Richard III, so uniting the two warring factions. Edward IV had already admitted his wife, sister and three daughters as Ladies of the Garter ten or so years before. In symbolic celebration of the end to the feud he created the Collar of the Order of the Garter, a chain with 26 enamelled roses in which the red rose of Lancaster is blended with the white rose of York to create the Tudor rose. The roses are formed within garters and linked with gold knots. From the chain hangs an 'image of St George on horseback, who, having thrown the Dragon upon his back, encounters him with a tilting spear'. The Collar was worn over the mantle and secured with white ribbons, as it is to this day. In 1488 Henry VII created his mother Margaret Beaufort, Countess of Richmond and Derby (who was 13 when she gave birth to Henry), a Lady of the Garter, the last woman to be admitted until Queen Alexandra, wife of King Edward VII, in 1901.

The quaint ceremony of 'degradation' – when a Garter knight was removed from the roll for one of a variety of offences – is described in manuscripts by Elias Ashmole, the Windsor Herald to Charles II, in relation to Edward, Duke of Buckingham, condemned for treason and beheaded by Henry VIII in 1521. The Garter King of Arms first demanded that he return the badges of knighthood. His banner was taken down from St George's Chapel, then:

Above: Richard III
Below: George V wearing the regalia of the Order of the Garter

'*he read aloud the instrument of degradation; after which one of the heralds, who was placed ready on a ladder set to the back of the convict knight's stall, at the words "expelled and put from among the arms", took his crest, and violently cast it down into the choir, after that his banner and sword; and ... all the officers of arms spurned [literally kicked] the achievements out of the choir into the body of the church ... so out of the west door, thence to the bridge, and over the ditch.*'

And there they lay amongst the rubbish in the open sewer the ditch had become.

Today, the insignia of the Garter is once more the gift of the sovereign and every year in June when The Queen is in residence for Ascot Week the members of the order meet at Windsor Castle. After a lunch in the state apartments they process on foot to St George's Chapel wearing the blue robes, insignia and plumed hats of the order to take up their position in their designated stalls for the Garter Service. No formal ceremony of degradation has been held in recent years – the last being The Duke of Ormonde in 1716 – though several members, including Kaiser Wilhelm and Emperor Franz Joseph I of Austria during

the First World War, had their appointments annulled, and Emperor Hirohito, during the Second World War, had his banner removed from St George's Chapel. The latter was reinstated on the Emperor's state visit to Britain in 1971.

To help those knights who had served with him with their own feudal retainers at Crécy but had been captured and impoverished by the need to sell their estates to raise ransom money, Edward III also established in 1352 the Alms Knights – known until 1833 as the 'Poor Knights' after which date they were given the formal title of the Military Knights of Windsor. They received an annual stipend and accommodation in the Lower Ward in return for daily prayer in the chapel for the monarch and the Garter knights and for their souls after death. They still exist and today wear the ceremonial scarlet uniform of army officers of the early nineteenth century. They must parade at numerous official functions as well as the Garter ceremonies and state visits. It is estimated they are on parade some 50 times a year.

The Military Knights of Windsor on parade

Above: Henry IV
Below: The Devil's Tower at Windsor Castle

Royal prisoners and rebuilding

Richard II was at Windsor shortly after his accession in 1377 and celebrated the Christmas of 1378 there. After his marriage to Anne of Bohemia at Westminster in 1382 it was recorded that The King 'carried the Queen to Windsor, where he kept an open and noble house'. During his 20-year reign Richard spent a great deal of money in maintaining an opulent court to reinforce the status of the monarchy. With Windsor Castle furnished with a series of suitably lavish apartments he turned his attention to the Palace of Westminster where he commissioned the rebuilding of Westminster Hall with its extraordinary 240-foot-long hammer-beam roof, the largest medieval timber roof in Northern Europe, which still survives over 600 years later.

On his accession in 1399, Henry IV ordered Richard's child queen, Isabella, daughter of King Charles VI of France (whom Richard had married aged six in 1396), to move out of The Queen's apartments. Henry celebrated Christmas that year at Windsor when an attempt was made to murder him by Richard's supporters but the plan was betrayed and Henry escaped to London unharmed.

By 1404 the castle was in dire need of repairs and mentioned in a petition to The King that year by the House of Commons as amongst the castles that were 'ruinous'. Seemingly the money assigned for its repair had, instead, been granted by Henry IV to his supporters. Henry preferred the Palace of Eltham to the dilapidated Windsor during the latter part of his reign and the castle was used mainly as a prison. On his accession Henry had quickly captured Edmund, Earl of March, then aged seven and the heir presumptive to Richard II, and his younger brother, and kept them throughout their childhood at Berkhamsted and Windsor Castles. Edmund was released after Henry

James I of Scotland

IV's death in 1413, the same year that the Welsh warlord, Owain Glyndower was imprisoned there.

Perhaps the most famous prisoner was James I of Scotland, who was captured on his way to France in 1405 at the age of 11. After two years in the Tower of London he was brought to Windsor where he remained for the next 11 years. He was allowed £500 a year (approx. £350,000 today) and to keep a retinue of Scottish nobles with him. His captivity continued after the accession of Henry V in 1413 and two years later he was joined by The Dukes of Bourbon and Orleans and other French noblemen who had been captured at the Battle of Agincourt. While at Windsor he was kept in an octagonal tower known then as the Maiden's Tower – now called Devil's Tower – in the south-west corner of the Upper Ward. There he famously fell in love with Joan Beaufort, the niece of Richard II, whom he observed from his tower walking in the garden below, which he described affectingly in his poem the 'King's Quair'. This is one of the few descriptions of formal gardens at Windsor in the Middle Ages, a garden 'made fast by the tower's wall' beset with shaded alleys, green arbours at each corner and planted with hawthorn hedges and sweet juniper. The poem continues:

And therewith cast I down my eye again,

Where as I saw walking under the tower,

Full secretly, new comyn her to plain,

The fairest and the freshest younge flower

That e'er I saw, methought, before that hour;

For which sudden abate, anon did start

The blood of all my body to my heart.

Joan was to become, in due course, Queen of Scotland. James I of Scotland's captivity was not onerous, he was made a knight at Windsor in 1421 and attended Queen Catherine's coronation at Westminster as a guest the same year.

The most celebrated visitor to Windsor during the reign of Henry

The Great West Window of St George's Chapel, Windsor

V was the very grand and very glamorous Sigismund of Luxemburg, who had become King of Hungary in 1387 and was made Holy Roman Emperor in 1433. Intending to help heal the longstanding rift between England and France, Sigismund landed at Dover in May 1416 with a fleet of 400 ships, which in turn disgorged an entourage of 1500 dignitaries. Henry rode out from London to greet Sigismund with his own entourage of some 5000 nobles and knights. The sight of such a huge number of mounted nobles must have been extraordinary. Sigismund bore a gift of either the heart of St George or an image of St George in pure gold (the records are unclear) and was accompanied to Windsor by the Garter knights 'each booted and spurred and in his habit', where he was inducted into the Order of the Garter in St George's Chapel.

The induction was followed by an enormous and elaborate feast, which must have strained the resources of the castle catering staff. The Black Book of the Order of the Garter records: 'The finery of the guests, the order of the servants, the variety of courses, the invention of the dishes, with the other things delightful to the sight and taste, whoever should endeavour to describe would never do it justice.' As one writer aptly describes it: 'during the personal and ritual reign of monarchs, statecraft is very much the art of ostentation and largesse'. By the end of Sigismund's four-month stay of ceremonial entertainment Henry had persuaded him to support his claim to the French throne.

It was at Windsor in 1421 that Henry's wife, Queen Catherine, gave birth to the son who would soon become Henry VI. The infant Henry remained behind at Windsor when Catherine travelled to France the next summer to be with her husband. Their time together would be only too brief. Henry V had achieved what English Kings had fought for since the days of Edward III, and had become the recognized heir to the Kingdom of France, but he died of dysentery at the Château de Vincennes on 31 August 1422 at the age of 35.

After an unhappy reign, deposition, bouts of madness, and the beginning of the Wars of the Roses, Henry VI was probably murdered by his successor, Edward IV, in the Tower of London in 1471. Fourteen years after his death Henry's body was moved from Chertsey Abbey to St George's Chapel at Windsor Castle, where he had been born, for reburial. He became popularly regarded as a martyr and miracles began to be ascribed to him, culminating in the compilation of a book of miracles attributable to his intercession at St George's Chapel. Henry had been a considerable patron of architecture, but he devoted most of his energies to his magnificent foundations of the nearby 'The Kynge's College of Our Ladye of Eton besyde Windesore', usually known as Eton College, and 'The Kynge's College of Our Ladye and Saint Nicholas' in Cambridge, now known as King's College.

Edward IV, who became King in 1461, used the castle regularly for magnificent pageants, particularly to mark the feast of St George. During his reign, in 1475, work began on the new St George's Chapel, to the west of the old one, together with the horseshoe cloister and lodgings for the college community. Several existing buildings, including three towers, were demolished to make way for it. Directed by the master mason, Henry Janyns, who had served his apprenticeship at Eton College chapel, and supervised by the Bishop of Salisbury, this was to be the most ambitious church-building project in Western Europe in the latter half of the fifteenth century. Much of the funding needed was plundered from the estates of a variety of aristocratic houses whose titular heads were minors and therefore wards of the Crown.

By the time of Edward IV's death in 1483 a great portion of the chapel had been completed, the celebrated choir stalls were in place and the choir nearly finished. The building was finished under the direction of the indefatigable Sir Reginald Bray who also provided, and bequeathed, some of the money necessary. Edward IV directed that his body should be buried in his new chapel. His coat of mail, adorned with gold, pearls and rubies, hung above his tomb until it was stolen by Cromwellian soldiers during the Commonwealth (1649–59).

Edward IV

Little new building work took place at Windsor for the next 200 years. Henry VII, who reigned from 1485, completed the roof of his father-in-law Edward IV's chapel, and created a small chapel to the east from the remains of Henry III and Edward III's chapel to serve in due course as a shrine for the now venerated Henry VI. In 1506 the Great

West Window was finished, one of the largest in England. Henry VII also added a three-storey tower with decorative oriel windows.

Henry VII preferred his palace at Sheen (later renamed Richmond Palace) to Windsor, though he continued the tradition of keeping the feast of St George there in as opulent a way as before. Ambassadors were entertained there and treaties signed. A record exists of the time of King Philip and Queen Joanna of Castile's visit to the castle in 1506. They had been shipwrecked off the Dorset coast and kept as hostages by Henry – though with due deference to their status, Henry's own chambers, lavishly furnished, in the new tower were accorded to Philip – until he had signed a defence pact and a trade agreement heavily biased in favour of English interests. This record describes in detail the furnishing of the castle and the entertainments provided for Henry VII's 'guests', which included hunting in the park, dancing, masques, tennis playing (The King of Castile won his set on a wooden tennis court in the Round Tower ditch, which had a gallery for spectators and was later rebuilt in brick), and 'baiting a horse with a bear' in the courtyard. The opportunity was taken to invest The King of Castile with the Order of the Garter with its accompanying pomp and ceremony.

Henry VIII at Windsor

Henry VII died in 1509 'the richest prince in Christendom' and the following year his son Henry VIII paid his first visit to Windsor Castle as monarch. Seventeen when he inherited the throne, Henry VIII was much admired for his zest, e n e r g y and accomplishments. He is described during that first visit as exercising himself daily in 'shooting, singing, dancing, wrestling, casting of the bar, playing at recorders, flute, virginals, in setting of songs, and making of ballads', and his tennis playing was 'the prettiest thing in the world'. Henry was much attached to the castle and the recreation afforded by the woods of the Great Park. He was described by an ambassador as drawing 'the bow with greater strength than any other man in England, and jousts marvellously', which, allowing for courtly obsequiousness, indicates that

Right: Henry VIII

Windsor Great Park he was an accomplished sportsman.

At the very beginning of his reign, to aggrandize the approach to the castle, Henry VIII rebuilt the gateway into the Lower Ward, creating the imposing structure that now bears his name. According to tradition it was from this gate that Henry VIII rode out in 1532 to meet Anne Boleyn before leading her into the old presence chamber of the castle to endow her there with the title of Marquess of Pembroke – a title in her own right – to give her the required status before she became his Queen.

The Garter ceremonies were now extravagant, ostentatious and very costly, with great calvacades of riders accompanying the knight or knights elect to Windsor. Elias Ashmole wrote, 'this proceeding on horseback was generally set forth with exceeding pomp ... the great number ... on gallant coursers ... the multitude of their own attendants well mounted, the richness of whose apparel, jewels, gold chains, rich embroideries, and plumes of feathers of their lords colours, even dazzled the eyes of the beholders'. By contrast, in the summer of 1517, when the plague was at its height in London, Henry VIII escaped to Windsor with only his physician and three of his favourite courtiers in attendance.

In May 1519 the crowd of courtiers, heralds, servants, messengers, trainbearers, swordbearers, prelates, bishops and the knights of the Garter riding two by two who accompanied The King to a St George's Day ceremony at Windsor was so enormous that the retinues had to be restricted by rank. Sixty horsemen were allowed for each duke, 50 for each marquess and so on down to 16 for an ordinary knight. The subsequent feasts on the eve of St George's Day and on the day itself consisted of 28 and 36 different dishes.

At Windsor in 1522, two years after the glamour and extravagance of the Field of the Cloth of Gold where the Kings of England and France met near Calais, Henry entertained The Queen's nephew, Charles V, Holy Roman Emperor and King of Spain, whose parents had been 'guests' of Henry VII at Windsor in 1506. The object was to cement their alliance and a series of masques were performed laden with symbolic meaning, and the usual competitive outdoor pursuits were indulged in, followed by gargantuan feasts.

In 1524, in the days when he was still *persona grata* in Rome and a few years after he had been granted the title *Fidei Defensor*, or Defender of the Faith, Pope Clement sent Henry at Windsor a three-foot high golden rose tree in a golden pot, the uppermost rose a 'fair sapphire'. In the 1530s Henry built a terrace of wood, in fact a vast 'deck', over the cliff edge below the royal apartments, where a target was set up 'for the Kyng to shott at with his hand-gonne'. He also created a huge arbour painted in the Tudor livery colours to use as a banqueting house.

In 1536 the uprising known as the 'Pilgrimage of Grace' broke out in Yorkshire, prompted by a combination of economic, political and religious grievances. Henry VIII hunkered down at Windsor and directed operations himself against the insurgency, writing detailed instructions to his commanders. By now he had become grossly fat and ropes and pulleys were installed in his various palaces to help him up and down stairs. Shortly before his death in 1547, a study of his late armour kept at the Tower of London showed he had a 52-inch waist, making him somewhere between 20 and 25 stone in weight.

The fate of Henry VIII's tomb

Henry VIII's third wife, Jane Seymour, whom he adored, died at Hampton Court after giving birth to his longed-for son, in due course to reign as Edward VI. She was buried in a vault in the middle of the choir aisle of St George's Chapel at Windsor. Henry directed in his will that he should lie by her side in an imposing vault. For such a powerful monarch whose intemperate policies changed the face of England forever, his final resting place is anything but imposing.

The memorial stone in St George's Chapel, marking the tomb of Henry VIII and Charles I

Henry had intended to create a tomb of great splendour based on the work already done by the disgraced Thomas Wolsey, who was a Canon of Windsor in 1511 before becoming a cardinal five years later. The lady chapel of Henry VIII's father had been granted to Wolsey and in the early 1520s he commissioned a Florentine artist to design his tomb for the chapel. It was to be a black marble sarcophagus on which his effigy was to lie, raised two feet above a black and white marble base. At each corner was to be a pillar of copper on which an angel held a candlestick. The design called for groups of angels and children to adorn the sides of the tomb holding up the Cardinal's arms. Wolsey died in disgrace at Leicester in 1530 and was buried in the abbey there, but by then Henry had earlier sequestered Wolsey's tomb and set about aggrandizing it for himself.

The sarcophagus was now to be raised five feet above its base rather than two and, instead of four pillars, it would have eight ten-foot high pillars adorned with the figure of an apostle. A further eight, nine-foot tall pillars would act as candlesticks. The intricate and opulent design incorporated a canopied altar with myriad cast and gilt figures of angels and children, the whole 'all in copper carven and curiously inlayed'. A life-size statue of Henry VIII on horseback under a triumphal arch was to stand beside it. The work went ahead slowly, though Henry's will assumed it would be completed and that masses would be said there daily 'as long as the world shall indure'.

It was not to be. The King's body, when he died in 1547 at Whitehall Palace, rested there, embalmed and encased in lead, for two weeks before being taken with due pomp and ceremony in a chariot drawn by eight horses to Windsor for burial, the train of mourners trailing for four miles behind the bier. As was usual at the time a life-like effigy of the dead King, dressed in his robes, was placed on top of the huge coffin. At Syon House, previously a monastery suppressed by Henry VIII, the cavalcade stopped for the night. It is alleged that Henry's body, in an advanced state of putrefaction and bloated with gas, burst, opening the seams of the lead coffin and allowing his blood to pool on the floor. This description was apparently repeated by the plumber called in to mend the coffin and another eyewitness, William Greville, though most scholars attribute this course of events to the body of William the Conqueror.

At Windsor, a magnificent coffin bearer was already positioned over the opened vault where Jane Seymour had been interred. The next day, after due ceremony, 16 Yeomen of the Guard 'let down the coffin into the vault (near unto the body of Queen Jane Seymour)'. The grandiose tomb, for whatever reason, was never finished. A hundred years later, when Oliver Cromwell's men took over Windsor Castle in 1649, they sold off all the cast bronze and brasswork. One of Henry's great candlesticks, dated 1530 and bearing the Tudor rose, still survives in St Bavo's Cathedral, Ghent, and a pair, copied from the originals, was presented to St George's Chapel in 1930 by King George V and Queen Mary and now flank the high altar. At the same time as Cromwell's men were removing 'scandalous monument and pictures' from the chapel, they also unceremoniously dumped the coffin of the decapitated body of Charles I in the same unmarked vault as Henry VIII and Jane Seymour.

In 1804, when George III commissioned a royal burial vault to be excavated in 'Wolsey's tomb house', the great black sarcophagus and its marble base were removed. The next year Admiral Lord Nelson died on HMS *Victory* at the Battle of Trafalgar, and about ten years after his interment in St Paul's, Wolsey's – and Henry's – sarcophagus was taken from

Admiral Lord Nelson

Windsor and placed on top, surmounted by a marble cushion holding Nelson's viscount's coronet. The connection between Nelson and Windsor was furthered in 1842, when the family of William Beatty, the surgeon on Nelson's HMS *Victory*, presented Queen Victoria with the musket ball that had killed Nelson. It is now amongst the treasures at Windsor Castle and can be seen in a glass case at the top of the main staircase.

Nelson's tomb at St Paul's Cathedral

The subsequently unmarked vault at Windsor bearing the coffins of Henry VIII, Jane Seymour, Charles I and an infant child of Queen Anne was discovered in 1813 – the skeleton of Henry VIII clearly visible. On the orders of William IV in 1837 the tomb was covered with a slab of black marble.

Edward VI

The reigns of Henry VIII's children

The young King Edward VI – he was nine when his father Henry VIII died in 1547 – did not care for Windsor. When rebellion threatened he was hurried from the indefensible Hampton Court to the security of Windsor by his uncle, Protector Somerset. Edward wrote in his diary: 'Methinks I am in prison ... here be no galleries, nor no gardens to walk in.' A year after his accession the Garter ceremony was purged 'of all papistical and superstitious practices' and greatly simplified. The lavish feasts at Windsor on St George's Day were discontinued; in future they were to take place wherever the monarch happened to be.

The one advance made at Windsor during Edward VI's reign was the piping of water from Blackmore Park, five miles away. Until this point in its history the castle had depended on wells and rainwater cisterns to cater to the considerable body of men and animals housed there. The conduit, completed in 1555, two years into Queen Mary's short reign, used pipes fashioned from lead salvaged from the dissolved monasteries of Woburn and Reading, and stone intended for further works to St George's Chapel. The resulting fountain sounds spectacular – in the middle of the Quadrangle, according to William Harrison Ainsworth writing in the mid-nineteenth century, a canopy was 'raised upon columns, gorgeously decorated with heraldic ornaments coloured and gilt, and a dragon, one of the supporters of the Tudor arms, casting the water into the basin underneath'.

Edward VI died aged 15 in 1553 from tuberculosis. The next year his sister, now Mary I, married her cousin, King Philip II of Spain, at Winchester and set out on the ten-day journey from there to Windsor, where Philip was invested with the Order of the Garter and was declared joint sovereign. In 1558 her royal arms were joined with those of the Hapsburg arms of Philip, carved in a decorated panel on a tower in the Lower Ward. She also added some further lodgings there for the Poor Knights made from stone quarried from Reading Abbey.

By the time of her accession in 1558, Mary's half-sister Elizabeth I found Windsor Castle cold and ruinous and began to make some necessary changes. By the end of her reign in 1603 she had spent more money on Windsor than any of her palaces (an echo of the reign of

Above: Elizabeth I
Below: James I of England and VI of Scotland

Edward III 200 years earlier), using it as a centre for diplomatic entertainment. She replaced her father's rotted timber deck with a vast stone terrace, built a new picture gallery and gateway and spent months there at a time avoiding the plague, on one occasion translating 'one of the tragedies of Euripides for her own amusement'.

Elizabeth I was a considerable scholar and fluent in six languages. We know she attended many theatrical entertainments, including a number written by William Shakespeare, reputed to have been a member of the Royal Household. Towards the end of her reign, somewhere between 1598 and 1601, it is thought she commanded Shakespeare to write *The Merry Wives of Windsor*, packed with local allusions and names, which was first performed in a hall built in the early fifteenth century and which, from 1693, has been used as the library of St George's Chapel.

The Stuarts and the Interregnum

When Elizabeth I died childless the Tudor dynasty became extinct and James VI, King of Scotland since 1567, as a great-great-grandson of Henry VII through his mother Mary, Queen of Scots, had the best claim to the English throne. In 1603 the two kingdoms were united and James became James I of England and the first of the Stuart dynasty. James used Windsor for hunting – his favourite sport – and repatriated the Garter Ceremony to the castle. Some jostling for accommodation between the Scots and English members of court was reported as a result. Neither James nor his son Charles I left their mark upon the castle. Charles spent some time there as the spectre of civil war loomed. He returned only as a prisoner in 1647 and 1648, and the next year as a headless corpse.

In 1642 the castle was commandeered

Warrant to Execute Kinge Charles the First · AD 1648 ·

At the high Court of Justice for the tryinge and iudginge of
Charles Steuart Kinge of England January XXIXth Anno Dni 1648.

Whereas Charles Steuart Kinge of England is and standeth convicted attaynted and condemned
and others high Crymes, And sentence uppon Saturday last pronounced against him by this Court to be
putt to death by the severinge of his head from his body Of wch sentence execucon yet remayneth to be done. These are therefore
to will and require you to see the said sentence executed In the open Street before Whitehall upon the morrowe being the Thirtieth
Day of this instante month of January between the houres of Tenn in the morninge and Five in the afternoone of the same day wth full
effect And for soe doing this shall be yor sufficient warrant And these are to require All Officers and Souldiers and other good
people of this Nation of England to be assistinge unto you in this Service Given under our hands and Seales

To Colonell ffrancis Hacker, Colonell ffuncks and
Lieutenant Colonell Phayre and to every of them

by the Parliamentarians, followed by looting and some destruction. The Dean and canons were ejected, treasures were removed – including the plate from the chapel and the coat of mail encrusted with gems hanging above the tomb of Edward IV – and statues and some painted windows smashed. The same year Prince Rupert, the

senior Royalist general, attempted to recapture the castle, his cannon pounding the wall for seven hours, but was rebuffed. A year later the castle became a prison for captured Royalists who were crowded into the towers, gatehouses and dungeons. Many of them scratched their names and dates on the stone walls, still to be seen today.

A few years later, as Parliament sought to raise money, statues

Top: The death warrant issued for Charles I in 1649.
Above: Oliver Cromwell
Right: Charles I

and other objects were sold, including an equestrian statue of St George and the candlesticks and other brass, enamelwork and copperware from Wolsey's tomb. After an attempted mutiny in November 1647, the Council of the Army based itself at Windsor, whilst negotiations were held between Parliament, the Parliamentary Army and The King. Charles I spent Christmas 1648 at the castle and on 30 January 1649 he was beheaded. The second shirt he wore that day – to prevent shivering that might make onlookers think he was afraid – is now kept in the Royal Library at Windsor.

A map of Windsor Castle in 1650

The body was taken to Windsor and laid on an oak table in the Deanery – the table is still preserved there – and in due course taken through a

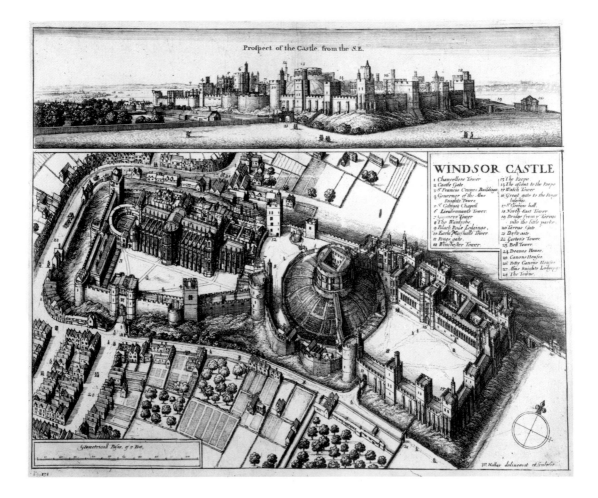

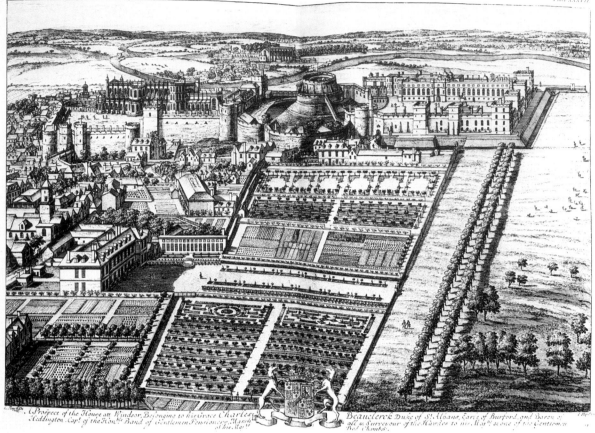

A Prospect of the House att Windsor, Belonging to his Grace Charles   Beauclerck Duke of St Albans, Earee of Burford and Baron of
Heddington Capt. of the Honbl. Band of Gentlemen Pencioners March   all Surveyour of the Hawkes to his Majty & one of the Gentlemen
of his Majty   Bed Chamber.

The Duke of St. Albans' House at Windsor, with a view of Windsor Castle from the South.
From Kip's Britannia Illustrata of 1709

A map of Windsor in 1709

snowstorm to the chapel where it was buried in the vault next to the coffins of Henry VIII and Jane Seymour.

In the 1650s, the House of Commons, always short of money, considered selling the castle but abandoned the idea and the Parliamentary Army used the castle as its headquarters throughout the Interregnum. The parks, however, were sold. The Little Park was bought back for Oliver Cromwell's exclusive use, and was returned to the Crown at the Restoration of the monarchy. The Great Park had been divided up and sold off in lots, and it was many years before it once again became Crown property.

Charles II was proclaimed King on Mayday 1660. The castle was once more a royal palace and stronghold. The diarist Samuel Pepys visited in 1660 and proclaimed it 'the most romantique castle that is in the world'. However, Pepys's fellow diarist, John Evelyn, writing four years later, noted that romantic as it might be, it was 'exceedingly ragged and ruinous'. Prince Rupert, who had attempted unsuccessfully to storm the castle 28 years before, was appointed Constable and Governor in 1670. He at once set about refurbishing the Round Tower and created much-admired arrangements of weapons and armour on the walls, which subsequently became the fashion.

Charles II

Prince Rupert and his first cousin, King Charles II, were Fellows of the Royal Society and, in the spirit of the times, both built laboratories at the castle and spent hours conducting experiments. Charles II enjoyed tennis and the country pursuits afforded by the parks but was only too aware of the 'ragged and ruinous' state of the castle and that his cousin Louis XIV was creating a vast baroque fantasy at Versailles. Accordingly he began work on aggrandizing the castle in the 1670s, principally altering the apartments and state rooms in the Upper Ward. The north front was rebuilt and the interiors of many of the rooms dramatically updated. The architect Hugh May collaborated with the celebrated Neapolitan artist Antonio Verrio and the wood carver Grinling Gibbons ('the greatest master both for invention and rareness of work that the world ever had in any age') to create some of the most revolutionary and dazzling interiors ever seen in England, a swirling mass of colour and gilding that in feats of baroque *trompe l'oeil* blurred the boundaries between art and reality. St George's Hall and the adjoining chapel were the richest and most extravagant examples of this new decoration, which was finished by the early 1680s.

The King's and Queen's royal apartments were comprehensively reworked but were preserved as before as parallel suites of rooms, The King's facing north and The Queen's south. Below The King's suite a new apartment was fashioned for his mistress, Louise de Kérouaille, The Duchess of Portsmouth, and their son, Charles, 1st Duke of Richmond. A backstairs linked the two apartments. Outside the walls a grand house with orangery and extensive formal gardens was constructed for his other principal mistress, Nell Gwynn, and their son, the 1st Duke of St Albans.

Other apartments were built for Charles II's brother The Duke of York (later James II) and his wife, and various towers were repaired or rebuilt. The exterior of the castle was also given a facelift. Ditches were filled in, the terraces extended and the Great Avenue, or Long Walk, just under three miles in length, was created in 1680–5 through the park from the south front of the castle; 1652 elm trees were planted in a double row on each side of the walk. The castle also benefitted from a new pressurized water system, a pump invented by Sir Samuel Moreland, created Master of Mechanics by Charles II for his efforts. In July 1681 water mixed with red wine to make it more visible was pumped from the Thames 20 metres (60 feet) into the air above the North Terrace, watched by The King and Queen and an estimated 1000 spectators. A large reservoir to hold the pumped water was excavated under the North Terrace and this in time fed, via copper pipes, a marble bath for The Queen as well as providing a new pressurized supply for the castle. On top of the reservoir was placed an equestrian statue of Charles II on a huge marble base carved by Grinling Gibbons.

Charles II on his accession determined to restore the pomp, glamour, music and colour of the monarchy, after the drab monochrome of the Commonwealth with its all-day prayer meetings. One of his first acts was to restore the choir of St George's Chapel to its 'former lustre and dignity', to reinvigorate the Order of the Garter and its attendant ceremonies and feasts and to make the costume and regalia worn by its members even more spectacular. In April 1661, 13 knights were installed. Three-day feasts became the norm but soon proved a financial drain and were discontinued after 1674. As Celia Fiennes on visiting Windsor some 20 years later remarked sagely, 'Some of these foolerys are requisite sometimes to create admiration and keep up the state of a kingdom and nation'. Elias Ashmole, the Windsor Herald, compiled a monumental record of the Order, its members, ceremonies, regalia and dress and commissioned Wenceslaus Hollar to illustrate it. It is from this record we draw so much of our knowledge of what the castle looked like before the changes wrought by Charles II and his architect Hugh May.

After Charles II died of a stroke at the age of 55 in 1685, his brother James II did little to the castle except substitute his own priests in place of the Dean and chaplains at St George's Chapel, pay for expensive vestments, candlesticks and other accoutrements of the mass and introduce 'Roman' services. This unpopular move was compounded by his receiving a papal emissary, the Papal Nuncio, at the castle in 1686. The birth of a Catholic son – and heir – to James II was too much for a Protestant country. As a result of opposition on all sides James II threw the Great Seal of England into the Thames and fled abroad. His Protestant daughter Mary and her husband William of Orange, James's nephew as well as son-in-law, were offered the Crown as joint monarchs by Parliament, and were crowned in 1689, thereby becoming King William III and Queen Mary II.

In 1692 William III ordered Sir Christopher Wren to make a survey of the castle and suggest proposed changes in its design, but Wren's extensive work at Hampton Court and the new palace he was building for The King at Kensington absorbed most of William's time.

The lion of England, one of the heraldic Queen's Beasts of Windsor

Wren produced a series of dramatic plans, one for the reconstruction of the castle as an Italianate palace and the other, already produced for Charles II, of a beautiful domed mausoleum – a smaller version of the dome of St Paul's – to hold the body of Charles I, still languishing in the simple vault beneath the nave of St George's Chapel. Neither plan saw the light of day. Perhaps Wren's only visual contribution to the castle was to advise on the taking down of the serried ranks of decaying heraldic beasts from their pinnacles above the chapel. These pinnacles remained unadorned for another 250 years.

After the deaths of first Mary II and then William III, James II's younger daughter Anne became Queen in 1702. Anne spent a great deal of time at Windsor but left little mark upon the castle apart from completing the grand staircase, preferring a little brick house beside the Rubbish Gate where she 'daily withdrew from the royal lodgings'. In 1698 her stillborn son was placed in the vault with Henry VIII, Jane Seymour and Charles I.

But Queen Anne has left one enduring legacy: she was responsible for the institution of the Ascot races. Horse racing was The Queen's favourite sport and, while driving through the countryside in the early summer of 1711, her eye alighted on the Common at Ascot. The *London Gazette* of 12 July that year announced: 'Her Majesty's Plate of 100 guineas will be run for round the new heat on Ascott Common, near Windsor, on August 7th next, by any horse, mare or gelding, being no more than six years old the grass before'. The meeting is now held in June, but Queen Anne must be credited for its very existence.

Above: Queen Anne
Below: George III

The House of Hanover

The early Hanoverians, beginning with George I after the death of the final Stuart monarch, Anne, in 1714, were occasional visitors to Windsor but preferred to live elsewhere. The keep became briefly a state prison but quaint customs were nonetheless maintained. Every year on Easter Sunday, as required by Charles I's grant in 1632, two arrows were delivered to the Governor, by virtue of which gift Lord Baltimore held the province of Maryland in North America. On New Year's Day 1753, two uncured and presumably smelly beaver skins were received on behalf of Richard and Thomas Penn, who held Pennsylvania from the Crown. By the 1760s, devoid of the lustre of royalty, the castle was shabby and neglected, divided into a warren of grace-and-favour apartments. A series of famous watercolours painted around 1770 by Paul Sandby show picturesque but clearly down-at-heel views of the castle.

George III's Queen, Charlotte of Mecklenberg-Strelitz, whom he married in 1761, came to the rescue and fell in love with the castle. Initially Queen Anne's old retreat was bought and enlarged by Sir William Chambers but as their family expanded (they had 15 children) George III bought, in 1777, Nell Gwynn's old house in the Great Park from her grandson, the 3rd Duke of St Albans. By the next summer the royal family was established at Windsor, with Queen Charlotte especially favouring the house at Frogmore which was bought for her in 1792 (and which subsequently became the home of Queen Victoria's mother, The Duchess of Kent). Fond of flowers and botany, Queen Charlotte had one of the principal rooms decorated by the artist Mary Moser to resemble a floral bower. Today Frogmore House is occasionally used by the royal family for entertaining and The Queen is especially fond of the gardens – dog bowls can be found in the summer house adjacent to the lake; an indication that it is a favoured spot.

Over the next few years, in deference to its renewed royal status, the castle was slowly spruced up, the old moats and ditches filled in and the drawbridge – last raised as a precautionary measure in 1765 – dismantled. On Sunday evenings in summer the royal family

LE RETOUR DE WINDSOR,
a New
SONATA,
for the
Piano Forte,
With or Without the Additional Keys,
With an Accompaniment for a Violin (ad Libitum)
Composed & Dedicated to
Miss Olympia Cazalet
By Mr LATOUR.
Op. 9
Pr. 4s

London Printed & Sold at Bland & Wellers Music Warehouse, 23, Oxford Street

Le Retour de Windsor, a sonata composed for George III in 1808

would walk through the crowds (anyone could attend) on the terrace as a band played. The choir of the chapel was restored.

In 1796 James Wyatt was appointed surveyor to the castle and began to remodel Charles II's apartments in the Gothic idiom. However, after a few years, with the expense of the Napoleonic Wars, work ceased. By 1804 sufficient remedial work had been undertaken for the royal family to move into the castle proper, where The Queen wrote to a friend, 'I have changed from a very comfortable and warm habitation to the coldest house, rooms and passages that ever existed.'

The same year two guards' barracks were built to serve the castle and protect the monarch but the large numbers of soldiers quartered there had, within a few years, led to a major problem of prostitution in the town. George Street and Peascod Street, opposite the castle, were full of boarding houses of ill repute and there were even reports of soldiers selling their services along the Long Walk. The areas with the worst reputation were knocked down in 1839 and a decade later the Royal Mews and Windsor Central Station were built over them. Combermere Barracks is today the headquarters of the Household Cavalry Regiment.

Despite the simplicity and strict regularity of his day-to-day existence King George III held a glittering house-warming party in 1805 and on St George's Day that year installed seven new knights, the first installation for over 30 years – it was to be the last for the next 150. After the

A view of Windsor Castle from the Thames, by William Raymond Dommerson, c1880

traditional feast the leftover food was taken out to trestle tables set up in the Quadrangle and the castle gates opened to an onrushing horde of hungry townspeople.

The King's Golden Jubilee was celebrated in Windsor in 1809 with fireworks, feasts, illuminations and a spectacular water pageant on the lake at Frogmore. The King, by now blind and going deaf, did not attend and shortly afterwards was stricken with insanity – now thought to be caused by a genetic disorder called porphyria – which virtually confined him to the castle for the next ten years, at times constrained by being 'wrapped in a winding sheet'. In 1820 he was the first sovereign to die at Windsor and his heavy casket was propelled along a specially made trackway to the new Royal Vault he had commissioned where he would lie beside his Queen and four of their fifteen children.

George IV and late Georgian taste

George IV

George IV, who had been Prince Regent for nearly a decade before becoming King in 1820, was a very different animal to his father, George III. A big man in every sense he was an architect manqué, a collector of art and furniture and a man of refined but flamboyant sensibility possessed of great taste and energy. He had already built, in the 1780s and 1790s, Carlton House, a spacious and opulent palace beside St James's Park. At roughly the same time he had begun the Royal Pavilion in Brighton, an extraordinary pleasure palace with an amalgam of Moorish or 'Saracenic' exteriors and Chinese interiors. He also began the ambitious remodelling of his father's Buckingham House to turn it into the palace that would become the primary residence and workplace of successive reigning monarchs. It is no wonder then that after a two-month stay, following his first visit in 1820, he decided extensive works were required at Windsor.

Following a competition Jeffry Wyatt, the nephew of James Wyatt who had worked with George III at Windsor, was selected. In 1823 work began. A Grand Corridor over 150 metres (500 feet) long was designed to ease circulation, a new gateway was opened centred on the Long Walk and buildings were raised and crenellated (including the Round Tower which was doubled in height

A chromolithograph of Windsor library, designed by Jeffry Wyatville, 1838

and increased in girth). Towers were taken down and rebuilt and the Hugh May interiors dating from Charles II, the apogee of the baroque style in interior decoration, were destroyed, apart from three rooms. The chapel was demolished and added to the once-magnificent St George's Hall to make one enormously long, and unsatisfactory, room. Nonetheless the silhouette of the castle – now so instantly recognizable – benefitted enormously from Wyatt's changes. He changed his name, too, in 1824, to Wyatville to distinguish himself from a plethora of family members in the building trade with the same name. He was knighted in 1828.

The internal decorations, painting, plasterwork, gilding, woodcarving, carpets and furniture, were not Wyatville's responsibility although he contributed some lavish plaster ceilings for the principal reception rooms. The decorating and furnishing of the new interiors was personally supervised by The King (who had already worked with a trusted team of artists and craftsmen at his other major building projects) with the help of cabinet makers Nicholas Morel and George Seddon, a partnership formed to take on this daunting task. Among their workforce was the precociously young Augustus Welby Northmore Pugin, who at the age of 15 designed furniture and fittings in the Gothic style for the castle.

Carlton House was demolished in 1825 and the huge collection of paintings, furniture, fixtures and fittings, which had accumulated in over 40 years of ceaseless collecting, was divided between Buckingham Palace and Windsor, and many of the interior schemes were designed to accommodate particular pieces or suites. The results of these labours was summed up by Hugh Roberts in his submission to the Options Report after the Great Fire of 1992:

'The area that Wyatville remodelled presented, before the fire, a superb and unrivalled sequence of rooms widely regarded as the finest and most complete expression of later Georgian taste. The three styles of architecture selected by Wyatville and King George IV – Classical, Gothic and Rococo – were deliberately and carefully orchestrated throughout the building to emphasize the function of the different rooms and to harmonize with the furniture chosen or designed for them.'

As Guy Francis Laking, Keeper of The King's Armoury, noted in *The*

Furniture of Windsor Castle (1905), 'it is to King George IV's fine taste and appreciation that the nation must be ever grateful for the real treasures now existing at Windsor Castle and Buckingham Palace'. Many of these treasures are of French origin – gilded and decorated in extravagant style and still adorning the state rooms of the castle. They were acquired after the Revolution by a King well aware of their beauty and the quality of their craftsmanship and of their ability to impart a richness and grandeur synonymous with that of a reigning monarch. Furniture from the reign of Louis XVI was especially favoured, and French royal cabinet makers were also shipped over the Channel to work directly for the British King.

George IV towards the end of his life was a vastly fat, heavily rouged, blind old man addicted to laudanum to combat constant pain and prone to fantasy. At his death in 1830, much was still to be completed and the work was carried on by his successor, his younger brother William IV. Where George IV, the artist-king, was described as 'capricious, luxurious and misanthropic', William IV was 'a plain, vulgar, hospitable gentleman, opening his doors to all the world, with a numerous family'.

William IV took possession of Windsor the day after his brother's funeral, arriving in a carriage with his wife Queen Adelaide and two of his illegitimate daughters by the actress Dorothea Jordan. William and Dorothea had five boys and five girls in the 20 years they were together (1791–1811). William was then Duke of Clarence and all the children were given the surname FitzClarence. By 1837, when William IV's young niece Victoria inherited the throne (as a young girl she called William 'Uncle King'), the great works initiated by George IV at Buckingham Palace and Windsor Castle were virtually complete. William IV's contribution was to

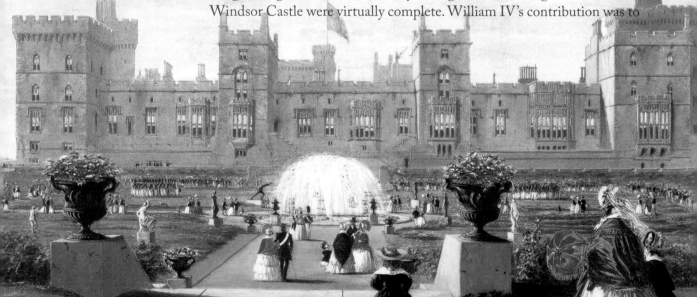

turn the Long Gallery of Elizabeth I into the Royal Library. Both brothers were buried in the new Royal Vault in St George's Chapel.

The Victorian castle

Victoria took possession of the castle in August 1837 (where she was to encounter two of her uncle's bastards, the FitzClarences, as one was Constable of the Castle and another Ranger of Windsor Little Park). Her cavalcade approached via the Long Walk through a triumphal arch and under the new King George IV Gateway. That evening a Mrs Graham, 'the only English female aeronaut', provided the entertainment by ascending in a balloon named 'Victoria' to mark the auspicious occasion.

Margaret Graham was an intrepid woman. In later balloons she survived several falls ('although the ground was very hard there was an evident impression of her form upon it') and a fire, severely injuring herself and becoming as famous for her near-death escapes as her aeronautical skills. She lived nonetheless to old age.

Victoria and Albert's Uncle Leopold, King of the Belgians, had much the same relationship with Victoria and Albert as Lord Mountbatten with the younger royals in the 1960s. It was Leopold who proposed his nephew Albert of Saxe-Coburg-Gotha as a prospective husband for Victoria. Albert's initial visit in 1836 was followed by a second, to Windsor, in October 1839 and this time Victoria was smitten. Albert being of inferior rank it was she who had to propose, which she did five days after his arrival with the words, 'Could you forsake your country for me?'

Above: The young Queen Victoria receives guests at Windsor, 1844

Left: A chromolithograph of the gardens at Windsor Castle, by J. B. Pyne, 1838

They were married the following February, an event which gave her great joy: 'he clasped me in his arms & we kissed each other again and again! His beauty, his sweetness and gentleness – really how can I ever

Queen Victoria and Albert, Prince Consort, 1861

be thankful enough to have such a *husband*!' The honeymoon was at Windsor. Nine months later, in November 1840, their first child, Victoria, was born and the following month they were at Windsor for Christmas. This was celebrated with Christmas trees and presents in the German manner – Queen Charlotte and Queen Adelaide had already introduced the custom decades earlier – which soon became fashionable. The Queen later wrote she was pleased that the custom had become 'so generally adopted in this country'. Windsor became the preferred place to spend Christmas. In 1842 the future Edward VII spent his first Christmas there and afterwards was baptized in St George's Chapel.

Victoria preferred Osborne and Balmoral to Windsor, but she would rather be there than in London itself, which she hated, and it was close enough to the capital – particularly once the opening of the railway made the journey so much quicker – to make it useful. In this way Windsor became 'the seat of authority, and an indispensable wheel in the machine of government'. Although Albert had made good use of the fledgling railway, he and Victoria made their first joint journey by train from Slough to Paddington in June 1842 – the Windsor line opened in 1849 – in a train driven by the great engineer Isambard Kingdom Brunel, who had built the railway. The journey took half an hour. By 1852 the Privy Council was coming down to Windsor by special train.

Albert was indefatigable. He was instrumental in the design and construction of both Osborne and Balmoral and in creating the formal and landscaped gardens that surround them. At Balmoral he diverted public roads to ensure greater privacy and he did the same at Windsor, turning his attention as Ranger of the Parks (he was also Constable of the Castle – thus replacing both FitzClarences) to the improvement of the parks and farms. In due course he divided the Home Park into public and private areas, the latter for the exclusive use of the royal family. Under his direction the old music room beside St George's Hall was converted by Edward Blore, who also worked at Buckingham Palace, into a new Private Chapel. It was in this room that the disastrous fire started, just over 150 years later.

Windsor was host to a spectacular series of state occasions and royal relations from most of the monarchies of Europe were constant visitors to the castle. In 1844 it was the Tsar of Russia, when 4000 soldiers were reviewed in the Great Park with the elderly Duke of Wellington attired as a Russian Field Marshal once more at the head of his old regiment. From 1842 the German court painter Franz Xaver Winterhalter spent several months of each summer at Windsor painting Victoria and Albert, their growing brood of children and scenes of court life as well as giving Victoria – a good amateur painter in her own right – lessons. In 1844 he painted the reception accorded Louis Philippe of France at Windsor. Victoria revived the full ceremonial of the Garter in Louis Philippe's honour. In 1855 it was the turn of Napoleon III, the nephew of Napoleon Bonaparte, England's implacable enemy for so many years, to be inducted into the Order. Another military review took place in the Great Park and this time a Napoleon charged with the English cavalry, rather than against it. His Empress, Eugenie, chic and beautiful beside the dumpy Victoria – who had little dress sense – made a strong impression with her love of jewellery and her crinoline skirts, the first ever seen in England.

The Winterhalter portrait of Queen Victoria and Prince Albert with their children Victoria, Edward, Alice, Alfred and Helena

The defining moment of Victoria's reign was the death of her beloved Albert from typhoid fever in 1861. He died at Windsor in the Blue Room overlooking the park where both George IV and William IV had died. Thereafter she was submerged in grief and allowed the very Germanic cult of death to take her over. Albert's body was stored in the Royal Vault at St George's Chapel, while a large Italianate mausoleum was built in the corner of his favourite garden at Frogmore. His room, until her death 40 years later, became a shrine, kept exactly as it was when he died, with fresh clothes laid out and hot water provided

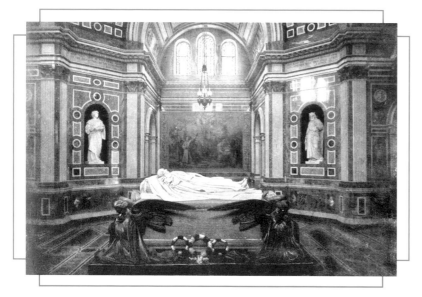

daily. Every year on the anniversary of his death she would place flowers on his bed and the family would attend a memorial service in the mausoleum. Dressed from that moment in the deepest mourning she shut herself away and later became known, from Kipling's poem, as 'The Widow at Windsor'.

Above: Prince Albert's tomb at Frogmore
Below: Frogmore Mausoleum

Still stricken with grief, she attended in 1863 the wedding of The Prince of Wales to the eighteen-year-old Alexandra of Denmark at St George's Chapel. By all accounts it was a magnificent spectacle, which she watched hidden behind thick velvet curtains. The great west door was used and since this was before the construction of its imposing flight of steps in 1871, a temporary structure of oak in the Gothic style was constructed to provide an entrance way and separate rooms in which The Prince and Princess could wait before the service began. Later that year George Gilbert Scott began work in converting what had become known, despite its sequestration by Henry VIII, as 'Wolsey's Tomb House' into a memorial chapel for Albert. A dazzling high-Victorian tour de force in coloured marble with a recumbent Albert clad in armour, it was completed in 1874.

While George Gilbert Scott was working in the chapel the architect Anthony Salvin was at work on various parts of the castle including the walls, repairing and restoring several towers including the ancient Curfew Tower, with its old clock tower that also doubled as the bell tower of St George's. The characterful bell-cage and dome, dating from the time of Edward IV, was encased by Salvin in a replica of the Tour de la Peyre in Carcassonne, the Gothic architect Eugène Viollet-le-Duc's fanciful idea of what a medieval tower should look like.

Edward VII

As the years passed so Victoria's grief slowly abated and in due course acting companies and other entertainers were invited to Windsor to perform. She threw herself wholeheartedly into supporting the troops during the Second Anglo–Boer War, which began in 1899, giving up her holiday at Osborne to entertain the families of the troops at Windsor. The next year, aged 80, in an extraordinary whirlwind of activity, she went to Ireland, to thank her Irish troops for the part they had played in the war, welcomed The King of Sweden and the Khedive of Egypt on state visits, attended innumerable court functions and held her last Privy Council at Windsor.

In December 1900 she moved to Osborne and died there on 22 January 1901. Brought across the Solent on the ship *Alberta*, her body was then transported alternately by train and gun carriage to the railway station at Windsor, resting in St George's Chapel before being interred in the mausoleum at Frogmore. The giant bell, taken from a church in Sebastopol at the time of the Crimean War and rehung in the Round Tower of the castle, tolled during the funeral, as did the bell of the restored Curfew Tower. The matching effigy Victoria had ordered to be carved at the time of Albert's death was placed over her coffin in the huge granite sarcophagus she shares with her beloved husband – in her coffin various mementoes of Albert and in her hand a photograph of her faithful servant John Brown, placed there on The Queen's express instructions by her physician Dr Reid.

The twentieth century at Windsor

Both Edward VII and George V preferred Sandringham to Windsor. Edward had little regard for the niceties of style and decoration, unlike George V's consort, Queen Mary, who knew a great deal about furniture and paintings and their settings.

Edward VII set about de-cluttering and updating the castle with unsophisticated zeal, thinning out furniture, sending ornaments to storage and recovering frayed curtains and worn upholstery, but not necessarily in quite the sensitive way they had been restored before – so diluting Jeffry Wyatville's vision. He reopened the suite of rooms kept for so long as a shrine to his father, Prince Albert, redecorating them for his own use and

including a smoking and billiard room, two of his favourite pastimes. Electricity, heating, bathrooms and telephone lines were installed and the castle drainage updated. An ardent admirer of women, one of Edward VII's first acts was to revive the practice, dormant since medieval times, of admitting ladies to the Order of the Garter.

Royal occasions at Windsor were once more enormous, lavish affairs, like the three-day wedding of Edward VII's niece, The Princess of Albany, to Prince Alexander of Teck in 1904, with visitors and their entourages dispersed among the castle's many bedrooms and entertained to vast meals.

On the death of Edward VII in 1910 nine monarchs and innumerable princes and princelings accompanied The King's funeral cortege as it was pulled by naval ratings from Windsor station to St George's Chapel. There he was interred, his terrier Caesar included in his effigy, carved beneath his feet.

George V, a stickler for order, punctuality, stamp collecting and high standards, kept a staff of over 600 busy whilst at Windsor. Queen Mary was instrumental in the acquisition or reacquisition of artworks and pieces of furniture for the state rooms. Her visits to country houses were anticipated by their owners with a degree of apprehension since The Queen was famous for 'admiring' various trinkets and bibelots that the owners would then feel obliged to bestow upon her as a gift. Wily chatelaines would put away their most treasured possessions to avoid embarrassment. In acknowledgement of The Queen's interest in interior decoration Princess Marie-Louise, her husband's first cousin, commissioned the architect Sir Edwin Lutyens to design a vast miniature neo-classical house for her, the largest 'dolls' house' in the world. It was completed in 1924. Now one of the great attractions of the castle, it contains over 1000 objects, all crafted at 1:12 scale by the leading designers of the 1920s, and includes hot and cold running water, flushing lavatories, working lifts, electricity and a pretty formal garden designed by Gertrude Jekyll that slides out from underneath the house.

An enlarged replica of one of the miniature books created for Queen Mary's Dolls' House in Windsor Castle

The Prince of Wales, the future Edward VIII, was inducted into the Order of the Garter in 1911 and a Garter service was held once more at St George's Chapel, the first since the reign of George III. In deference to the anti-German sentiment following the First World War, in 1917 George V decreed the name of the royal family should change from the House of Saxe-Coburg and Gotha, Prince Albert's Ducal House, to the House

Above: Queen Mary's Dolls' House being packed up for delivery to Windsor

Below: The heraldic Queen's Beasts, here celebrated in stamp form: the lion of England, the griffin of Edward III, the falcon of the Plantagenets, the black bull of Clarence, the white lion of Mortimer, the yale of Beaufort, the white greyhound of Richmond, the red dragon of Wales, the unicorn of Scotland, and the white horse of Hanover.

of Windsor. At the same time innumerable royal relations with German surnames anglicized their names too and renounced their German titles, so the Battenbergs became the Mountbattens. In 1960 'Mountbatten' was joined to Windsor by royal proclamation to create the surname Mountbatten-Windsor for all the descendants of Queen Elizabeth II and Prince Philip. The first time it was used officially was in 1973, in the marriage register, when Princess Anne married Captain Mark Phillips.

It was during George V's reign that St George's Chapel was discovered to be dangerously unsafe: the foundations were moving and the huge beams spanning the roof above the vaults were failing. A ten-year programme of restoration was undertaken, finally completed in 1930. At the same time, due to the generosity of a Putney builder, the 76 heraldic beasts, which had adorned the parapets of the chapel from Tudor times until the 1680s, were replaced, those on the north side representing the House of York, those on the south the House of Lancaster. Both George V and, in due course, Queen Mary, were buried in St George's Chapel.

Edward VIII's short reign in 1936 had little impact on the castle. His preferred country residence was Fort Belvedere in Windsor Great Park.

Originally a folly built in the 1750s for the younger son of George II, it was extended by Wyatville for use as a hunting lodge and also, with a battery of 31 guns, for royal salutes, with a resident bombardier. In 1911 it was converted into a house and in 1929 given to The Prince of Wales, after which it became a fashionable venue for parties. It was there that Edward VIII had his fateful final meetings with the Prime Minister, Stanley Baldwin, and signed the Instrument of Abdication in December 1936. The document was also signed by his brothers, The Dukes of York, Gloucester and Kent. The following day he broadcast to the nation from the castle: 'you must believe me when I tell you that I have found it impossible to carry the heavy burden of responsibility and to discharge my duties as King as I would wish to do without the help and support of the woman I love'.

It was Edward's wish to return to live at Fort Belvedere after his marriage to Wallis Simpson, but this was not allowed. However, George VI proposed that his brother should adopt the title 'Duke of Windsor' and this title was created for him in March 1937. He and Wallis are buried in the Royal Burial Ground beside the mausoleum at Frogmore.

The Duke of Windsor had included in his abdication speech the phrase, 'my brother ... has one matchless blessing, enjoyed by so many of you and not bestowed on me – a happy home with his wife and children'. His brother, as Duke of York, had taken out a lease on 145 Piccadilly and this was the family's London house until his accession as George VI. It was destroyed during the Blitz, its ruins subsequently demolished to

make way for the InterContinental Hotel. The couple's country house was initially White Lodge in Richmond Park, from which they moved to Royal Lodge in Windsor Great Park in 1932. Even after George VI's accession in 1936 the family preferred the relative cosiness of this home to the castle. However, in May 1940, with the threat of a German invasion a real possibility following the retreat from Dunkirk (the sound of gunfire and explosions could be heard in Windsor), Princesses Elizabeth and Margaret were moved to Windsor Castle for the duration of the war. The castle became a fortress once again, its dungeons pressed into service as air-raid shelters, its paintings and chandeliers removed, the furniture shrouded and glass-fronted cabinets turned to face the walls. Three hundred bombs fell in Windsor Great Park during the war, but mercifully not one of them fell on the castle itself.

Princess Elizabeth and her mother Queen Elizabeth at the Windsor Horse Show, 1935

The King and Queen lived at Buckingham Palace during the week, returning to Windsor Castle on Friday afternoons when the Royal Standard was raised above the Round Tower to denote that the monarch was once more in residence. The Princesses were schooled at the castle, living in the Lancaster Tower, and Princess Elizabeth, to help prepare for her future role, continued to receive lessons in Constitutional History from Henry Marten, then Vice-Provost of Eton College.

There was no central heating, merely small and ineffective electric stoves in the bedrooms and log fires in the sitting rooms. In winter the children's nanny described it as a feat of endurance to travel the icy corridors between the heated rooms. Entertainment was provided by amateur theatricals and pantomimes on the stage Queen Victoria had erected in

Princess Elizabeth and the Welsh Cottage

the Waterloo Room (one of the performances was watched by a young Prince Philip, at home on leave from the navy), outings with the Girl Guides in Windsor Park and parties with the young Guards officers stationed at the castle. Princess Elizabeth was also instructed in carriage driving and in two consecutive years, 1943 (also the first year she rode out with a hunt) and 1944, she won first prize at the Royal Windsor Horse Show with her own pony and trap. On her sixteenth birthday she registered at the Labour Exchange in Windsor and subsequently joined the Auxiliary Territorial Service (ATS), commuting from the castle to her detachment in Camberley every day. The sisters' incarceration in the castle ended in May 1945 when they were taken to Buckingham Palace to join in the celebrations of Victory in Europe Day. After years of blackout, the castle was floodlit to celebrate the end of hostilities.

In 1948 George VI revived the formal Garter installation with a full ceremonial investiture at Windsor – the first time it had been seen since the reign of George III in 1805. It was exactly 600 years since the foundation of the Order in 1348 and it has been an annual event ever since. Apart from the annual round, when the court moved to Windsor Castle for Easter and again for the Ascot races and Garter Day – always the Monday of Royal Ascot Week – the royal family at this time reverted to using Royal Lodge as their country retreat.

The reign of King George VI was regarded as being both a triumph and a stabilizing influence during the troubled years of the Second World War, but The King was left weak and exhausted. After intermittent illness George VI died at Sandringham on 6 February 1952, aged 56. The Sebastopol Bell in the Round Tower at Windsor tolled at one-minute intervals, one toll for each year of The King's life. He was buried at St George's Chapel, as were his father and grandfather before him.

The royal family today

The Queen and Prince Philip have made the castle their weekend retreat – their real home, in effect – and an escape from the interminable bustle of London. From time to time, however, state visits take place at Windsor Castle rather than Buckingham Palace, and a number of investitures are also held there. The Queen has hosted over 100 state visits of monarchs or heads of state, including six French presidents, three German presidents and three US presidents. The 105th state visit of The Queen's reign – of President Higgins of Ireland and his wife Sabina – to Windsor Castle in April 2014 was an historic occasion, the first official state visit of an Irish head of state. It was a return match after her successful visit to Ireland in 2011. The traditional state banquet is always held in St George's Hall and a table 55.5 metres (182 feet) long is used to seat up to 160 guests.

The Queen has left a lasting legacy to the castle. It is not something she would have undertaken had it not been forced upon her, but it is every bit

The Windsor Castle fire, 1992

The Queen visits her home after the 1992 fire

as important to the fabric of the castle as the work of her illustrious predecessors, Edward III, Charles II and George IV. At about 11.30 on the morning of 20 November 1992 in the Private Chapel, picture specialists working on paintings, which had been dismounted during a programme of rewiring, smelled burning. Simultaneously, workmen on the roof of the Waterloo Chamber at the other end of the St George's Hall spotted white smoke pouring from roof vents. The castle, built by so many different monarchs over so many centuries and containing priceless treasures and historic interiors, was on fire. Almost certainly started by a spotlight overheating and setting fire to curtains in the Private Chapel, the fire took hold and spread quickly.

It was to burn for 15 hours and was fought by over 200 firefighters, using more than 30 fire engines from 7 different brigades. It destroyed a total of 115 rooms, including many of the most sumptuous reception rooms in the castle. The extraordinary salvage operation that swung into action as the fire raged, involving the Household Cavalry from nearby Combermere Barracks with their Bedford trucks, fleets of hired removal vans and another army of palace staff and residents, including several members of the royal family, meant that very few of the many thousands of paintings and other priceless fixtures and fittings were lost.

The fire spread widely through the labyrinth of interconnected roof spaces and after battling an increasingly fierce conflagration – the heat at the foot of the Brunswick Tower was later calculated to have reached an astonishing 820°C (1508°F) – the fire brigade commander decided the best course was to hold the fire at a certain line and allow it to burn itself out. But the firefighters' attempts to douse the flames had a major effect later. The thousands of gallons of water used in the attempt to save the building soaked into the ancient, porous fabric of the walls and added to the weight of ceilings, which later collapsed and made the task of restoration and repair much more difficult.

Committees were at once set up chaired by The Duke of Edinburgh and The Prince of Wales to oversee the general restoration of the destroyed interiors and to decide on whom should be the architects and designers of any new work. Debate raged about restoration and reinstatement of the old versus the opportunity for entirely new and contemporary interiors. After the salvage teams from English Heritage had done their work it was discovered that a remarkable number of interiors had survived in a state that could be reasonably restored. Since the furniture originally designed for those interiors had also been saved, the decision was taken to restore, where possible, Wyatville's interiors for George IV. Where the fire had destroyed the fabric beyond repair – the roof of St George's Hall and the Private Chapel, for example – the fabric would be renewed entirely.

It was nevertheless decided that the designs for these two areas should stay within the Gothic craft tradition, so much a part of the castle's history, and the new roof of St George's Hall is an enormous green oak hammer-beam structure – the largest constructed since the Middle Ages. It gives this vast space a much more impressive feel than Wyatville's shallow, oppressive, wood-grained plaster roof of 1828. The Private Chapel – the original seat of the fire – was given a new circulation space. An octagonal two-storey structure, with a delicate array of laminated oak columns rising to form rib vaults (designed by computer technology), now support a central lantern. The effect, described as 'organo-Gothic', is a triumph of modern design. A new Private Chapel was built, with stained glass bearing images of Windsor Castle rising anew from the fire, based on designs drawn up by The Duke of Edinburgh.

Over the years George IV's interiors and the later ones of the 1850s had degraded with each revamp of the curtains, paintwork or upholstery and the original vibrancy of the colours had become muted. With the evidence from watercolours of the original interiors and archaeological work on surviving fragments the decision was taken to recreate as far as possible the original designs. There is no doubt the restored interiors are stunning through the interplay of colour and the extensive use of gilding.

There were other pluses too. The warren of staff bedrooms on the upper floors and the accretions of assorted buildings that had choked Edward III's Kitchen Court had been destroyed. The opportunity was taken to modernize the accommodation and to clear the jumble of buildings in the Kitchen Court, which revealed the fourteenth-century gateways and

The Green Drawing Room at Windsor Castle, which was completely restored after the fire in 1992

stonework of Richard III. A new building was inserted into the space, which allowed the old walls to be seen. In the Great Kitchen, the original timbers of the lantern were uncovered and in doing so the realization dawned that the kitchen was the one that had been built in 1259. In continuous use for nearly 800 years, it is one of the oldest still-working kitchens in the world. The fourteenth-century vaulted undercroft beneath St George's Hall has emerged once more from a warren of subdivisions and gloss paint.

Managed by the officers of the Royal Household with the royal family constantly consulted – after all this is The Queen's 'home' – the whole extraordinarily complicated exercise was completed in five years, within the time allowed and under budget. On the site of the fire in the old Private Chapel the reredos behind the altar was restored and reinstated and now bears an inscription, 'The Fire of 20th November 1992 Began Here', and goes on to record that the work was finished on 20 November 1997, the fiftieth anniversary of the wedding of The Queen and The Duke of Edinburgh. The restored Windsor Castle helped to lay to rest some of the ghosts of five years before when The Queen had spoken of 1992 as being her *annus horribilis*, 'not a year I shall look back on with undiluted pleasure'.

The castle has witnessed a number of poignant family events since the fire. In June 1999 Prince Edward was married to Sophie Rhys-Jones at St George's Chapel. After the ceremony they rode in an open carriage to

The newly married Duke and Duchess Of Cornwall pose for their official wedding photograph with their children and parents. From left to right: Prince Harry, Prince William, Laura and Tom Parker-Bowles. Front: The Queen, Prince Philip and Bruce Shand in the White Drawing Room at Windsor Castle, 2005.

the reception for 550 guests in St George's Hall. Over 200 million viewed the wedding on television.

On 9 February 2002 The Queen's sister, Princess Margaret, died and her funeral was held at Windsor on 15 February, the fiftieth anniversary of the funeral of her father, George VI. After resting overnight in the nave of the chapel and following the service in the choir, attended by 37 members of the royal family (including The Queen Mother, who was determined to be there), Princess Margaret's coffin was taken to the waiting hearse as the Curfew bell tolled and pipers played the lament. While the 400 mourners had tea in St George's Hall the hearse left the castle by the King Henry VIII Gate en route to Slough Crematorium. The princess's ashes were buried with her father in the Royal Vault. Two weeks later, on 30 March 2002, The Queen Mother died at Royal Lodge in Windsor Park, aged 101. Her funeral service was held at Westminster Abbey on 9 April and her coffin taken by road to Windsor and interred with her husband and daughter in the Royal Vault.

On a happier note, on 23 April 2008 Prince William was announced as the 1000th member of the Order of the Garter. He was invested by The Queen as a Royal Knight Companion at Windsor on 16 June. Three years later, in 2011, The Duke of Edinburgh turned 90 and on 14 June a service was held in St George's Chapel followed by a champagne reception at the castle for 750 people.

Today the ancient castle, which has provided the stage for so much of England's history, is not just home to The Queen and The Duke of Edinburgh but also either home or office to some 500 people; and a huge tourist attraction with approximately a million people visiting annually. It is open almost every day, when visitors can admire the state and semi-state apartments and, sometimes, even the historic kitchens.

Above: The Queen and The Duke of Edinburgh at the Royal Windsor Horse Show, 2013

Below: The Queen and The Duke of Edinburgh at the Royal Windsor Horse Show, 1974

The Great Park is a remarkable example of an ancient deer park and driving through it gives some idea of its scale: at 5000 acres (2020 hectares) it is an open space that, at its highest parts, offers views of far distant London.

The Duke of Edinburgh planted an oak avenue in the private Home Park, which consists of 655 acres (265 hectares) and was formerly known as the 'Little Park'. Finding that the royal family had nowhere to sit out close to the castle, he also created a 'sitting-out garden' by having a road along the South Slopes moved and laying out a small garden under the south wall of the East Terrace. He later planted a hornbeam avenue in the Home Park.

The Great Park itself offers welcome respite from the duties of monarch and The Queen rides there regularly in the company of her groom, Terry Pendry, during the kinder months of the year – in a headscarf rather than a hard hat. The Royal Windsor Horse Show is staged in the Home Park directly under the castle ramparts annually in May, when The Queen can be found, usually in headscarf and mac, quietly walking among the other visitors and watching the competitions in the equestrian arenas. The Duke of Edinburgh, stopwatch in hand, will most likely be timing competitors at the water-splash on the carriage-driving course. This informality – and the relaxed attitude of the monarch and her consort – surprises many visitors to the show, but then, as The Duke once told me, 'This is our back garden.'

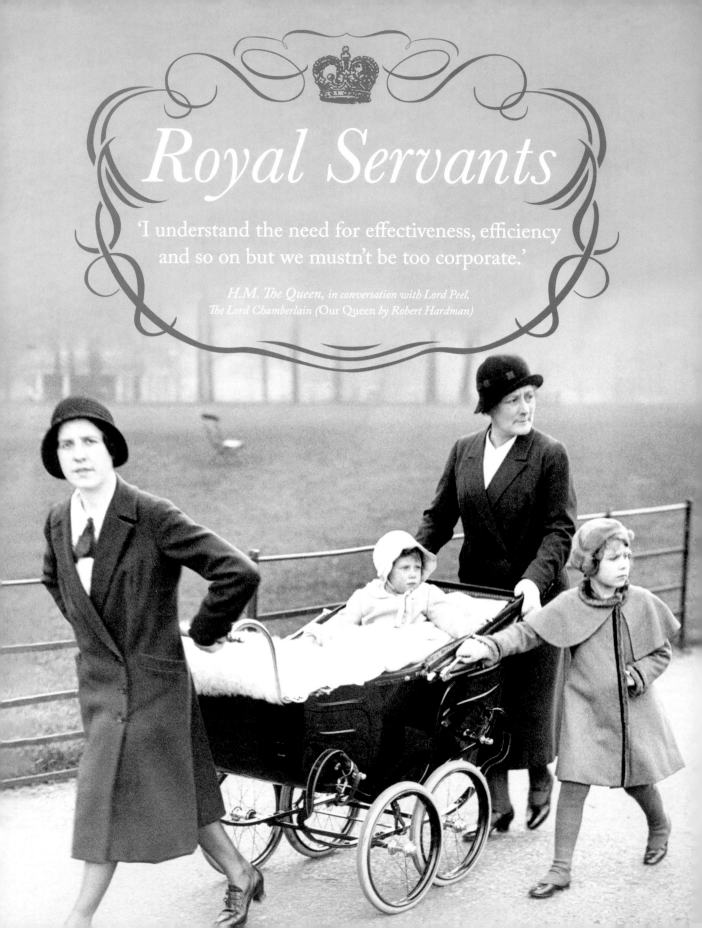

Royal Servants

'I understand the need for effectiveness, efficiency
and so on but we mustn't be too corporate.'

H.M. The Queen, *in conversation with Lord Peel,
The Lord Chamberlain (Our Queen by Robert Hardman)*

Above: The young Princesses Elizabeth and Margaret with Margaret 'Bobo' MacDonald

Opposite page: The young Princesses and their nannies

To day's royal servants (though the term 'staff' is now more usually employed) are a highly efficient and modern body of men and women whose working lives are regulated by contemporary management practices and the most up-to-date communication systems available, but they retain titles with a decidedly archaic ring. Look at any list of royal functionaries and then try to guess what each does. You will quickly drown in a sea of historical obfuscation. Many of the titleholders of the first rank are honorific, or political appointments, or have them by virtue of inheritance or by some historical anomaly, the actual work being carried out by professional 'deputies'. Walter Bagehot, the economist and political commentator who first turned a spotlight on the nature and practices of Parliament and the monarchy in the 1860s, famously wrote, 'Royalty is to be reverenced, and if you begin to poke about it you cannot reverence it ... In its mystery is its life. We must not let daylight in upon its magic.' Royal servants and their historic titles are perhaps part of that mystery too, but with a bit of digging around it is possible to trace them from their emergence in the mists of antiquity.

A good place to start is 1483, when Richard III appointed The Duke of Norfolk to be Earl Marshal with instructions to prepare Westminster Abbey for his coronation, a job The Dukes of Norfolk were to retain over the centuries. Four hundred and seventy years later, in 1953, Bernard Marmaduke Fitzalan-Howard, 16th Duke of Norfolk, took charge of Westminster Abbey to organize the coronation of the present Queen. An historic title it may be, but in the case of the 16th Duke it was blessed by a man with a formidable organizational ability. The schedule devised by The Duke called for The Queen to be crowned at 12.34 p.m. on 2 June. When the crown was placed on Her Majesty's head by the Archbishop of Canterbury the time was noted at 12.33.40, 20 seconds early ... Even as you read this the 18th Duke of Norfolk will have to hand a number of alternative plans for the coronation of the next monarch; it's what he does. As well as being hereditary Earls Marshal, The Dukes of Norfolk are also hereditary Marshals of England, in charge of all heraldry and grants of

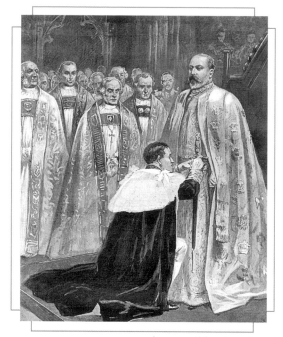

Above: Edward VII with his Lord Chamberlain, the Marquess of Cholmondeley, 1902

Below: Vice Admiral Sir Peter Ashmore, Master of the Household of Queen Elizabeth II 1973-86

arms.

The Earl Marshal was the third of the 'great offices of the realme' listed by an Act of Henry VIII in 1539, which included, in order of precedence, 'the great chamberleyn first, the constable next, the marciall third, the lorde admyrall the fourth, the grand maister or lorde stewarde the fiveth, and the Kinges chamberleyn the sixt'. In medieval times, when the business of ruling the country was more precarious, the monarch would surround him- or herself with supporters from the more powerful families who would take charge of the organization of the household. The Great Officers of the Household – as opposed to the Officers of State – in due course were reduced to three.

The most important is the Lord Chamberlain who is always a Privy Councillor as well as being a peer and is now the part-time chairman of the executive committee that runs the Royal Household. In the past, his department dealt with the ceremonial and social life of the court, organizing royal ceremonies and, until 1968, administering the licensing of theatres and theatrical performances countrywide, ensuring they were 'fitting for the preservation of good manners, decorum or of the public peace'.

The Lord Steward's department dealt by contrast with domestic and culinary matters (often described as 'below stairs') – provisioning, feeding, cleaning and security – and was the 'engine room' of the household. The Lord Steward, together

Sir Henry Guildford, Master of the Household for Henry VIII

with the Treasurer, the Comptroller, the Master and the Cofferer of the Household, with their clerks, constituted the 'Board of the Green Cloth', a committee that regulated the workaday parts of the Royal Household. They took their name from a table or 'board' covered with a green cloth, around which their predecessors had met since it was constituted in the reign of King Edward IV in the fifteenth century. The Board of the Green Cloth made the contracts with suppliers and paid their bills. Provisioning accounts were calculated by using piles of tokens, which were pushed backwards and forwards across the table, representing goods in and out. The board was also responsible for maintaining discipline with judicial responsibility for all offences committed in, or within a prescribed distance from, the court, wherever it might be. Typically it might concern itself with disobedient or dishonest servants or pickpockets and prostitutes who haunted the palace courtyards.

Punishments could be harsh for servants caught stealing from the royal palaces. In 1731, a servant named as Sarah Matts was imprisoned for 'feloniously stealing a quilt' from a palace guard room. A servant of long standing, Catherine Pollard, who had been for 30 years in the silver scullery at Kensington Palace, was found guilty at the Old Bailey and condemned to death for stealing four silver plates and of selling them on to a dealer. In her defence she protested, 'I believe there was a spell set upon me, or else I was bewitch'd.'

The last of the reduced Great Officers of the Household is the Master of the Horse, one of the 'officers of the Household Without' and his remit originally encompassed being in charge of the royal stables and for arranging for horses in time of war as well as for transport for the sovereign and the Royal Household (see 'The Royal Mews' chapter). He was the personal body servant of the monarch once he or she was outside the palace walls. All three titles now, largely, have ceremonial roles only and appear in a splendid uniform on state occasions, the Master of the Horse – currently Lord Vestey – shadowing the monarch, as of old.

So much for the first rank of royal servants. It is a much more difficult business to throw light on the lives of individuals lower down the scale. But there is one tantalizing glimpse of the actual faces of past royal servants who still look down on us today. In the 1720s William Kent

Above: William Kent's painting of servants at Kensington Palace peering over The King's Grand Staircase

Below and right: Staff of the Royal Mews at Buckingham Palace

ROYAL COACHMAN

painted the portraits of 45 of them (including himself) looking over a painted balustrade on The King's Grand Staircase at Kensington Palace. They included some of the Yeomen of the Guard, the comedian Ulric Jorry, a Polish dwarf who entertained the court, The King's two Turkish grooms of the chamber, and a 'Wild Youth' who was found in the forests of Hanover and brought over as a curiosity in 1726.

Another rare glimpse comes from Gabriel Tschumi, who was appointed in 1898 at the age of 16 as an apprentice in the royal kitchens and worked for the royal family for over 40 years. He left a rare first-hand account of his time in royal service. On his first day he was surprised to find 'only thirty or forty' servants at dinner in the servants' hall at Buckingham Palace. When he was despatched to Windsor Castle the next day, where Queen Victoria was in residence, he felt he had 'never seen such a vast collection of people ... it took me a long time to discover what the duties of many of these servants were, and in some cases I did not ever find out'. At that time there was 'an indoor staff of more than three hundred, and a permanent kitchen staff of forty-five'. He felt that with such a number supervision was lax and 'a good deal of laziness resulted' – except in the kitchens which were run by the Royal Chef, M. Ménager, a Frenchman who was 'a stickler for perfection'. He never did find out the duties of many of the staff as there was a complete reorganization of the Royal Household after the death of the old Queen in January 1901.

If servants had become somewhat towards the end of that very long reign, at the beginning things were a great deal worse. When Victoria

ROYAL FOOTMAN.

ROYAL POSTILLION

inherited the throne in 1837 the way in which the household went about its business was decidedly shambolic. Servants were inexplicably absent when required and seemed to answer to no one. A typical example was the obstacle course encountered by those invited to Windsor Castle. As often as not there would be no servant to greet them, to take their coat and luggage or to direct them to their quarters. There were many instances of guests wandering the maze-like corridors of the castle trying doors at random in order to find someone to guide them. The premier of France on one such expedition opened a door to find, much to his consternation, The Queen having her hair brushed by a maid.

Victoria's uncle Leopold, King of the Belgians, sent help to Victoria in the form of his trusted adviser and sometime physician, Baron Stockmar. A man with a rigorous, logical intellect he advised Victoria, and in due course Prince Albert (whom he had accompanied on his Grand Tour of Italy), on a range of issues, perhaps most importantly through his memorandum on the reform of the Royal Household, which he deemed 'unpractical and confused resulting in disorder and discomfort'. His enquiries quickly uncovered the fact that 'there is between departments no proper system of cooperation and concurrence, insuring unity of purpose and action. The work is parcelled out in a ridiculous manner among them ... so as to impede the satisfactory progress of business'. His 'Observations on the present state of the Royal Household' was just the ammunition Prince Albert required and he immediately undertook the realization of the majority of Stockmar's proposed reforms. So ingrained was the way things were done, or not done, among the servants of the household that it took him many years to effect the necessary reforms.

Stockmar had realized that at the heart of the servant problem lay the fact that although the Royal Household nominally divided into three great departments under the Lord Steward, the Lord Chamberlain and the Master of the Horse, these three luminaries, the highest court officials, were appointed for their political loyalty and not for their administrative gifts. What's more they changed with every new government, so none of the main officers of the household remained permanently at court. Neither did they have a permanent deputy in post to whom they could delegate any responsibility in their absence. As a result there were no links to bind the departments efficiently together, and the respective limits of what they

Christmas preparations in the kitchen at Windsor Castle, 1857

did and did not do were wholly arbitrary, and in many roles unspecified: 'It is quite undecided what parts of the palace are under the charge of the Lord Chamberlain and which under the Lord Steward.' Stockmar discovered more than two-thirds of all servants 'are left without a master in the house. They can come and go as they choose, commit any excess or irregularity', with no one to 'observe, correct or to reprimand them'. With a degree of indignation he went on, 'if smoking, drinking, and other irregularities occur in the dormitories, where footmen, etc., sleep ten and twelve to each room, no one can help it'.

Some of his more absurd discoveries of departmental inefficiencies are often quoted: 'The writer of this paper, sent to complain by Her Majesty

to Sir Frederick Watson, the Master of the Household, that the dining-room was always cold, was answered: "You see, properly speaking, it is not our fault, for the Lord Steward lays the fire only, the Lord Chamberlain lights it'"; and, 'the Lord Chamberlain provides all the lamps, and the Lord Steward must clean, trim, and light them'. The inside cleaning of windows was part of the Lord Chamberlain's departmental responsibilities but anything outside was the responsibility of the Department of Woods and Forests, so an understanding between the two was required in order for any light to be let into the palace – the London air was laden with sooty particulates from coal fires which settled quickly on the outside of buildings.

Things came to a head when one night a boy was discovered asleep under a sofa in a room next to The Queen's bedroom. He had simply walked in, as had the French premier, and wandered around undetected. The subsequent enquiry could find no department had direct responsibility for security. Baron Stockmar laboured to make the point:

'there was no person in the Palace on whom such responsibility could rightly be fixed; for it certainly did not fall on the Lord Chamberlain, who was in Staffordshire, and in whose department porters are not; nor on the Lord Steward, who was in town, and who has nothing to do with the disposition of the pages and other parties nearest the royal person; nor finally on the Master of the Household ... On whom does it then fall? Entirely on the absence of system, which leaves the royal palace without any responsible authority.'

Extravagance, a certain mayhem and periodic retrenchment were nothing new in the Royal Household. Go back almost 250 years to the Restoration in 1660 and you will find that the years of asceticism that had characterized the drab-suited Commonwealth were swept away in an orgy of excess by Charles II who was determined to bring back the gaiety and style of his father's court. A massive number of new appointments were made, 1200 by October 1660, of which 800 were in the Lord Chamberlain's department and nearly 300 in that of the Lord Steward. Two years later the complement had reached over 1350. The diarist John Evelyn commented that Charles II, 'brought in a politer way of living, which passed to Luxurie and intolerable expense'. Amongst the list of appointments is a Royal Comb-Maker for Life and after the years of misrule a Master of the Revels makes his reappearance. A Printer for The Oriental Languages, a Flourisher and Embellisher, a Master of the Art of Defence, a Rat-Killer and a Mole-Taker, a Master for each of Harriers, Hawks, Staghounds and Buckhounds, a Marker of the Swans, three Distillers of Strong Water, a Periwig Maker, a Sempstress to the Person and a Strewer of Herbs were amongst the long list of those found essential to the household. The Strewer of Herbs was named as one Mary Dowle and her vital role was to walk before The King when in procession and scatter herbs, specifically known (or assumed) to counter the plague, in his path. Mary Dowle was still strewing herbs when William and Mary came to the throne.

The Sempstress to the Person, Dorothy Chiffinch, was charged with

CHARLES II,
'BROUGHT IN A
POLITER WAY OF
LIVING, WHICH
PASSED TO LUXURIE
AND INTOLERABLE
EXPENSE'

making sure The King was well stocked with linen and had plenty of shirts into which to change to counter the constant smell of ordinary life in the mid-seventeenth century. Here is the list she was handed: '108 Shyrts, 54 half-Shyrts, 12 dozen of Pocket Hankerchers, 18 Night-Caps, 18 Pillow cases, 12 Payres of Great Sheets, 3 Payres of Tamise Sheets, 18 Payres of Lace Stockings, 3 Trunks to carry it', and she was also required to give the whole lot a first wash.

Not only did Charles II appoint such a vast array of servants and officers, he also granted them free 'diet' and very shortly the principal officers had begun to keep 'open table' for family and friends at the expense of the Crown, and other abuses were rife. The strain on the royal finances of this laissez-faire system could not last and free food for all, apart from The King and Queen and the immediate royal family, was rescinded two years later. The 90 cooks no longer required were sacked.

Continuing fluctuations in household costs meant the Treasury stepped in and demanded a degree of control over budgets and expenditure. After years of part measures, in 1680 swingeing cuts were implemented. All salaries were reduced by at least a quarter and most by two-thirds; the budget for the Lord Steward's department was sliced nearly in half. By the time James II came to the throne in 1685, action was once again needed and the staff totals were cut by almost a half with 'useless offices' being abolished and more productivity demanded from his remaining servants.

There were mitigating forces that made it difficult sensibly to reduce the cost of maintaining the court. Alongside a need for economy was the requirement to keep the trappings of monarchy, the splendour of the court itself and the possibilities for patronage at a suitable level. In 1690 the new incumbents to the throne, William III and Mary II, despite their perceived frugality, needed urgently to establish their legitimacy by maintaining the royal state. They raised the staffing levels of the Royal Household once more, at the same time purging a large number of James II's servants and officers because of their Catholicism or association with the old regime. This resulted in an influx of inexperienced servants and administrators, which in turn caused inefficiency, waste and, in due course, corruption. The state of royal finances was further exacerbated by the inadequate settlement granted the Crown by Parliament and the costs of prosecuting a war. Before long the household found itself unpaid. By 1691 servants below stairs were nine months in arrears and purveyors to the Crown were

The young Princesses out for a drive with their nanny, 'Bobo' MacDonald

threatening to cut off supplies. Four years later servants were 16 months in arrears of pay and in 'a starving and wretched condition'. By the time of his death William III owed his servants and suppliers a full year's wages and payments.

At the beginning of the eighteenth century Queen Anne encountered the same economic stringency with yearly cost overruns unsupported by parliamentary grants. As a result her household numbers were cut back, mostly in the departments of the Lord Chamberlain and the Master of the Horse. In the latter part of her reign, as the Civil List declined once again, servants and suppliers suffered. The result of this chronic underpayment was that most servants resorted to corruption of one kind or another simply to get by.

With the coming of the Georges, Parliament agreed to guarantee The King's income for the first time. But with household costs rising inexorably the Treasury stepped in once more and in 1718 demanded tighter controls on spending. To no avail; departmental debts were increasing by the end of the reign of George I in 1727. Sir Robert Walpole engineered a generous Civil List payment for King George II but parliamentary reluctance to inquire into what were considered The King's private affairs meant that financial scrutiny of household spending was not as stringent as it might have been and midway through the reign of George III the debts had risen once more.

In 1782 a Bill was enacted to allow the debt to be discharged while imposing swingeing cuts and abolishing a large number of offices and departments. The names of those made redundant – some of them delightfully arcane – give an insight into the wide-ranging nature of eighteenth-century life at court. Letters of dismissal were sent out to, amongst those in a very long list, the Deputy Examiner of Plays, the Vocal Performer in Extraordinary, the Furner to the Pastry and the Turncock and Keeper of the Buckets.

The balancing of the royal books swung perilously into the red once more over the following reigns, and is to this day still an issue. But here is Gabriel Tschumi again, as he gives us a vivid picture of servant life

The young Princesses with their nanny 'Crawfie'

under Queen Victoria towards the end of the nineteenth century as a kitchen apprentice on £15 (approx. £1500 today) a year. We left him commenting on the lazy ways of his fellow servants but he exempts the royal kitchens, 'the centre round which the whole life of the Royal Household revolved'. In the kitchens were prepared 'every day the meals for all the lower servants, as well as the breakfasts and ten- or twelve-course luncheons and dinners served to the Queen, the Royal Family, their guests, and the lords and ladies-in-waiting who were in residence'. Besides the Royal Chef, 18 master cooks sported immaculate white uniforms with the royal cipher and chef's toques and, of these cooks, eight had their own tables preparing 'the most elaborate and difficult dishes on the day's menu'. Gabriel, with admirable ambition, worked in the kitchens of the big London hotels during his time off and judged the royal kitchens 'vastly superior in every way'.

Each senior member of Queen Victoria's kitchen staff had his own set of utensils, which no one else used, and which were kept sharp and in gleaming order by the kitchen-maids. When the Royal Household moved from house to house nothing was lost or mislaid, and everything functioned just as smoothly whichever the kitchen. The kitchens had 'the discipline of a barrack room'. Every copper pan was numbered and once finished with immediately washed and burnished and hung in its place. No one sat down – as a result a high proportion of long-serving staff developed fallen arches from standing on stone floors all day and spent their hour off resting in their rooms. There was no talking, except for the giving of orders, because 'the standard of cuisine insisted on by M. Ménager demanded intense concentration'. Such was the standard of perfection sought by him that the master cooks and chefs 'brought their dishes to him at various states of preparation to be passed before they could go on to the next stage'. Barons of beef and scores of chickens were roasted in front of open coal ranges. All the bread was baked daily by the bakers as were buns, rolls and cakes. Whenever Kaiser Wilhelm I came to stay, his favourite raised pie consisting of 'a turkey stuffed with a chicken, inside the chicken a pheasant, and inside the pheasant a woodcock' was made for him.

Tschumi paints a delightful portrait of the Royal Chef – on £400 (approx. £40,000 today) a year plus a living-out allowance of another

Kitchen staff at Windsor Castle, 1887

£100 (approx. £10,000 today) – with his bushy moustache, coming to Buckingham Palace each day by hansom cab wearing an immaculate frock-coat and top hat. A quote from Tschumi sums up the royal cooks' devotion to their task:

> *'A chef is an artist. And like an artist he strives constantly for perfection. But he has as difficult a task as any man who creates beauty from wood or stone, and there are no memorials to his art. His triumph is a momentary one, between the serving of a dish and the minute when the last few mouthfuls are taken. To*

achieve that short triumph he must expend all his skill and experience.'

Gabriel Tschumi worked through the reigns of Edward VII and George V to be pensioned off when economy cuts were once again made to the Royal Household. He was then appointed Royal Chef to Queen Mary at Marlborough House from 1943 until he retired in 1952.

By the end of Queen Victoria's reign there were just under 600 domestic servants working at Buckingham Palace; today it is half that. Of

Above: Princess Elizabeth (centre) walks her dog with nanny Marion 'Crawfie' Crawford (left)

Below: Princesses Elizabeth and Margaret with 'Crawfie'

Opposite page: The Queen creates Angela Kelly a Lieutenant of the Royal Victorian Order (LVO)

that number a very few have become known to the public. Margaret MacDonald, always known as 'Bobo' was one. She served Queen Elizabeth II for 67 years, initially as a nursery maid and latterly as her dresser. She died in 1993 aged 89 in her suite at Buckingham Palace and The Queen came down from Balmoral for her funeral service at the Chapel Royal, St James's Palace.

The governess to The Queen and Princess Margaret, Marion 'Crawfie' Crawford, served the royal family devotedly for over 20 years, delaying her own wedding for a year when, on the brink of Princess Elizabeth's marriage to Lieutenant Philip Mountbatten, The Queen said to her, 'Does this mean you are going to leave us? You must see Crawfie, that it would not be at all convenient just now. A change at this stage for Margaret is not at all desirable.' In retirement Crawfie wrote a series of uncritical articles about her life with the young Princesses, later collected together as a book. While the revelations could in no way be ranked as scurrilous, the action was regarded by the royal family as a complete breach of trust. It is not really surprising. When the majority of one's life is spent in full view of the media, the ability of close associates to keep confidences is especially valued. Long-term stalwarts of the Royal Household are most revered for their ability to remain low key and to avoid the limelight – people like The Queen's long-serving and trusted page Paul Whybrew ('Big Paul') who was seen alongside Her Majesty, and her corgis, in the filmed sequence for the 2012 London Olympic Games.

From the private secretaries to the press secretaries, the accountants to the cleaners, the pages to the footmen and the chamber maids, how do such members of staff (the term servants is avoided nowadays) come to be appointed? Most often they answer advertisements in the press and many of them remain in post for a long time. Mark Flanagan, The Queen's chef, has undertaken that role since 2002 and many other members of staff have been with her for much longer. While the rates of pay may be less than extravagant, the loyalty of staff, the provision of central London accommodation and a huge pride in working for a monarch whom they respect are contributory factors.

Perhaps The Queen's closest confidante is Angela Kelly, who now holds the compendious title 'Personal Assistant, Adviser and Curator to Her Majesty The Queen (Jewellery, Insignias and Wardrobe)', the first to hold such a title. Angela Kelly's dress design and fashion sense has transformed

The Queen's 'look' in her later years and her affection for The Queen is clearly evident. Her remark, 'we have ... a lot of fun together', has caused much comment. She says of her boss: 'I love The Queen and everything about her, I adore her – but then so does everyone else.' It's a fact that's true of generations of servants, of whatever rank, over her long reign.

Buckingham Palace

'Living above the shop.'

HRH The Duke of Edinburgh

Today if you stand looking through the railings at Buckingham Palace you will see the imposing but slightly bland Portland stone facade of the east-wing extension, 108 metres (354 feet) in length. The guardsmen, resplendent in their red tunics and shining boots, topped off with black bearskins, are in their black-and-gold sentry boxes, ramrod straight.

Three arches pierce the facade; those to left and right give access to the palace and the larger central arch takes carriages and cars through to the inner courtyard. The right-hand arch is used for the day-to-day business of the palace though most of the 800-odd domestic staff who work there use an entrance on the south side (having first shown their passes to the policemen at the gate).

At first-floor level in the central block is the famous balcony, at which, since 1851, so much emotion has been directed in times of national or royal celebration by the seething masses swirling around where you now stand. Is the Royal Standard flying from the flagstaff above the central block? If so, Her Majesty The Queen is in residence, which she is every weekday except for certain fixed times of year when she is at Windsor Castle, Balmoral on Royal Deeside, Sandringham in Norfolk or Holyroodhouse in Edinburgh. At these times, and at weekends, the Union Flag will be hoisted in place of the Royal Standard.

Buckingham Palace is The Queen's office where 'the firm' that is the monarchy conducts its business and where she carries out the official and ceremonial duties required of her as head of state. It is the 'youngest'

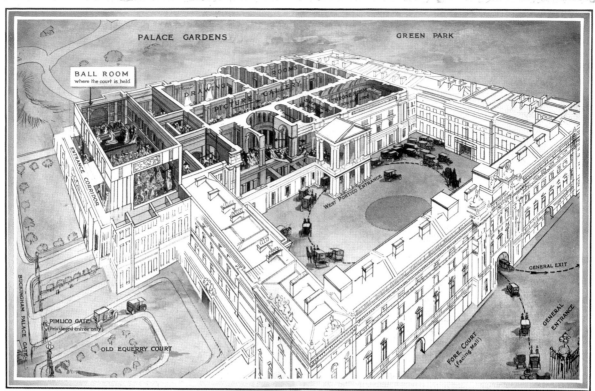

PALACE GARDENS GREEN PARK

BALL ROOM
where the court is held

A DIAGRAMMATIC VIEW SHOWING THE PROGRESS OF THE DÉBUTANTE FROM THE MOMENT SHE ENTERS BUCKINGHAM PALACE TO THE TIME SHE LEAVES

A map showing the progress of a debutante through Buckingham Palace, 1912

of the royal palaces, having been transformed from a country house by George IV in the 1820s. He never got to live there, dying before its completion. His brother William IV chose not live there, preferring the comparative seclusion of Windsor Castle. So it was George and William's niece, Victoria, who really made it the formal seat of monarchy and the court, and her husband Prince Albert who had much to do with its mid-nineteenth-century aggrandizement.

Behind the building directly in front of today's visitor lies the courtyard of an older building, which in turn, at its centre, envelops the old eighteenth-century house transformed by George IV with the help of the architect John Nash. The wine vaults below it date from 1760. The whole structure now has a floor area of nearly 80,000 square metres (860,000 square feet), and is pierced by over 1500 doors and nearly 800 windows (each one cleaned every 6 weeks). Seven hundred and seventy-five rooms jostle for space, some huge like the 19 state rooms where the various events requiring pomp and ceremony take place (the biggest, the ballroom, is 36.6 metres [120 feet] long), and others very modest, like many of the 188 staff bedrooms. There are 52 bedrooms allocated to the royal family and their personal and official guests, and 78 bathrooms service the bedrooms. Ninety-two offices complete the room count, used to administer the personal and very complex official life this family leads.

Behind the inner courtyard, furthest from where the onlooker stands, outside the palace railings, is the garden front, a handsome range of buildings in yellow-coloured stonework, which faces a large expanse of lawn – an excellent space to contain the 8000 guests who attend each of the three annual garden parties, gazing over a large lake and a mix of woodland and herbaceous planting, the whole garden stretching to nearly 40 acres of prime London real estate. But it was not always like this. To find out how it grew into such a recognizable national icon we need to go back 400 years ...

Origins of the palace

It is the late 1620s, and beside a dusty road at old Eye Cross, a sluggish river runs; well, more of a stream than a river to be accurate. The road is uneven, cut with iron wheels of carts and carriages in times of rain. No one could fail to notice the smell, the pungent, gut-heaving stink, a mixture of dead matter and human excrement, intensified by the heat. The Tyburn River is an open sewer. Smells are a fact of daily life, with very few people bathing regularly, and most not at all. The rich wear perfume to mask the constant smell and change their clothes frequently. The poor just stink.

To the right, a little bridge takes the road over the Tyburn and then curves north towards Chelsea, following the east bank of the river. Passers-by are a little nervous – until recently the swampy area behind them featured crocodiles introduced by the late King, James I, together with camels and an elephant. He had landscaped the park, making elegant walks, surfaced with crushed seashells, and he had also created a mulberry garden in 1608. The whole area had been purchased 200 years before from Eton College by Henry VIII, who then turned Wolsey's grand York House into yet another of his palaces, to be renamed Whitehall. The land here was his hunting park attached to the palace.

Almost upon the road and bounded by the smelly river to its east is a newly built house, facing due south, a bit rambling, of modest size but clearly with pretensions. The new cracks in the plaster infills between the studwork beams show signs of haste in building. Surprisingly, this unassuming house in this stench-filled area stands on the site of the future Buckingham Palace, which will become one of the most famous buildings in the world.

The house was built by a William Blake on wasteland beside the road for his son, also called William, and his new bride. Unlike the present-day palace, it faced south as opposed to east. Blake House went up very quickly because the Blakes were, in effect, squatting on the site. The freehold of the land belonged originally to the Crown and a reversionary lease was granted on it by Elizabeth I, due to expire in 1675. The land had passed by dubious practices through various unscrupulous hands until 1623 when Charles I's Lord Treasurer, Lord Cranfield, used nominees to disguise his purchase of the lease and also the freehold of nearby Ebury Manor. The purchase excluded James I's mulberry garden, which extended to some four acres. Cranfield was impeached for corruption the next year and his estates were required to stand surety for the fine imposed on him.

In 1626 the lawyer, moneylender and rich skinflint Hugh Audley (known as 'The Great Audley' because of his wealth) bought the lease and the freehold of Ebury cheaply from the distressed Cranfield and attempted to oust the Blakes, who refused to quit. Somehow old Sir William Blake, another fraudulent character in a litany of unscrupulous men connected with this site, had managed to acquire a deed to supplement whatever squatter's title had accumulated. Audley contested this for the next 20 years but meanwhile the Blakes, father and son, had died, and Blake House had been sold in 1633 to Lord Goring, later 1st Earl of Norwich, another avaricious and unscrupulous courtier. The early years of what we know as 'Buckingham Palace' were far from uneventful.

Goring enlarged Blake House, by all accounts adding to it rather than demolishing the original, creating a desirable gentleman's residence renamed Goring House. He negotiated with Audley to buy a further 20 acres of land around his new house, which are now part of the palace gardens. From these acres he evicted a number of smallholders, planted an apple orchard and enclosed the whole area with what became known as 'Goring great garden wall'.

Goring approached Charles I to buy out the Crown freehold of the mulberry garden, the only remaining Crown lease. This he agreed in 1640, but before the required legal document could be executed Charles I had fled London. By this date Lord Goring had accumulated nearly all of what was to be the future site of Buckingham Palace, apart from mulberry garden to the rear and the area circumscribed by the Tyburn and the Chelsea Road to the immediate front. Goring was reduced to ruin when all the sinecures granted by The King were annulled by the Long Parliament of November 1640. Consequently he defaulted on the payments still owing to Audley and therefore Audley tenanted Goring's great garden.

In March 1643 Parliament ordered a defensive ring known as the 'Lines of Communication' to be thrown up in an 18 km (11 mile) arc around London to prevent it being retaken by Royalist forces. The lines featured intermittent 'forts', probably earthen ramparts palisaded with timber stakes intended to hold cannon. One such fort, labelled 'A Court of Guard at Chelsea Turnpike' in the John Rocque plan of 1738, was erected in the grounds of Goring House. A later survey required that this should be strengthened: 'at the corner of Lord Goring's brick wall next the fields a redoubt and battery where the (guard post) now is; at the lower end of Lord Goring's wall, the brete work to be made forwarder'.

While Goring was abroad on royal business in November 1644, Parliament seized the empty Goring House, at first using it as a barracks for Parliamentary troops, then as a residence for the French Ambassador and finally for the Speaker of the Commons, William Lenthall. On his return, Goring failed to wrest the house back from Parliament and, after leading a Royalist revolt, was eventually captured and executed, his death sentence having been commuted on the casting vote of Speaker Lenthall ... the tenant of Goring House.

In 1650 Speaker Lenthall's son vacated Goring House, which was once more used by the Parliamentary Army as a barracks, eventually leaving after seven years of occupation. The ramparts were demolished – but not all traces vanished. In the 1670s the garden is described as 'having therein a mount set with trees', the remains of the old Great Goring Fort. A plan of 1675 shows this feature just beyond the garden terrace, which would place it in the back garden of Buckingham Palace today. In 2006 a survey by Channel 4's *Time Team* with Oxford Archaeology using a gradiometer survey found anomalies west of the palace 'that may be associated with the Civil War defences and the Goring Great Garden'.

In 1653, the Great Audley, after years of patience as befits a master property speculator, finally bought Goring House and repossessed the land he had sold to Goring but for which he had never been paid. With all tenants finally removed he set about restoring the dilapidated house so 'meanly and improvidently built' and 'in so great decaye that £1500 [approx. £210,000 today] would not putt itt in repayre'. By the Restoration of the monarchy in 1660, repairs were complete and Audley began to let out the house as a venue for weddings and parties of all sorts. Pepys records in his diary attending a wedding there that year. By 1662 Audley was dead.

So much for the house. But what of the mulberry garden that lay immediately behind it? During the Commonwealth it had been sold, along with so much Crown property, to a private individual to aid the state coffers. In the 1650s it devolved on a Mr Chipp who opened it as a 'place of entertainment' where John Evelyn, the diarist, records in 1654 it was a place 'for persons of the best quality to be exceedingly cheated at'. In 1660 the lease reverted to the Crown and Mr Chipp was confirmed as lessor. In 1668 Pepys described the garden as 'a wilderness, somewhat pretty but rude' – inferring that by night it was a haunt of prostitutes. So successful was this pleasure garden that Mr Chipp leased further land from what had been Goring's Great Garden.

Audley's nephew inherited Goring House, which he leased to Sir Henry Bennet, a leading minister and a friend of King Charles II. In 1665 the indefatigable Evelyn went to visit and records: 'went to Goring House now Mr Secretary Bennet's, ill-built but capable of being made a pretty villa'. Bennet, having obtained the title Lord Arlington, married in 1666 and thereafter seems to have kept a splendid house Pepys described as 'a very fine house and finely furnished'. Alas, all was to perish in a fire in 1675, which entirely destroyed the house and all its rich contents.

Outside the house, work was going on to transform St James's Park, now fast becoming a playground for the new court. A canal was dug to help drain the swampy land in 1660 (the precursor of the present informal lake), and The Mall was constructed not long afterwards. It was a good time to purchase, as fashionable London began to surround the site of old Goring House. Arlington duly bought the freehold in 1677 and rebuilt the house with some speed, with steeply pitched roofs and a central cupola as was then the fashion. He turned 'Arlington House' 90 degrees from the old, and it now looked east over St James's Park, as Buckingham Palace does today. It had a long gallery which overlooked the park with nine tall sash 'picture' windows for strollers to enjoy the view. He was also granted a 99-year lease on the old mulberry garden site by The King, so at last the house and garden were united, with consequences for the future. In 1682 Arlington diverted the Westminster-Knightsbridge Road further away

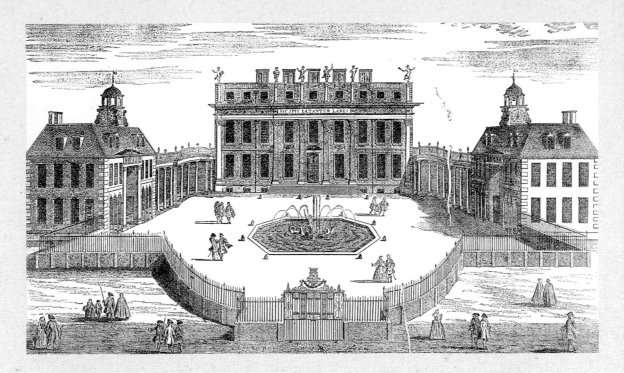

Buckingham House in 1705

from what were now his front windows and enclosed the old verge and the wasteground beside it to form his forecourt – an illegal act for which he was never challenged. Arlington died in 1685.

Buckingham's house

John Sheffield, who would become The Duke of Buckingham in 1703, bought Arlington House from Lord Arlington's grandson in 1702. Buckingham was a remarkable, multi-talented man, who cleverly married three times, each time to moneyed women. He was also a notorious womanizer, despite being described as short, sour, lofty and shallow. In 1704 he married his third wife, Lady Catherine Darnley, the daughter of James II by Catherine Sedley.

Prior to this last advantageous marriage, he quickly began laying out the formal gardens, which would form the setting for his new house. The new ground plan determined that, for the first time, a house on this plot would be built over the old mulberry garden site, for which he did not own the freehold. The freehold and the leasehold were to become inextricably mixed, with disastrous consequences for the future with the Crown lease due to revert some 50 years hence.

Buckingham made a second grand decision. The portly Queen Anne, always putty in his hands, informally agreed to let him alter his front boundary to encompass a portion of St James's Park. He leveraged this agreement shamelessly, demolishing a royal lodge to the park and the boundary wall, pushing his forecourt into the park in a great semi-circle. The roadway was shifted away from his original boundary by some 20 metres (70 feet) or more. The new, illegal, forecourt was enclosed with baroque railings by the master smith Jean Tijou and a wildly extravagant ornamental central gate was surmounted by the ducal coronet and the Buckinghamshire coat of arms (Sheffield had been created Duke of Buckinghamshire to distinguish the title from earlier Dukes of Buckingham but this was widely ignored, not least by him). It was recorded 'the Queen notes that the Duke of Buckingham hath gone further into the park than had leave ... to do'. But she did nothing about it.

The Duke and his wife, a descendant of royalty, held court in their new Buckingham House, completed in 1708, and it was described as 'a new palace come to town'. The Duke died in 1720 but his wife, dubbed 'Princess Buckingham' by Horace Walpole, who described her as 'more mad with pride than any mercer's wife in Bedlam', kept a stifling, regal court at Buckingham House for the next 20 years. On the yearly anniversary of the execution of Charles I the whole house went into deep mourning and there she sat in a chair of state to receive equally mad Jacobites who felt it their duty to make obeisance to someone supposedly purified by Stuart blood. She made her ladies in attendance vow that on her deathbed they were to stand in her presence until after she was dead, even though she might be insensible. She duly died in 1743 and her ladies at last sat down.

The legitimate son of the Buckinghams had died of consumption in Rome in 1735 and his half-brother, Edmund, inherited Buckingham House. Made a baronet by George II and adopting his father's name, he became Sir Charles Sheffield (Samantha, Prime Minister David Cameron's wife, is the daughter of the 8th Baronet). Moving into Buckingham House about 1745 and knowing that the Crown lease on the old mulberry garden site, now firmly buried under the new house, was due to revert in less than 30 years' time, he opened negotiations with the Crown to purchase the freehold or extend the lease. The Surveyor General duly did his measurements and marked on a plan of the house where the old garden had been. It clearly showed that if no agreement was reached it made the whole property untenable. And no agreement was forthcoming.

Knowing he was over a barrel, in 1761 Sheffield opened negotiations for sselling the whole site and a sale was agreed for a knock-down sum of £28,000

George III and Queen Charlotte

(approx. £3.8 million today).

The Queen's House

George III bought Buckingham House for his wife, Queen Charlotte, settling it on her for life and by Act of Parliament changing its name to The Queen's House. George III and his wife Charlotte lived in 'The Queen's House', and all but the eldest of their 15 children were born there in the 20 years from 1763 to 1783.

The house they bought, as George III told a contemporary, 'not meant for a Palace, but a retreat', was a modest affair. The architect Buckingham had hired at the beginning of the eighteenth century is likely to have been William Talman with the actual construction under the control of William Winde. Talman was a pupil of Sir Christopher Wren, with whom he had worked on the rebuilding of Hampton Court, and was Comptroller of the Royal Works under William III. He worked on many of the grand country houses of the late seventeenth and very early eighteenth centuries, the most famous of which is Chatsworth House.

Buckingham's house was a simple, square-profiled, brick-built block with four giant pilasters framing the entrance door and with one at each end of the facade. These rose through the attic storey to culminate in six figures that broke the skyline. On either side, wings with hipped roofs culminating in centrally placed lanterns were joined to the main house by short, curved and columned arcades.

In 1762 George III commissioned his favourite architect, Sir William Chambers, fresh from designing the magnificent baroque state coach (still to be seen at the Royal Mews at Buckingham Palace), to undertake the 'necessary works and repairs' to turn Buckingham's and Talman's house into an up-to-date mansion fit for the monarch. Chambers had been appointed 'architectural tutor' to the 19-year-old George when Prince of Wales; Chambers and George II were friends, as well as architect and

George IV riding through Hyde Park, 1831

client, and had a close working relationship. Chambers was one of the towering figures of eighteenth-century architecture and from 1766, with Robert Adam, he was Architect to The King and then, in 1769–82, Comptroller of The King's Works. Widely travelled and experienced, he had published his influential *Treatise on Civil Architecture* in 1759, and following his work on The Queen's House, he would design Somerset House, his most famous building.

At The Queen's House over the next few years, Chambers simplified the house in a more austere neo-classical style to suit the unpretentious tastes of his patron. He toppled the statuary, refaced the house with smooth, new brick, rebuilt the north and south wings, added four libraries (George was an obsessive collector of books, maps, medals and coins) and a riding house, and altered much of the interior decoration. By 1774 nearly £95,000 (approx. £10.5 million today) had been spent in the transformation. The American Minister to England described the house in 1783: 'In every apartment of the whole house, the same taste, the same judgment, the same elegance, the same simplicity, without the smallest affectation, ostentation, profusion, or meanness.'

The four libraries, one of which was a two-storey octagon, were most impressive spaces and The King spent a great deal of his time there, poring over his collections, while Queen Charlotte was also an avid reader. The Royal Library, built up over several centuries, had been donated by George II to the British Museum and George III determined to replace it. At his death in 1820 his collection comprised some 67,000 volumes on which he had spent £120,000 (approx. £8.4 million today). It was removed to Windsor Castle and then donated to the nation by George IV. It has joined the earlier Royal Collection at the British Museum.

The Queen's House was not all an exercise in austerity. The Grand Staircase matched that at Chatsworth, and The Queen's apartments were much grander, despite the fact that Queen Charlotte was characterized as frugal, 'a severe and parsimonious lady', fond of knitting.

From the 1790s George spent less time at The Queen's House and commuted on a weekly basis between Windsor, The Queen's House and his mother's old house at Kew.

Now it was the turn of his son, The Prince Regent, soon to become King George IV, whose taste for art and architecture were extravagant in the extreme. Under his aegis, Buckingham House would, indeed, be transformed into a palace.

From house to palace

In January 1830, the view from the palace railings is of a building site, behind a new and elaborate arched entranceway still under construction. The railings curve round in two quadrants on either side to join the colonnaded wings of the palace. The palace under construction is wholly the work of the architect John Nash for George IV. He has been working on it for five years and it is not yet finished, and his patron is about to die. The new, bright-yellow Bath stone gleams, and the intricate detail of the carvings on the three pediments, one above the centre and two on each wing, are crisp.

The building is certainly beautifully constructed, but despite its symmetry is not quite harmonious (unlike the beautiful garden front which remains to this day much as Nash designed it). A small central dome appears out of scale and the tall, thin, columned constructions breaking forward from the main facade are too dominant and top-heavy. The wings, originally single storey with what appeared to be a pile of children's building blocks on top, have already been pulled down as wholly inadequate – shortcomings 'which could only be remedied by demolition'. They have been rebuilt in three storeys to provide more accommodation and to align with the three storeys of the front facade.

Very shortly a triumphal arch will rise from the building site, intended to commemorate the great British victories over the forces of Napoleon Bonaparte on land and sea. Already dubbed the 'Marble Arch' it is made of gleaming white Carrara marble and has three arches in the manner of a Roman triumphal arch. Above the attic storey a huge base is planned, with the winged angels of Victory at its corners and Britannia with her shield and trident seated in the centre. Atop this is to stand a great bronze statue of King George IV on horseback by Sir Francis Chantrey. (Given that towards the end of his life George IV, addled with too much laudanum and alcohol to the point he was convinced he had taken part in the Battle of Waterloo, had a 50-inch waistband and was a figure of general ridicule, the fine monument – the very model of martial hauteur – which now graces a plinth on one corner of Trafalgar Square, is a testament to Chantrey's tact.)

By this point, the building had already come in for a great deal of criticism, both for its suitability and its vast cost. Answerable to the Treasury for its expense but to his patron for his architectural ambitions, Nash had chosen to obey his patron and by 1828 the work was already vastly over budget. Three Parliamentary select committees met in successive years to investigate and Nash came in not just for severe criticism but his professional competence was questioned. A contemporary Thomas Rowlandson cartoon shows a glum John Bull reading a list of charges to Nash, imprisoned in the forecourt of his palace.

The eye-watering expense of the building was also queried in a time of national stringency, when 'poverty and distress abounded in the country'. An interesting and ingenious riposte was published in the new *Frasers*

Above: Architect John Nash
Opposite page: Marble Arch, early 1800s

Magazine in May 1830. After acknowledging that 'the completion of so costly a pile might have been postponed till a happier period', the writer goes on to say the erection of the building was a moral duty, not for the 'personal comfort of the King', but in order to employ the craftsmen 'not one of which ... could find employment if the works were suspended'. The writer then invokes the future: 'Can it be disputed that public edifices are the monuments of nations? Can it be denied that they are the only memorials by which posterity is enabled to estimate the worth and greatness of a people? What awakes the wonder and admiration of the traveller in Egypt, but the vast piles of human effort and ingenuity which he sees there?' It was – and is – a fair point.

John Nash was an energetic and visionary architect, first apprenticed in his teens to the sculptor and architect Sir Robert Taylor, then Architect of The King's Works. By sheer hard work and competence Nash attained celebrity status in London. He was in his sixties when The Prince of Wales (later George IV) was made Regent in 1811. Nash, in competition with others, was instructed to prepare plans for the development of a new road from Marylebone Park (an old royal hunting ground to be re-landscaped as Regent's Park) to The Prince's magnificent palace, Carlton House. The master plan he created involved the bold curve of Regent's Street linking twin circuses, to become Oxford and Piccadilly, and was regarded as both original and brilliant. The Prince Regent was suitably impressed – 'it will quite eclipse Napoleon,' he said – and thereafter Nash became his confidential adviser not just on architecture but on a wide range of the issues of the day. Nash's grandiose and very expensive scheme was accepted in 1813 and work continued until 1825 when the money ran out and the full objective was never achieved. Nonetheless, to Nash we owe one of the few wide processional routes in London, in the style of the boulevards of Paris, as well as a host of much-loved London buildings. He was also responsible for laying out what became in due course Trafalgar Square.

Nash was the perfect architect for The Prince Regent and after about 1810 worked almost exclusively for him. They shared an ambitious, grandiose and very showy vision for everything they conceived. Prior to Buckingham Palace, Nash had already worked on Carlton House (which had earlier been subject to a parliamentary commission to investigate the cost overruns in its construction) and a temporary polygonal ballroom with a tented roof, to house The Prince Regent's grand fête of 1814.

*The Prince Regent,
later George IV*

Nash's next task for The Prince Regent was to transform, from 1815–22, a large villa in Brighton into a palace in the style of an 'Eastern pleasure pavilion'. The result, the Royal Pavilion, is an extraordinary blending of the Classical, European Gothic, Mughal and Chinese traditions, its roof sporting a thicket of minarets and onion domes. Not everyone was ecstatic. The wife of the Austrian Ambassador was decidedly baffled, writing 'How can one describe such a piece of architecture? The style is a mixture of Moorish, Tartar, Gothic and Chinese. It has already cost £700,000 [almost £50 million today] and it is still not fit to live in.' Despite its exotic appearance, the building was technically advanced, with cast iron used to support the weight of the many domes and minarets and with gas lighting throughout as well as running hot and cold water, not then a usual attribute in domestic arrangements. Nash also rebuilt for The Prince Regent, with money provided by the Treasury, Lower Lodge in Windsor Great Park. It was transformed as Royal Lodge, a stuccoed, thatched and rather overlarge 'cottage orné', its disguise perhaps spoilt by its forest of chimneys.

When his father died in 1820 and the first public proclamation of the new King was made on the steps of Carlton House, the new King George IV began immediately to foster his architectural ambitions. The 'disgraceful littleness' of the royal palaces in London had been much commented on. There was nowhere suitable to house visiting royalty and other important guests, particularly after a fire in 1804 had destroyed a large part of St James's Palace. In *Tour of a Foreigner in England*, published in 1825, the author wrote:

> '*Though the royal or government palaces are among the most remarkable in London, they serve to show how little the dignity of the sovereign is respected in England in comparison with other countries of Europe. To say nothing of St James's Palace (which the present sovereign has not thought fit for his residence) there are in Paris many hotels preferable to Carlton House.*'

Mindful of these slights and the need for the British monarch to have a palace commensurate with his status, George IV first tried to rebuild Carlton House and Nash duly produced plans for a vast palace in both Gothic and Classical styles. A wary Treasury, knowing 'there appeared to be no limit to his desires, nor any restraint to his profusion', as one venomous biographer said of The King, refused the finance so St James's

Above: The interior of Carlton House, early 1800s

Below: Carlton House, 1809

Palace was accordingly upgraded to provide more state rooms for entertaining in the grand manner.

Before work had been completed The King had been diverted by the prospect of redeveloping The Queen's House. When he was informed that £150,000 (approx. £10.5 million today) over three years was 'the utmost sum' that could be found by Parliament from public funds, George, true to form, retorted that this was 'wholly inadequate' and that 'it will be safer to reckon on £450,000 [approx. £31.5 million today]'. In 1821 the new King appointed Nash as the architect for Buckingham House and building began a few years later. It was Nash who proposed the demolition of Carlton House and the redevelopment of the site and reuse of its fabulous contents to help defray the costs of the new works, which were nonetheless to be subject to Treasury scrutiny.

Because of the paucity of funding Nash was required to remodel and enlarge the existing house rather than start afresh, although the scope and ambition – and cost – of the new works increased significantly as time went on. Originally a brick-built house with colonnaded quadrants linking modest, matching pavilions joined by simple iron railings, Nash demolished the old pavilions and constructed wings in their place. The right hand, or north wing, housed the royal apartments and the one opposite was devoted to the household staff. Closing off the fourth side and enclosing the courtyard was the Marble Arch. In the centre, the hall of the old house remained, long galleries were built behind it, one above the other, and a new garden range was added beyond them. A new scheme to

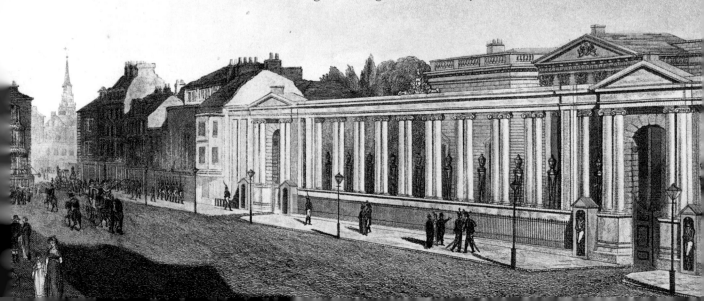

enrich the exterior with an extensive range of sculpture to commemorate the victories over Napoleon. Little by little, from what had begun as a grand gentleman's residence, The King, his architect and a band of artistic advisers had created a state palace, a monument to the glory of Britain and its monarchy.

The complexity of the exterior elevations was more than matched by the opulence of the interiors, commissioned from the leading craftsmen of the day. Moulded plaster, scagliola, marble in abundance, gilt bronze, mahogany as well as a variety of other decorative hardwoods, mirror-glass, opulent draperies in damask and other fine stuffs and gold leaf by the yard gleamed in gorgeous profusion. But all that was to be in the future. At the time of the disgrace of Nash and the death of The King in 1830 the works, although well advanced, were still not finished.

The ailing George IV died in January 1830 and immediately, with his patron and protector removed, Nash's enemies pounced, as The Duke of Wellington remarked with relish: 'to make a hash of Nash'. Nash was summarily dismissed from his contract and also from his position as architect to the Board of Works.

William IV

George IV's brother, The Duke of Clarence, succeeded him as William IV. The new King had spent a great deal of time in the navy, rising to the rank of Rear Admiral. He had been a great friend of Admiral Nelson under whom he had served, but speaking against the war with Napoleon in the House of Lords cost him any further command, despite his eventual titular rank of Lord High Admiral. He was also celebrated for his 20-year sojourn with the Irish actress Dorothea Jordan.

Although he had been born at Buckingham House, William IV, a rather ascetic individual, derided his brother's building mania and refused to move into the new palace, remaining at Clarence House (which had also been built by John Nash between 1825 and 1827), using St James's Palace for state occasions. Nonetheless the building works at the new palace continued, in a somewhat plainer style, under the new architect, Edward Blore. Twice William tried to rid himself of the building, once proposing it as an army barracks and secondly as the new Houses of Parliament after the disastrous fire of 1834. It was not easily adapted to a barracks and Parliament preferred the historic links to its traditional location. And so Buckingham Palace remained empty, a building site for most of William's short reign. After not quite seven years as King, William died at Windsor Castle, where he was buried. He was succeeded by his niece, until that point Princess Victoria of Kent, and the palace became at once the location for the extravagant presentation of monarchical display, for which it had been intended.

A map of Buckingham Palace and the surrounding area, 1869

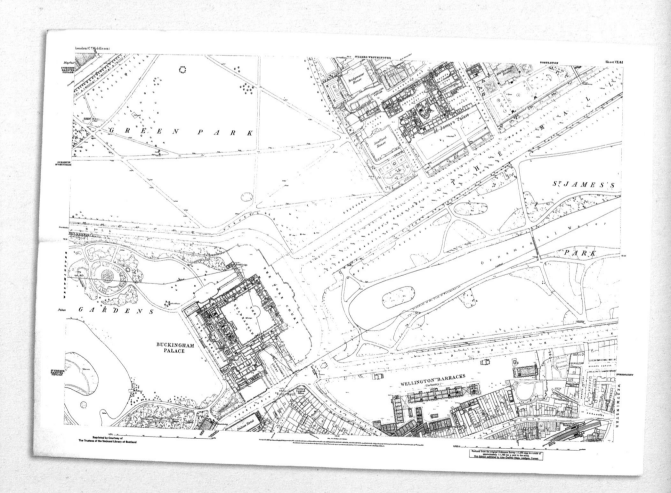

The race to provide an heir

The very existence of Queen Victoria was a direct result of the potential constitutional crisis precipitated by the death of Princess Charlotte, the sole child of The Prince Regent, in childbirth in 1817, three years before the Regent assumed the throne as George IV. There were no other legitimate heirs of her grandfather, George III, in the second generation now extant and so the spotlight of national expectation was turned on his numerous children, and an unseemly race to produce an heir began. The runners in this race to procreate were not necessarily particularly sound in wind and limb, nor young.

Consider the starters: Charlotte's father, The Prince Regent, despised his wife Caroline of Brunswick, who was approaching 50, therefore both were highly unlikely to produce further children. So he was out of the race to father a future monarch.

The next in line, Frederick, Duke of York, had married Princess Frederica Charlotte of Prussia some 26 years before. They had had no children and she now lived apart from her husband in Weybridge and had turned 50, so he was out of the race.

Next up was William, Duke of Clarence, who in due course, following the deaths of his two older brothers, George IV and The Duke of York, would succeed to the Crown at the age of 64 as William IV. William was certainly fecund: he had produced ten FitzClarence children from his 20-year liaison with the Irish actress Mrs Jordan. After an abortive search for a wife he finally married 25-year-old Princess Adelaide of Saxe-Coburg Meiningen in July 1818. Despite being half his age they were married happily for nearly 20 years. She accepted the numerous illegitimate FitzClarences and helped him sort out his straightened financial situation. But alas five pregnancies produced two short-lived daughters and three miscarriages. So William was, in effect, retired from the race.

The next potential runner was The Princess Royal, Charlotte, who had married the obese Frederick III, Duke of Wurttemberg, some 20 years before. They had only one stillborn daughter the year after their marriage, and she was now in her fifties. So she could be ruled out.

The fifth of the 12 surviving siblings was Edward, Duke of Kent. At one time Commander-in-Chief of the British forces in North America he had been for a year Governor of Gibraltar, where he had put down a mutiny with some brutality, before settling in Hampton Court Park. For many years he lived openly with his mistress, Julie de Saint-Laurent, but she was dispensed with when he married, at the age of 50, the 31-year-old Princess Victoria of Saxe-Coburg-Saalfeld, in May 1818. She had been married before to the late Prince of Leiningen, by whom she had two living children, so all looked set fair. A year after their marriage – on 24 May 1819 – they produced their only child, a daughter named Alexandrina Victoria, known as she was growing up as Drina. Some of George III's younger children did manage to have progeny who lived to reach their majority, but Drina became the rightful heir of her generation. Drina is better known as Victoria, Queen of England.

Princess Alexandrina Victoria, with her beloved dog Dash, 1833

Victoria's grand state palace

A ball at Buckingham Palace, 1856

Queen Victoria, unlike her 'Uncle King', William IV, who never lived there, embraced Buckingham Palace, moving in from her childhood home, Kensington Palace, in July 1837, two weeks after her proclamation. Within a very short time after she had taken possession of the unfinished new palace, what had been a vastly expensive white elephant had come into its own, a centre of court life and ceremonial, alive with dances and concerts. The young Victoria loved music, a good party and, most of all, to dance. At her behest it became known as Buckingham Palace, after the builder of the original house, parts of which, now altered out of all recognition, were buried deep within the new palace. To mark her arrival she gave a dinner party on her first night, followed by countless receptions, although many state functions were still held at St James's.

In June 1838 Victoria left Buckingham Palace for her coronation in Westminster Abbey, returning, as any teenager might, to greet first her pet King Charles spaniel, Dash, and give him a bath before assuming once more her new royal persona and entertaining 100 guests for a coronation dinner followed by fireworks. In the previous month, as part of a series of entertainments leading up to her coronation, she had held the first state ball, dancing until four o'clock in the morning, no doubt including the waltz especially composed by Johann Strauss the Elder in her honour (*The Times* reported that this 'new set of waltzes ... were much admired by Her Majesty').

Queen Victoria and Prince Albert in fancy dress, 1851

Successfully set up by her Uncle Leopold, less than two years later she married Prince Albert in the chapel at St James's Palace and returned to Buckingham Palace for the wedding breakfast, the first such celebration since the wedding of the first Queen Regnant, Mary I, to Philip of Spain in 1554. After a three-day honeymoon in Windsor Castle (Albert had proposed the honeymoon should be a longer one, but Victoria had retorted, 'You forget, my dearest Love, that I am the Sovereign, and that business can stop and wait for nothing') the royal couple returned to the palace, miles of cheering crowds thronging the route.

Four months later, while driving from the palace up Constitution Hill in an open phaeton with Prince Albert, a young man named Edward Oxford fired two pistols at her from the side of the roadway, perhaps 5 metres (16 feet) away. The first missed and Prince Albert, seeing the second pistol raised, pulled Victoria down inside the carriage and the bullet whistled over her head. As Oxford was seized she is reported to have stood up to show she was unhurt. For several days afterwards the parks around the palace were awash with people lining the roads and escorting her back to the palace, acting as her voluntary bodyguard. Shortly after the event the Houses of Lords and Commons came to the palace in a column of carriages several hundred long to present an address of congratulation for her safe deliverance from harm. At intervals throughout her long reign, as she left or was returning to the palace she was to be the subject of four further attempts to shoot her by deranged men.

In the early afternoon of 21 November 1841 the first of Victoria and Albert's nine children was born at Buckingham Palace, a girl who would be named Victoria, The Princess Royal. Less than a year later, to great rejoicing (but not by Victoria as she was not keen on babies, nor on giving birth so frequently: 'quite disgusting' – 'more like a rabbit or a guinea-pig than anything else ... not very nice') a prince was born, the future Edward VII.

The same year the royal couple gave the first of their famous fancy-dress balls at the palace. In 1842 the theme was the meeting between the two courts of Anne of Brittany and of Edward III and his Queen (and, of course, cousin) Philippa of Hainault. It was an impossible encounter

Continues on p.111

The Saxe-Coburg clan and the British royal family

As a child, Queen Victoria had been brought up by her mother, Princess Victoria of Saxe-Coburg-Saalfeld after the death of her father, Prince Edward, Duke of Kent and Strathearn, fourth son of George III (whose mother was Princess Augusta of Saxe-Gotha-Altenburg), before her first birthday. The Saxe-Coburgs were a peculiarly invasive family from the forests of Thuringia who were created Dukes in the sixteenth century and whose territories achieved independence in 1806 with the fall of the Holy Roman Empire. In 1826 the house of Saxe-Coburg-Saalfeld changed its name to Saxe-Coburg and Gotha following the merging of the two duchies of Coburg and Gotha. In 1871 it became part of the German Empire. Largely orchestrated by the match-making skills of Victoria's Uncle Leopold, by the early twentieth century Saxe-Coburg-Gotha was the name of the ruling families of Britain, Belgium, Portugal and Bulgaria as well as the original German duchy.

Prince Leopold and Princess Charlotte

In 1816 Princess Charlotte, the heir presumptive to the British throne as the only child of The Prince Regent, later George IV, married the 26-year-old Prince Leopold of Saxe-Coburg-Saalfield, brother of Princess Victoria of Saxe-Coburg-Saalfield, who was three years later to give birth to the future Queen Victoria. Victoria's Uncle Leopold (who was also her husband Prince Albert's uncle) was to be an important mentor to Victoria in the years to come. Leopold was a handsome and dashing soldier who had commanded a cavalry division against the forces of Napoleon in 1813. Leopold and Charlotte lived at Claremont House near Esher and in London in a house on Oxford Street and were very popular with the London crowds.

As the only heir to the throne in the second generation any child Charlotte would bear would secure the royal succession. She was soon pregnant and after two miscarriages her most recent labour was followed with great interest by the British public. The eventual birth in 1817 was traumatic, after a prolonged two-day labour that was fatally mismanaged by her doctors. Charlotte died from post-partum haemorrhage and the child itself – a boy – was stillborn. Leopold was understandably distraught as The Princess was taken to be buried with her stillborn child amongst her royal relatives in St George's Chapel, Windsor Castle. News of her death was accompanied by an outpouring of national grief not seen again until the death of Princess Diana exactly 180 years later. Haberdashers throughout the country were stripped of black crêpe to make mourning ribbons, shops closed in her memory and tickets for her lying-in-state were fought over. Lord Byron wrote from Italy that her death 'was a shock even here and must have been an earthquake at home'.

Leopold, although a minor German princeling, was now well known, both as husband of the late heir presumptive to the British Crown, but also for his military exploits. He was deemed capable and had excellent diplomatic and language skills; in due course he was offered the throne of Greece, which he turned down, and then in 1831 was chosen to be the first King of the Belgians by the National Congress formed after the Belgian revolution. The next year he married as his second wife Princess Louise-Marie, daughter of the French King Louis-Philippe. He was to lose her too at a young age, to tuberculosis, but not before he had secured the succession to the Belgian throne.

After Princess Charlotte's death there ensued a race among the brothers of George IV to marry and beget an heir – a race that would be won by the fourth son of King George III – Edward, Duke of Kent – whose daughter would become the longest-reigning British monarch to date.

In 1840 Queen Victoria married her only first cousin, Prince Albert of Saxe-Coburg and Gotha (they had even been delivered by the same midwife), second son of Ernest III, Duke of Saxe-Coburg-Saalfield and his wife – who was also *his* cousin – Louise of Saxe-Gotha-Altenburg, with the considerable encouragement of their joint uncle, Prince Leopold. In retrospect it is quite clear that Albert was groomed by his uncle to marry Victoria, and to become The Prince Consort of the British Queen, the very role denied Leopold by the death of his wife Charlotte.

In 1844 Ernest, Albert's elder brother, inherited the dukedom of Saxe-Coburg and Gotha, and in 1893 Victoria and Albert's second son Alfred, Duke of Edinburgh, a career officer in the Royal Navy, succeeded his uncle as Duke. After Duke Alfred's death in 1900, he was succeeded by his nephew, Prince Charles Edward, Duke of Albany, then at school at Eton, who was the only son of Victoria and Albert's youngest son, Prince Leopold. A general in the German army during the First World War he was stripped of his British peerages and princely title in 1919 (and two years before, in deference to anti-German sentiment, George V had changed the name of the British royal house from Saxe-Coburg-Gotha to the House of Windsor). After the November Revolution of 1918 and the abdication of Kaiser Wilhem II replaced the monarchy in Germany with a republic, the Duchy of Saxe-Coburg and Gotha split into the two independent states of Coburg and Gotha. In 1920 they merged with the states of Bavaria and Thuringia respectively and thereafter ceased to exist. The current head of the House of Saxe-Coburg-Gotha is Prince Andreas, who was born in 1943 and is a great-great grandson of Queen Victoria. He has dual British and German nationality and was largely brought up in the United States by his mother and American stepfather.

Queen Victoria attends the christening of Victoria, Princess Royal at Buckingham Palace, 1841

– the two lived a century apart – but that did not seem to matter. Prince Albert naturally assumed the role of Edward III and Victoria that of Queen Philippa. The Princess Augusta of Hesse-Cassel, who had married Victoria's uncle, The Duke of Cambridge, impersonated Anne.

Albert was to have a role to play in the establishment of Buckingham Palace as a grand state palace as opposed to a large domestic house, in much the same way as Edward III had at Windsor Castle exactly 600 years earlier. Everything about the ball was extravagant: The Queen insisted that the costumes should be as authentic as possible and James Planché, the author of a *History of British Costume* (1834), was engaged as adviser to all those invited – an astonishing 2000 people (he also contributed to the souvenir books, 'with illustrations printed in colour by chromolithography … in 20 numbers forming 2 volumes', published to commemorate the occasion). Planché stipulated: 'Tissues must be woven expressly – spurs, weapons, and jewelry modelled and manufactured on purpose … boots, shoes, gauntlets, hose, nearly every article of apparel must be made to order.' A commentator wrote:

> 'The wildest rumours of the extent and cost of the ball circulated beforehand. It was said that eighteen thousand persons were engaged in it. The Earl of Pembroke was to wear thirty-thousand pounds' worth of diamonds … He was to borrow ten thousand pounds' worth of diamonds from Storr and Mortimer at one per cent, for the night. These great jewellers' stores were reported to be exhausted. Every other jeweller and diamond merchant was in the same condition.'

Queen Victoria in costume as Queen Philippa of Hainault, 1843

The Queen's dress was designed under Planché's personal supervision and was copied from contemporary costumes worn by the effigies of Philippa and other women of the same period on their tombs in Westminster Abbey. Albert's costume was similarly a facsimile of that worn by the funeral effigy of Edward III. Sir Edwin Landseer was commissioned to paint the scene: the royal couple, in the high crowns and very pointed shoes of the mid-fourteenth century, stand beneath a canopy emblazoned with the Plantagenet arms in silver. Behind them are two elaborate Gothic chairs of the period.

The guests took The Queen and Planché's dress code seriously. Some 'appeared … in the very armour of their forefathers, others in costumes copied from family pictures, or in the dress of hereditary offices

*An invitation to a
royal garden party at
Buckingham Palace, 1984*

still held by the representatives of the ancient houses'. A writer some years later described the dazzling scene:

'At the appointed time King Edward escorted Queen Philippa to her throne, and they awaited with their Court the arrival of Anne of Brittany, who, led by Louis XII and accompanied by a suite of one hundred and twenty courtiers from France, Italy, and Spain, was to be presented before them. About half-past ten, marshalled by the heralds, the procession marched up the grand white marble staircase, through the gilded state rooms with their reflecting mirrors and glittering chandeliers, to the throne-room. The meeting of the two Courts formed a magnificent living picture of one of the most interesting periods in modern history, portrayed by the highest, the wealthiest, the loveliest, and the most honourable in the land.'

There was inevitably some comment about the extravagant cost, inappropriate at a time of economic hardship. The response from the palace was that by demanding that all the costumes should be British-made (Victoria and Albert's costumes were made by Spitalfields' weavers) those who could afford it were stimulating British commerce. The *Illustrated London News*, not usually noted later for its political or social comment, reported tartly in its first ever edition,

'never did sovereign and Prime Minister coincide in their measures more happily ... The latter taxes us to relieve the commonality; our gracious and lovely sovereign ... amerces her nobles through their pleasures and ... spend over £100,000 [approx. £8 million today] to revive languishing trade! This is the healthful ingredient which lies at the bottom of the overflowing cup of pleasure. This is one of the wholesome conditions by which affluence and rank should preserve their distinction amongst us.'

The evening was judged such a success that it was followed in 1845 by the Georgian *bal poudré* (so-called because of the white powder used on wigs) where the dress code was of the period 1740–50. The diplomatic corps 'adopted the uniform of their respective nations within the prescribed dates' and the ladies wore 'the greatest magnificence of embroidered and jeweled decoration consistent with propriety'. The last of the great series of costumed balls was the Restoration Ball held in May 1851 with costumes from the period of Charles II. In between these extravagant occasions, there were other parties, receptions, concerts – and balls.

An invitation to a Children's garden party at Buckingham Palace, 1909

In April 1849 the Strauss orchestra performed once more at a state ball for 1600 guests. Johann the Elder (in one of his last public performances, he died that September) performed the 'Alice Polka' for the first time, in honour of the six-year-old Princess Alice, Victoria and Albert's third child. On three occasions in the 1840s the composer Felix Mendelssohn played at the palace. After a dinner in 1842 he enraptured the royal couple with a rendition of the Austrian national anthem with his right hand whilst playing 'Rule Britannia' simultaneously with his left. The elaborate marquetry-decorated piano Mendelssohn played is still displayed in the White Drawing Room. On another occasion the couple played and sang together on the organ and piano (Albert played the organ and Victoria the piano) and Mendelssohn reported, 'the only really nice, comfortable house in England … where one feels completely at home, is Buckingham Palace'.

Comfortable it was not, in reality, given the growing royal family (Victoria and Albert were to have nine children between 1840 and 1857), entertainment on a vast scale, and the sheer number of retainers and courtiers required to service the new court. The Queen petitioned her Prime Minister, Sir Robert Peel, in 1845 for its enlargement. She wrote to him of the 'urgent necessity of doing something to Buckingham Palace' given:

'the total want of accommodation for our little family, which is fast growing up … A room capable of entertaining a larger number of those persons whom the Queen has to invite in the course of the season of balls, concerts etc is much wanted. Equally so, improved offices and servants' rooms, the want of which puts the departments of the household to great expense yearly.'

Space was not the only problem. The chimneys smoked, the drains were badly laid and a revolting smell pervaded many of the basement rooms, notably the kitchens. The plumbing was inadequate. When Victoria's uncle George IV had died in 1820 and John Nash was sacked for gross overspending, the job of finishing off the remaining works was given to an architect known for his careful, detailed, unspectacular work. Edward Blore was at the opposite end of the spectrum to the theatrical talents of John Nash – his professional work was briskly dismissed by the celebrated architectural historian John Martin Robinson, who wrote the official guide

*Buckingham Palace
as seen from a hot air
balloon, 1905*

to Buckingham Palace, as exuding 'a dull competence, healthily free from any spark of genius'. Blore had worked his way through the palace in the main using a simplified version of Nash's plans but also adding an attic storey to the central block to provide more space. On the front face of this new storey he embedded some of the carved triumphal reliefs destined for the Marble Arch, which was in consequence much simplified (other reliefs, together with the victory statues, were used on William Wilkins's National Gallery in Trafalgar Square). His attic storey also abolished Nash's much-derided central dome, which became the roof to the Music Room.

When Sir Robert Peel received The Queen's plea for more space Parliament voted £150,000 (approx. £13 million today) for modifications to the palace, but that was not enough to provide the scale of accommodation now required, so she looked for an additional source of income.

The Queen had never liked the Brighton Pavilion – it was cramped and was too open to public scrutiny. Instead she purchased land on the Isle of Wight and between 1845 and 1851 Albert supervised the building of Osborne House to replace it as the royal family's rural retreat. The Pavilion was sold in 1850 to the town of Brighton. The house was converted into assembly rooms and the adjacent stables became a concert hall – the Dome. The interior furnishings, fittings and fireplaces were removed and stored in Kensington Palace for reuse. The selling price of over £100,000 (almost £10 million today) was added to the government grant to complete the work at Buckingham Palace.

Work had already begun at the palace in 1847 on a new east range joining the two wings and closing off the old open court, converting it into a closed courtyard. As a result Nash's Marble Arch, standing in the centre of this new planned range, was dismantled and rebuilt by Thomas Cubitt – by now the preferred royal builder – as a ceremonial gateway to the north-east corner of Hyde Park. There it has remained but the widening of Park Lane in the early 1960s has marooned it incongruously in the middle of a large traffic island.

The building of the new east front was constantly disrupted by a parsimonious Treasury withholding the payment of bills, but despite that, the careful work of the architect Edward Blore and the efficiencies of Cubitt brought the new building to completion under budget. Built of soft Caen stone, which would prove to weather badly in the acidic air of a London of countless coal fires belching soot into the atmosphere, the new east facade was generally derided as being closer to the architecture of railway hotels than to the splendour required of the monarch of the most powerful nation on earth.

Blore made no attempt in style and decoration to marry his new facade with Nash's existing building. It had, however, one important innovation – a new ceremonial balcony placed in the centre at first-floor level. This was to become an emotional rallying point for monarch and people in the years to come. It was used for the first time in 1854 when Queen Victoria stood on the balcony to watch the Guards regiments march past on their way to the Crimea. She reported to her Uncle Leopold: 'We stood on the balcony to see them ... They formed line, presented arms, and then cheered us very heartily and went off cheering. It was a touching and beautiful sight.' There was to be a reprise on the return of the survivors two years later.

Prince Albert had taken a lead role in the modernization of the palace. In 1843, John Nash's south conservatory had been converted into a chapel under his guidance (the chapel was destroyed by German bombs in the Second World War). Shortly after his marriage, recognizing that his wife lacked any knowledge of art history, Albert became involved, now that the initial structural work was nearing completion, in the decoration of the palace and the acquisition and hanging of pictures. He hired Ludwig Gruner, an expert in ornamental art, as a paid artistic adviser. Gruner was an accomplished engraver and an outstanding networker who had trawled the country houses of Britain in the early 1830s in search of paintings by Raphael to engrave. Gruner was to stay in The Prince's service for 13 years from 1843 to 1856 and in 1845 he was given title of 'Adviser in Art' to The Queen, a new post intended to regularize his position in the household, on £200 (approx. £17,000 today) a year. Known in England as Lewis Gruner, he was to have a strong influence on the decoration of state buildings and the display of public art. After his formal appointment he took over the direction of the new decoration commissioned by Prince Albert at Buckingham Palace.

The old Houses of Parliament were destroyed by fire in 1834 and after an architectural competition Albert was appointed President of the Royal Fine Art Commission overseeing the internal decoration of the new building being built to the designs of Charles Barry and Augustus Pugin. The new building was erected, as Lewis Gruner described it, 'upon a scale of unusual splendour'. To further the design of the intended painted interiors the commission took the bold step of proposing the establishment of a British school of history painting using the fresco technique, portentously described as 'in connexion with a great national monument ... an affair of national importance'. Accordingly, in 1844 Albert and the painter and art historian Charles Eastlake (soon to be the first director of the National Gallery), under the direction of Gruner, created a Garden Pavilion in the gardens of Buckingham Palace as a laboratory for rediscovering this old technique. Eight British artists were chosen to decorate it in fresco – among them Daniel Maclise, Edwin Landseer and Eastlake himself. This jewel-like building unfortunately succumbed to dry rot and was demolished in the 1920s.

In 1852 Thomas Cubitt was called upon once again (he had also by then built Osborne House) to build the new Ball and Concert Room and the Ball Supper Room nearby. The unfortunate Blore was dispensed with and Cubitt worked to the designs of James Pennethorne, who had served as an assistant to Nash during his work on the palace. The Ball and Concert Room was 37 metres (123 feet) long and 18 metres (60 feet) wide, a cavernous space that could hold several thousand revellers in comfort. Viewed from the lawns to the rear, its vast and inelegant bulk, resembling the fly tower of a theatre rearing up behind the southern conservatory, destabilized Nash's delicate garden front.

The interior was a different matter: masterminded by the Albert–Gruner partnership, a team of artists created a rich, complex, polychrome scheme of sculptured plaster and painted panels. Gruner himself painted the enormous ceiling. The Ball Supper Room was in many ways more spectacular, with its domed ceiling painted to resemble a vast tent. Beneath these new buildings much-needed service rooms were contrived including a new kitchen. So avant-garde were these spectacular new rooms the palace was dubbed the 'Headquarters of taste' by the magazine *The Builder*.

With the completion of Osborne House in 1851 and Balmoral in the Scottish Highlands in 1856, the royal family now had a chance to

Above: Queen Victoria attends Diamond Jubilee Dinner Party thrown in her honour, 1897

Below: Queen Victoria and her son Albert (later Edward VII), and his son George (later George V), and his son Edward, the future King Edward VIII

spend more time away from Buckingham Palace; it was a chance they took. After Prince Albert's early death in 1861 at the age of 42 Victoria virtually abandoned the palace, preferring the seclusion of her new houses and, when needing to be in London, Windsor Castle. Twenty-six years later there was a very brief flowering of the glittering social life that had characterized the palace in the 1840s and 1850s when a galaxy of European royals came to stay to celebrate Victoria's Jubilee in 1887 and again ten years later. Victoria died at Osborne House in 1901. Buckingham Palace had been left as it had been before Albert's death 40 years before. In the meantime the grimy, heavily polluted London air had slowly settled in every crevice and on every painted surface of the interior.

Twentieth-century developments

Edward VII, the new King, set about personally supervising the redecoration of Buckingham Palace. Referring to the Italianate marbling in the entrance hall – blackened by half a century of grime – as 'a sepulchre', he brought light into the palace, banishing tables overloaded with his mother's beloved knick-knacks, and packing up Prince Albert's mountains of books. King Edward VII was not a great reader.

The King's private apartments consisted of four adjoining rooms on the first floor looking out over the garden. His bed was vast and heavy, the walls of his chamber hung with portraits of his female relatives. In his sitting room, alongside his neatly ordered desk, his ill-tempered French bulldog, Peter, lay in its basket and two cages of canaries provided a musical accompaniment.

He employed theatre designer Frank Verity under whose watchful eye plasterwork of the

The Grand Staircase at Buckingham Palace, 1895

state rooms was painted white and the mouldings gilded. Crimson velvet was hung in generous swags. Critics compared the effect to that of the Ritz Hotel, but it suited The King who introduced evening courts (as opposed to those of his mother, held in the afternoon) at which he and The Queen would sit side by side on a dais in the ballroom as debutantes were presented wearing elaborate trains carried by pages. The first of these, on 14 March 1902, proved, without doubt, that glamour had come back to the palace.

In the period before the First World War the east wing of the palace – the 'front' facade – was smothered by scaffolding as an army of masons refaced the old yellow Caen stone, crumbling badly in the acidic air of the sulphurous city, with the denser white stone from Portland, creating the monumental facade that has become so familiar. It was to be completed in a record 13 weeks. The *Sphere* commissioned an ingenious engraving of how the refaced palace would look, one wing as it was and the rest as it would be, though somehow it looked a bit more interesting than in reality it turned out to be.

The architect, Sir Aston Webb, was commissioned to reface the facade erected by the architect Edward Blore in 1847 and to formalize the ceremonial approach to the palace in memory of Queen Victoria. Between 1911 and 1914 he designed and built the Admiralty Arch to provide a triumphal gateway leading to Buckingham Palace via the wide ceremonial roadway known as The Mall. Directly in front of the palace he placed the

842 H.M. PRIVATE SITTING-ROOM, B. PALACE.

Private sitting room,
Buckingham Palace, 1895

great statue by Thomas Brock of the late Queen sitting impassively on her great white obelisk surrounded by the swirling statues of lesser beings. The whole ensemble was very impressive, its architectural pomp echoing the might of empire.

But for Edward VII's successor George V, King from 1910, the palace held little thrall, causing him to confess to Viscount Esher that he would happily pull it down and sell off its garden as a public park, using the money to rebuild Kensington Palace to his own less flamboyant taste. Content to use the palace as an office and headquarters, he was happier at Balmoral in autumn and Sandringham in winter. Queen Mary, too, betraying her German ancestry, remarked that 'Buckingham Palace is not so *gemütlich* [cosy] as Marlborough House', their previous London base. For a year after Edward VII's death, the palace remained gloomy and silent, a victim of court mourning, Queen Mary gradually banishing what she referred to as 'this surfeit of gold plate and orchids'. Comfort she enjoyed, but not extravagant luxury. On George V's death in 1936 she moved into her much preferred Marlborough House to make way for King George VI and his consort Queen Elizabeth who were to live in the palace, most memorably, during the Second World War.

On 14 September 1940 a delayed-action bomb, dropped the previous morning, finally exploded. The raid on 13 September had deliberately targeted the palace. With poor weather over the south-east, major daylight operations were cancelled by the Luftwaffe in favour of 'nuisance'

Above left: Bomb damage to the North Lodge of Buckingham Palace, 1941

Above right: Winston Churchill and The King and Queen inspect the bomb damage after an air raid on Buckingham Palace, 1940

raids. A lone aircraft dropped a single bomb on the garden of 10 Downing Street and then a stick of five high-explosive bombs on Buckingham Palace. Queen Elizabeth was in residence with The King and wrote later to her mother-in-law, Queen Mary, that at about 11 a.m., as she was 'battling' to remove an eyelash from The King's eye, she heard 'the unmistakable whirr-whirr of a German plane' and then the:

> 'scream of a bomb ... It all happened so quickly that we had only time to look foolishly at each other when the scream hurtled past us and exploded with a tremendous crash in the quadrangle. I saw a great column of smoke and earth thrown up into the air, and then we all ducked like lightning into the corridor. There was another tremendous explosion ...'

The bombing of Buckingham Palace gave rise to one of The Queen's most famous sayings: 'I am glad we have been bombed. Now we can look the East End in the eye.' The attack on Buckingham Palace was discussed that day in Cabinet, which quickly saw the propaganda value The Queen had already spotted. The Cabinet duly invited the Prime Minister to send a message on their behalf to The King: 'The War Cabinet offer their hearty congratulations to their Majesties on their providential escape from the barbarous attack made on their home and Royal Persons.' It was also agreed that, 'subject to His Majesty's consent', the fullest possible publicity should be accorded the message. Of the five bombs dropped, two hit the inner courtyard, one landed on the Royal Chapel to the west and the other two dropped either side of the railings of the forecourt. By chance the bombs fell in such a way that major damage – apart from to the Royal Chapel – was largely avoided. A great number of windows were blown in, causing damage from flying glass to paintings hanging opposite them, and a water main was ruptured.

Above: Crowds outside Buckingham Palace, VE Day 1945

Below: The royal family wave to the crowds from the balcony of Buckingham Palace, VE Day 1945

The chapel, originally one of four conservatories built by John Nash in the 1820s (one of which was later removed to Kew Gardens by William IV and now much used as a wedding venue), was converted in 1843 by Douglas Morison. Despite a great deal of red plush and twin pulpits, its exposed steel girders and cast-iron columns continued to betray its horticultural origins. It was never rebuilt as a chapel and in due course, after an initiative from The Duke of Edinburgh – so often the guiding light in such matters – it became The Queen's Gallery, opened in 1966 to show off work from the Royal Collections in rotating exhibitions. In 1999 it was closed for renovation and opened again in time for the Jubilee of 2002, with a new and striking Greek temple portico and more than three times the exhibition space it had previously. It is now one of the most successful exhibition spaces in London.

The palace had been bombed before the explosion of the delayed-action bomb, on 8 September 1940 and again on the following day, when the swimming pool was destroyed and the north wing damaged. On 15 and 17 September it was again targeted, bombs dropping on the lawns as well as destroying a bathroom. Further damage occurred in October from a parachute mine, which once more blew out a considerable number of windows. The attrition didn't stop: the next month a bomb dropped on the lawns, its explosion damaging a bedroom and a number of windows and another in the courtyard of the Royal Mews; in March 1941 the North Lodge was partly demolished and a policeman killed, and the forecourt bombed again. And finally, in June 1944 a V1 flying bomb hit the garden wall near Constitution Hill, badly damaging a summer house.

On Victory in Europe (VE) Day, 8 May 1945, a hot summer's day, thousands of men in uniform and girls in thin, bright cotton dresses – most of them happily inebriated – celebrated the fact that the war was over. Late in the afternoon the royal family came out onto the balcony and the

Above left: A Beefeater and palace staff watch the spectacle on Coronation Day, 1953

Above right: Crowds in London celebrate the coronation of Queen Elizabeth II, 1953

crowd – 20,000 or more – cheered and shouted. Amongst the crowd were the two Princesses, Elizabeth and Margaret, who had slipped out of the palace to see what it was like on the other side. The future Queen Elizabeth II wrote later, 'we stood outside and shouted, "we want the King", and were successful in seeing my parents on the balcony ... I think it was one of the most memorable nights of my life'. Eight times The King and Queen, eventually joined by the Princesses (and later by a beaming Winston Churchill), reappeared to appease the crowds, experiencing the 'heartfelt expressions of joy' as the Pathé News commentator described it. A drunken Australian waved his slouch hat from atop the palace gates in an effort to orchestrate the cheering. A couple, perched precariously on traffic lights, kissed and received a round of applause. Every lamp post was festooned with people and the Victoria Memorial became an anthill, dark with swarming bodies. As darkness fell searchlights lit up the palace, finally ending the dreary blackout that had been in force since 1939.

On the death of King George VI in 1952, Queen Elizabeth The Queen Mother, as she would now be known, knew that she would have to move out of Buckingham Palace. She found the prospect distressing but there was no alternative. Queen Elizabeth II and Prince Philip, Duke of Edinburgh moved out of Clarence House and into the palace. The Queen Mother made the reverse move.

In the 1950s, the road that led to the palace was, like every other road, the deep grey tone of asphalt. David Eccles, a Conservative politician who as Minister of Works had helped organize the coronation in 1953, ordered the transformation of The Mall the next year by the application of iron oxide pigment to create a giant red carpet, underlining its purpose as a ceremonial route. So it has been for over half a century, each year punctuated with royal occasions complete with horses and carriages and cheering crowds. It has been witness to intense jubilation – a million people thronged The Mall to celebrate The Queen's Golden Jubilee in June 2002 – and great sadness as the route for royal funeral processions, mostly

recently The Queen Mother and, before her, Princess Diana. As you stare down the broad red carpet lined with giant flagpoles you can feel the recent history of the nation swirling around you.

The Queen in residence

'Living above the shop' is how The Duke of Edinburgh has referred to life at Buckingham Palace and, indeed, it is the working week that is spent there from Monday until Friday when the family retreats to Windsor.

During the present Queen's reign the palace has seen a number of changes – not least the summer opening when the public are allowed to view the state rooms. Silver and Golden Jubilees have been marked by processions down The Mall and, most recently, The Queen's 60 years on the throne were celebrated in an event held on the Queen Victoria Memorial or, as it is known within the palace, 'the wedding cake'.

It was 4 June 2012 – a bank holiday – when the Diamond Jubilee Concert took place. Organized by Take That singer Gary Barlow, my wife and I found ourselves sitting in a stand just outside the palace where we witnessed an A-list of performers giving their all for The Queen. Robbie Williams sang with the drummers and trumpeters from the Coldstream Guards, Cliff Richard, Annie Lennox, Tom Jones and many others belted for Britain before the interval. Grace Jones sang while rotating a hula-hoop around her waist and, in the row immediately behind us, the parents and sister of The Duchess of Cambridge joined in with the fun and waved

their Union Jacks along with the rest of us; the royal family did the same a little further back in the Royal Box. The atmosphere was one of joyous celebration and good humour. The Queen arrived at 9 p.m. to be greeted by 'Sing', specially composed by Andrew Lloyd-Webber and Gary Barlow in her honour. Barlow was joined on stage by a band from the Commonwealth, the Military Wives and their choirmaster Gareth Malone. Shirley Bassey came and went, a film of The Queen's reign was screened with excerpts from the coronation and her wedding

The Mall is illuminated for the Diamond Jubilee Concert, 4th June 2012

to Prince Philip, and there followed another roll call of the great and the good ... Elton John, Paul McCartney, Stevie Wonder amongst them as well as Madness who sang 'Our House' perched on the roof of the palace – transformed into a row of terraced houses by some clever projection.

The spirit of the occasion was summed up in an emotional speech by The Prince of Wales: 'as a nation this is our opportunity to thank you and my father for always being there for us ... and for making us proud to be British'. The national anthem followed, before The Queen lit the last in a chain of beacons which had been lit across the nation as excerpts from national favourites – including 'Land of Hope and Glory'– were played by an orchestra, all guaranteed to stir the patriotic heart. It was a fitting celebration of a 60-year reign, but also a little slice of the ongoing history of a royal residence that dates back four centuries.

And what of the old mulberry garden whose existence delivered the site into royal hands? Despite legends to the contrary, no original trees from the old 1608 garden have survived at Buckingham Palace (although one specimen is thought to be some 200 years old), but there is still one of James I's original plantings to be found at Charlton House in Greenwich (built between 1607 and 1612 for the Dean of Durham, tutor to Prince Henry, James I's eldest son) a scion from which has recently been planted in the west section of Buckingham Palace Garden. In 2000, The Queen's Head Gardener, Mark Lane, asked Her Majesty's permission to establish a definitive collection of mulberry trees in the palace garden. The work began with the searching out of trees initially from British nurseries and then from further afield. The collection was granted Full Collection Status in 2005. The Queen is now the named holder of the National Mulberry Collection with 29 species so far planted at Buckingham Palace where most of the collection is housed – a few are held at Kensington Palace and Marlborough House. A limited edition book: *The Queen's Mulberries* – with illustrations by the botanical artist Alysia Hunt – was produced in 2012.

The Buckingham Palace gardens themselves – occupying some 39 acres

(16 hectares) – contain an extraordinarily wide range of cultivated plants as well as 350 species of wild flower plus fungi, insects and birds and a lake that plays host to a variety of waterfowl. There are no flamingos any more – the foxes saw to that – but

Above: Inside Buckingham Palace, The Queen greets Australian Prime Minister John Howard, 2005

Below right: The Queen and The Duke of Edinburgh inspect the gardens at Buckingham Palace

from the Waterloo Vase and the Rose Garden, to the mound designed by William Aiton to mask the smell of the 'arisings' from the Royal Mews, there is much within their confines to give a clue to the rich and varied history of the palace itself, and of its present incumbents: every couple of hours a small group of corgis and 'dorgis' (corgi/dachshund crosses) will be walked around by a footman. If you have to live over a shop, then this is an especially accommodating one.

A State Banquet at Buckingham Palace

'The tables were an explosion of damask, silver gilt, glass and flowers ... By the serving tables stood batteries of footmen ... The impact on entering can only be described as dazzling.'

Sir Roy Strong, Diary, 1976

A state visit – when one head of state visits another – wherever it may be in the world, follows the same time-honoured pattern. The incoming head of state walks down the steps of the presidential or royal aircraft onto a red carpet, newly rolled out and hoovered, is greeted by his or her counterpart, the visitor's national anthem is played by a band, a guard of honour is inspected, ceremonial salutes are fired and then a limousine or open carriage will take the two heads of state back to the presidential or royal palace.

If the head of state is also the chief executive he or she will conduct business over the next few days; trade and political pacts of one kind or another will be begun, advanced or concluded and relationships strengthened. The *Japan Times* noted that US President Barack Obama's state visit to Japan in April 2014 came at a 'crucial time ... with defence and trade issues still to be resolved [the state visit] is a high-stakes game for both sides'. If the head of state is a royal, he or she will be accompanied by a band of politicians and businessmen and women, who will conduct

President Ronald Reagan speaks at a state banquet in 1982

business. As the centrepiece of the visit there will always be a state banquet, a show of lavish entertainment aimed to honour, and perhaps slightly overawe, the visitor. Speeches will be made, toasts drunk and the national anthem played.

In the United Kingdom, who comes when is a matter for the government of the day, and more specifically the Foreign and Commonwealth Office, depending on the political or economic issues in play with a particular country. The serious buttering-up of a state visit – the highest form of diplomatic contact between two nations – can potentially advance national interests. Usually no more than two countries a year are accorded a state visit to Britain and the cost is met by the Treasury.

The Queen has been the host, accompanied by The Duke of Edinburgh, at over a hundred state visits throughout her reign, roughly two per year, occasionally three – no head of state, alive or dead, can have presided over more. The great majority of the incoming heads of state have been entertained at Buckingham Palace, around 20 at Windsor Castle (used more often recently, especially now the kitchens and other service rooms have been completely rebuilt following the fire in 1992) and a very few at Holyroodhouse in Edinburgh.

In Britain great emphasis is placed on the part the royal family plays in the unfolding drama of a state visit. Pomp and ceremony, executed with verve and precision, make for an impressive backdrop to the serious matters in hand. The monarch, and the deference paid her, the gloriously uniformed royal guards who surround her and the undeniable grandeur

The Queen and The Duke of Edinburgh accompany President Obama and First Lady Michelle Obama on their state visit to Britain, May 2011

of her palaces smack of history, stability, power and prestige – all the things that subconsciously should impact on and stay in the mind of the visitor as he or she begins her rounds of negotiations over the following days. It was ever thus. We know that the protracted, elaborate and very costly entertainments that Henry V provided for Sigismund of Luxemburg at Windsor Castle in 1416 paid dividends, with Sigismund subsequently supporting Henry's claim to the throne of France. It is unlikely that other state visits have yielded quite such a tangible bounty but their unseen benefits are inestimable.

Once the invitation to a foreign head of state has been accepted, the Master of the Household's Department, with over 250 employees the largest sector of the Royal Household, swings into action. The position of Master of the Household was first created in 1539 in a drive for efficiency. Like so many of the great offices of state it became a sinecure until the 1840s when Prince Albert purged the inefficient, wasteful and often fraudulent arrangements by which the royal palaces were run and reorganized them. The Master once more became an executive officer and was put in charge of the entire domestic establishment, masterminding his empire from offices on the first floor of the south wing of Buckingham Palace. Another sweeping reorganization in the 1980s brought further efficiencies and removed many of the old anachronisms: separate food preparation for royals and others, five different dining rooms according to staff grades and so on.

The department today encompasses a bewildering array of specialist staff, many with wonderfully arcane titles derived from historic precedents, amongst them the housekeepers and their staff of housemaids at the five royal residences; the Page of the Chambers responsible for all the pages; the Yeoman of the Royal Pantries in charge of all the plate, glass and china, some of which is literally priceless; the attendant under-butlers; the Palace Foreman who looks after a range of crafts skills; the French polisher, carpet planner, locksmith, fendersmith, gilders, cabinet makers and upholsterers; and the Royal Chef with his staff of sous-chefs, cooks and porters.

The department organizes everything, from greeting and looking after the guests and members of the royal family, the guest lists and seating plans (confirmed by The Queen and the Foreign and Commonwealth

Office) to checking dietary requirements. Before the Obama state visit the Foreign Office would have been in touch with the White House some six months in advance to check likes and dislikes. Much thought and care goes into the preparation, cooking and service of the meal on the day. However, although the footmen in tailcoats would be recognized by their Georgian forebears, their modern wireless earpieces would not.

The Royal Household is a highly efficient organization and runs with clockwork precision – it has to. The Queen disarmingly says of it all, 'I understand the need for effectiveness, efficiency and so on, but we mustn't be too corporate ...'

The state visit of US President and Mrs Obama in May 2011 is a good example of the brilliantly choreographed, set-piece theatre, full of pomp and ceremony but run to a precise, rehearsed schedule, which characterizes a typical state visit and its climax, the state banquet. Arriving in Ireland, the President paid a quick visit by helicopter to the ancestral lands of

Above: The Duke and Duchess of Cambridge meet the Obamas

Opposite page: A State Banquet in St George's Hall, Windsor Castle, 2009

the 'O'Bamas' to drink (and pay for) a symbolic pint of Guinness before the presidential armoured limousine managed to get stuck exiting the US Embassy in Dublin and had to be abandoned; not a perfect start to his visit. Leaving Ireland the night before his scheduled departure to avoid the ash cloud erupting from an Icelandic volcano, the President and his wife arrived at Stansted Airport from Dublin aboard the presidential plane Air Force One and were whisked by limousine to Winfield House in Regent's Park, the American Ambassador's residence, for their first, unscheduled, night.

The next morning they were welcomed to the UK by The Prince of Wales and The Duchess of Cornwall on behalf of The Queen. All four climbed into the 'Beast', the President's armoured car, more of a fortress than a limousine, and in a 19-car motorcade flanked by motorcycle outriders made the trip from Regent's Park, down Constitution Hill, into

the forecourt of Buckingham Palace and through the central arch of the east wing to the inner courtyard. An open carriage for the President of the United States was vetoed by his security staff with so many potential threats to guard against only three weeks after the killing of Osama Bin Laden.

The Queen and The Duke of Edinburgh were on hand to welcome them at the Grand Entrance to the palace. A brief meeting with The Duke and Duchess of Cambridge, married barely a month before and just back from their honeymoon – and Kate's first role as a member of the royal family – in the 1844 Room (named in honour of a state visit by Tsar Nicholas I in 1844) was followed by a ceremonial welcome on the West Terrace. Stepping out from the bowed front of the Music Room into the blustery sunshine, the President and The Queen stood two steps in front of The Duke of Edinburgh and Mrs Obama, who was holding her skirt down lest the gusts of wind should render her reminiscent of Marilyn Monroe in *The Seven Year Itch* (The Queen has her dressmaker sew tiny weights into her hems to discourage them lifting). As the Guards band played the American national anthem a 41-gun salute reverberated over the music from the guns of The King's Troop Royal Horse Artillery lined up in Green Park nearby. Twenty-one guns is the standard salute for heads of state but an extra 20 are added when the salute is given from a royal park. The President and The Duke of Edinburgh, accompanied by the major commanding, inspected the ceremonial guard of honour of 1st Battalion Scots Guards before the massed ranks moved off to the sound of the pipes and drums.

The Queen and The Duke then took the presidential couple on a tour of American-themed items from the Royal Collection, which had been assembled in the Picture Gallery, including a photograph of HMS *Resolute*, timbers from which were used to make the desk in the Oval Office in the White House. A trip to Westminster Abbey to lay a wreath on the Tomb of the Unknown Soldier was followed by a visit to Prime Minister David Cameron at 10 Downing Street and a game of table tennis against Southwark schoolboys, the Cameron–Obama axis being soundly beaten – which required a 'high-five' to cement the Special Alliance. A return to Buckingham Palace saw a courtesy call by the Leader of the Opposition and then it was time to get into white tie and tails ready for the state banquet, the President and the First Lady retiring to their suite in the Belgian State Apartments. This suite of interconnecting rooms was named after Victoria

Opposite page: A State Banquet in St George's Hall, Windsor Castle, 1855

THE GRAND STATE BANQUET IN ST. GEORGE'S HALL, WINDSOR CASTLE.

Above: A view of the ballroom at Buckingham Palace, prepared for a State Banquet in 2008

Below right: A member of staff prepares the banquet table for use, 2009

and Albert's uncle, Leopold, King of the Belgians, on the ground floor of the west-facing garden wing at the foot of the Minister's Staircase. These rooms also formed the suite used by Edward VIII during his brief tenure at Buckingham Palace before his abdication in 1936.

As the presidential couple got ready there would have been a purposeful bustle below stairs and in the ballroom where the table had been laid (preparation for the dinner had begun some three weeks before). Since 1914, all state banquets held at Buckingham Palace have been held in the ballroom, a vast room 36.6 metres long, 18 metres wide and 13.5 metres high (120 x 59 x 44 feet). When it was first built between 1853 and 1855 it was the largest room in London. The first event staged in the ballroom was a ball to commemorate the end of the Crimean War. In the centre of the room a huge horseshoe table had been constructed, a giant jigsaw puzzle of interlocking bases and tops, all adjustable to fit the numbers required – 172 on this particular night. For a state banquet the top of the horseshoe, where the guests of honour sit, is usually 8.5 metres (28 feet) across. It can seat 15, and is dressed with damask festoons, a tradition dating back to George IV's coronation banquet in 1821. The table is covered with seven fine damask linen tablecloths with the royal cipher of George IV woven at intervals, all sewn together to ensure they lie flat, and together extending over 60 metres (200 feet). At Windsor Castle a magnificent single 50-metre (175-foot) long mahogany table stretching the length of St George's Hall, dating from 1846, with 68 separate leaves and seating 160 people, is used for state banquets. It is left without tablecloths and polished to a high shine by staff standing on it using what appear to be padded croquet mallets.

At Buckingham Palace, with the tablecloths laid the table settings can

begin. The setting out of the table usually begins two full days before the banquet. The first to be set out are the table napkins embroidered with The Queen's monogram, folded into a Dutch-bonnet style by the Yeoman of the China and Glass Pantries. Candelabra holding over 100 ivory candles a foot high are placed at intervals, each candle topped with a miniature shade. They rest on mirrored stands, which reflect the candlelight and the gleam of gilt plate from the table settings. The very grandest, richly chased silver-gilt candelabra, depicting sculpted figures enacting stories from mythology, stand over 1.2 metres (4 feet) tall and hold 12 candles each. They are, like so many of the treasures on display, part of George IV's Grand Service of banqueting plate and cost nearly £3400 each in the early nineteenth century (approx. £240,000 today), a staggering sum. They are placed on either side of the 'top' table, just as it intersects with the two arms extending down the room. Over 30 flower arrangements take the royal florist and a team of arrangers the best part of 36 hours to create and are displayed on the tables and around the rooms. The flowers used for the Obama visit were predominantly roses, then in season, and the heady scent of their perfume permeated the air throughout the banquet.

The individual place settings measure 45 cm (18 inches) across and are laid according to the dishes to be served. For the Obama banquet over 2000 pieces of cutlery had to be individually polished and laid with perfect precision (according to the Butlers' Guild it should take about 15 minutes per place setting to get it absolutely right). Two knives and two forks were provided for the fish course (sole with crayfish and watercress with a béchamel sauce) and the meat course (new season's lamb from The Queen's Windsor farm with roast potatoes, roast radish, courgettes and green beans), a dessert spoon and fork for the pudding (vanilla charlotte with morello cherries eaten from Minton plates) and a butter knife. Fresh fruit is always displayed on the table (typically grapes, pineapples, plums and nectarines), each fruit or leaf polished to perfection, and a silver-gilt knife, fork and spoon also provided. The fruit is eaten from Tournai fruit plates, cut with a knife and eaten with a fork. Until recently a soup spoon had also been included but the soup course was abolished as the banquets were dragging on too long and the soup had taken at least 20 minutes to serve, consume and clear away. Four guests share a salt dispenser, a pepper caster and a mustard pot between them.

Six glasses are always set before each guest, one each for the white wine, red wine, water and port; there are two champagne glasses, one for the toast and one for the pudding course. The more than a thousand glasses on the table come from a set made at Stourbridge for The Queen's coronation in 1953 and are engraved with the EIIR cipher. All were cleaned, rinsed and polished immediately before laying to maintain their sparkle. The Yeoman of the Royal Cellars will have warmed and decanted the port (Royal Vintage, 1963), and checked the red and white wines and champagne (Veuve Clicquot Ponsardin Vintage) are at the right temperature. With rising temperatures as a consequence of global warming the alcohol content of British wines has now reached drinkable levels and that night a Fitzrovia Cuvée Merret rosé 2004 from the British winemaker Ridgeview was served. For the state banquet for the Irish President in April 2014 a Ridgeview Grosvenor Blanc de Blanc 2009 was chosen: 'Alluring and zesty, a sort of rustic Bollinger', according to wine expert Jancis Robinson. Some 5000 bottles a year are bought for the royal cellars for the more than 300 events held at Buckingham Palace and Windsor Castle. The more expensive wines served on state occasions are stored in the government cellars under Lancaster House.

A booklet was provided for every guest, bound with a red, white and blue ribbon, the colours of the American flag. Inside the timetable for the evening, the wine list, the menu (it is always in French, the language of gastronomy), the music played (selections from *South Pacific*) and a list of every guest attending was printed. At the back a seating plan folded out neatly with a coloured dot denoting the guest's seat, so anyone in doubt knew exactly where he or she should be seated.

Around the room tables covered in red fabric fringed with gold interspersed with tall buffets displayed the treasures from the Royal Collections, plate and china that is in many instances priceless. The gleaming plate, jugs, wall sconces, platters, dishes, tureens, basins and tankards in silver, silver-gilt and gold on display date largely from the time of George IV, who created the most lavish, theatrical backdrops of any monarch to the business of royal entertaining. At Carlton House in 1811, as Prince of Wales, he created one of his most spectacular *coups de théâtre*:

The Queen holds a banquet for the Royal Hospital Chelsea, 1965

a miniature waterfall fed a stream, lined with mossy banks, alive with swimming goldfish and studded with aquatic flowers, which ran down the centre of the dining table. The buffet at the Obama state banquet displayed a porcelain dessert service made for William IV between 1830 and 1837, at the Rockingham factory in Yorkshire, celebrating Britain's overseas territories and William's own naval background. The service, originally consisting of 56 large pieces and 12 dozen plates, may well be the most ambitious commission ever produced by an English factory.

With the table dressed and the chairs measured by rod to be at the correct distance, The Queen will have begun her pre-dinner check. Like any concerned hostess, she checks that all is well and her eagle eye can spot anything – a chair not in line, a candle not ramrod straight – a fraction awry. Below stairs (the kitchens were relocated directly beneath the ballroom when it was built) 20 chefs under Royal Chef Mark Flanagan had been hard at work preparing and cooking.

At the appointed time the Yeomen of the Guard, in their Tudor uniforms and carrying halberds, processed into the ballroom and took up their positions guarding the entrances, two standing directly behind where The Queen would sit. More discreetly the American presidential protection officers had stationed themselves around the building, earpieces connected to a command and control centre. The Queen with the President and The Duke of Edinburgh with the First Lady led the procession behind the sword-bearer, everyone governed by strict rules of precedence, into the ballroom. With all the guests seated the speeches began. That night there was a rare glitch. The band of the Scots Guards high on the balcony started to play the national anthem before the President had finished speaking. He gamely laboured on with his toast as the music played: 'To Her Majesty, The Queen, to the vitality of the special relationship between our peoples, and, in the words of Shakespeare, to this blessed plot, this earth, this realm, this England.'

With the toasts finished, the food service began. A hundred footmen under the direction of the Palace Steward are controlled by a system of traffic lights. When they turn from blue to green they pour in from all four corners of the room to serve the next course. When a zapper controlled from directly behind The Queen signals that she has finished they appear once more to clear the plates. Whether a guest has finished or not, that course is over. Queen Victoria was notorious for bolting her food and her older and slower courtiers managed to eat very little of their meal before it was removed. Petit fours, handmade chocolates and coffee are handed round before the end of the banquet is signalled by the arrival of the 12 pipers processing around the table, led by The Queen's Piper, Pipe-Major Derek Potter. The thirteenth Queen's Piper since Queen Victoria began the tradition after falling in love with the bagpipes in Scotland, his job, for four years until his retirement, was to play under The Queen's window at 9 o' clock each morning she was in residence. The tradition continues.

Above: President Obama and The Queen

Opposite page: The scale of a State Banquet reflects its history and significance

The day after the state banquet the visiting head of state will begin the serious business of advancing the agreed political and/or economic agenda. It may just be that the stunning display of hospitality that they have experienced, the finest food and wines served immaculately in a setting with an overwhelming history, might colour his or her attitude to the matters in hand. It most certainly cannot do any harm.

Balmoral Castle

'My dear paradise in the highlands.'

Queen Victoria

Above: The Queen and The Duke of Edinburgh relax in one of their private rooms at Balmoral, 1976

Balmoral Castle is The Queen's private Scottish residence and is, she has been overheard to remark, the only one of her houses in which she can spend two consecutive months sleeping in the same bed. It must come as a tremendous relief.

This is very much a home, rather than a palace – the entrance hall has a stone floor and fishing rods, waterproofs, wellingtons, and dog bowls are very much in evidence. The rooms have a 'Scottish country house' feel. It is, in short, a retreat, albeit a retreat where there is no escape from the continuous flow of red dispatch boxes and, in the middle of it all, a weekend stay for the prime minister of the day.

The sepia road signs in and around Ballater in Aberdeenshire proudly proclaim to travellers that they have entered 'Royal Deeside', but in spite of an influx of tourists in summer, this is a relatively quiet and secluded spot, the only bustle in evidence out of season being that of the River Dee, which snakes its way through the rugged landscape of an estate that includes one-sixth of all Scotland's remaining Caledonian pine forest.

Early history of the castle

Imposing in its grey granite livery, with towers and turrets a-plenty, Balmoral Castle has been owned by the royal family since 1851. Six hundred years before Queen Victoria and Prince Albert bought the estate, the founder of the Stuart royal dynasty, Robert II (an ancestor of the present royal family), owned a hunting lodge in the area. By the eighteenth century Balmoral was, appropriately, owned by the Farquharson family who lost the estate after fighting for the Jacobites, the followers of King James II, in the rebellions of 1715 and 1745. James Farquharson, known as 'Balmoral the Brave', was wounded at the Battle of Falkirk Muir in January 1746, a rare Jacobite victory, which took place during a violent storm.

A century later Victoria was to declare herself a Jacobite, too, as she embraced a highly romantic view of Scotland and its history, despite having 'Butcher' Cumberland, the victor of the Battle of Culloden (when the Jacobites were defeated), as a great-great uncle. After that battle, in April 1746, one of the Jacobite officers, Captain James Stuart, stayed at Balmoral on his way home.

The original castle, a square keep of the early sixteenth century with the addition of seventeenth-century turrets and a courtyard surrounded by a high wall, was partly demolished and extended in the mid-eighteenth century by the addition of a long, steep-gabled house with narrow windows set high in the walls. This was further extended in the nineteenth century and it was this patchwork building, set in a wild, picturesque landscape close to the ancient pine forest of Ballochbuie between the River Dee and the Cairngorm mountains, with which Victoria and Albert fell in love.

Their first visit to Scotland occurred purely by chance. In 1842, originally destined for a holiday in Brussels, Victoria

BALMORAL CASTLE.

fell ill and was advised by her doctor to go to Scotland as a less strenuous alternative.

Subsequent visits in 1844 and 1847 whetted their appetites. For Albert, the hills and forests reminded him of the landscape around his childhood home, Schloss Rosenau near Coburg. He wrote to his stepmother: 'We are all very well and live a somewhat primitive yet romantic mountain life, that acts as a tonic to the nerves and gladdens the heart …' Victoria was equally enchanted and later wrote in her diary, 'All seemed to breathe freedom and peace, and to make me forget the world and its sad turmoils.'

In 1847 The Queen and The Prince rented a house on Loch Laggan in Inverness-shire but the mist descended, it rained continually and they were beset by midges. Undeterred they returned the next year and, advised by The Queen's physician Sir James Clark, a graduate of Aberdeen University and an expert on climate and disease, they chose Deeside and took up a lease on Balmoral, its furnishings and staff, from Lord Aberdeen. Deeside

Balmoral in the 1850s

had reputedly the lowest rainfall in Scotland and 'bracing air'. In September 1848 they made their first visit and were immediately at home. Sarah Lyttelton of the household observed that leaving the Highlands produced 'actual red eyes' in Victoria. In later years she would dread going back to London and, like a child before being sent back to school, wrote in her diary, 'I wish we might be snowed up and unable to move.'

Balmoral, as the crow flies, is some 600 miles from London. Before the railways reached the Highlands, the royal couple and their entourage would embark at Woolwich on the new Royal Yacht *Victoria and Albert*, which had been launched in 1843, and sail up the east coast, followed by a long carriage drive. Balmoral must have seemed secluded, a world apart from the press and smell of London. In the capital, overflowing cesspits had caused cholera to become widespread in the 1840s and culminated in the Great Stink of 1856, when the stench of untreated human effluent in the River Thames was overpowering. Buckingham Palace, built over the culvert-contained Fleet river, did not escape from overflowing drains and a constant stench.

BALMORAL CASTLE

Kenneth Steel

ROYAL DEESIDE

SEE BRITAIN BY TRAIN

BRITISH RAILWAYS

By the late 1840s the railway line reached as far as Montrose, between Dundee and Aberdeen, and by 1853 Aberdeen itself. A branch line had also been built 16 miles to the West as far as Banchory, and then to Ballater, just five miles from Balmoral, by 1867. In the early days of train travel overnight stops were made for the royal party to sleep at Crewe and again at Perth but with the advent of the Royal Train in the late 1860s they slept on board. Typically the party would leave Windsor Castle after lunch, have tea at Leamington Spa, breakfast the next morning at Perth and be at Balmoral in time for lunch.

With his characteristic vigour Albert set to improving the house and grounds. The immediate landscape was a particular obsession and he enlisted the help of landscape designer James Beattie and painter James Giles. Giles was not only a famous landscape painter of the picturesque and sublime – and an Aberdonian to boot – but also had an extensive practice as a landscape architect working with the owners of Aberdeenshire estates. With these two to help him Albert planted a huge number of trees and attended to the layout of the gardens, including creating new parterres. He redirected roads and created new bridges – Isambard Kingdom Brunel designed one of them, a new bridge of 'functional elegance' over the Dee linking Balmoral to the local village of Crathie, in 1857.

But the house was quickly deemed too small for the royal couple, their three children, the Royal Household and 60 attendant servants so the architect of the most recent work to the old house, John Smith of Aberdeen, was commissioned with his son William to once more enlarge the castle.

The first phase of building included new estate buildings and offices and, in due course, a large pre-fabricated corrugated-iron structure to serve as a temporary dining room and ballroom – Albert had been much taken

Above: Queen Victoria and her family pose outside Balmoral, 1896

Opposite page: A British Rail poster publicizing the rail line to Deeside, featuring a painting by Kenneth Steel

Top: Abergeldie Castle, 1900
Above: Victoria and her son Bertie, 1894

with one he had seen at the Great Exhibition of 1851.

In November 1851, a chance presented itself to buy the estate outright. After protracted negotiations Balmoral and its estate of 17,400 acres stretching westward to the summit of Lochnagar was bought for £31,500 (approx. £3 million today), with the neighbouring estates of Birkhall, purchased at the same time for Albert Edward, Prince of Wales (known as Bertie, who would become King Edward VII), and Abergeldie, held on a long lease from the Gordon family.

Abergeldie was besieged during the Jacobite rebellion by John Farquharson of Inverey. When he was defeated at the Pass of Ballater, and the castle relieved, his lands were destroyed, the garrison commander burned everything in a 12-mile radius including up to an estimated 1400 houses. In Victoria's time Abergeldie Castle was lived in by various members of the royal family, including the future Edward VII (who had abandoned Birkhall as being too small), and Eugenie, ex-Empress of the French. Birkhall is now used by Prince Charles and The Duchess of Cornwall.

In October of the following year, 1852, The Queen and Prince Albert celebrated the purchase of Balmoral with what was to be the first of many cairn-raising ceremonies. Craig Gowan, a prominent position overlooking the house, was selected and the members of the royal family in residence, the household, servants, tenants and their families gathered in a circle to help build the cairn. Victoria wrote in her diary:

'I placed the first stone, after which Albert laid one, then the children, according to their ages. All the ladies and gentlemen placed one, and then everyone came forward at once, carrying a stone and placing it on the cairn. At last when the cairn, which I think is seven or eight feet high, was nearly completed, Albert climbed up to the top of it, and placed the last stone, after which three cheers were given. This took about an hour during which the piper Angus McKay played, whisky was drunk and merry reels danced on a stone opposite.'

Over the following decades a rash of cairns spread over the hills behind the house celebrating, commemorating or memorializing individuals and events.

The Balmoral Cairns

Eleven stone cairns commemorating important events in the domestic annals of the royal family are clustered on the summits of various hills on the Balmoral estate (with one on the neighbouring Birkhall estate) and a visitors' trail links those closest together. Victoria and Albert's inspiration for the cairns may have come from previous owners of Balmoral, the Jacobite Farquharsons, whose remembrance cairn, Cairnaquheen ('Cam na Cuimhne' or 'cairn of remembrance' was the old war cry of the Farquharsons), stands by the riverside about a mile or so above Balmoral. The cairn acted as a tally – as each member of the clan went off to war he added a stone to the pile. If he returned, he removed one; the stones still left were a poignant reminder of those killed or missing.

After Victoria and Albert's first cairn, the Purchase Cairn, was built in 1852, others followed to mark the marriages of their children, and what a diverse clan they commemorate. Nine children produced 40 grandchildren, including two kings, five queens and a member of the Reichstag representing the Nazi Party. The history surrounding these cairns is complex but fascinating – showing the interwoven nature of the royal families of Europe and the broad scattering of Victoria and Albert's progeny.

THE PRINCESS ROYAL The *Princess Royal's Cairn* marks the marriage of Victoria and Albert's eldest child, Princess Victoria, to the Crown Prince of Prussia, later German Kaiser Friedrich III, at St James's Palace in 1858. The belligerent Kaiser Wilhelm II, Britain's enemy in the First World War, was their eldest son. Their seventh child, Sophie, married Constantine I and became Queen of Greece.

ALBERT EDWARD *Albert Edward's Cairn* of 1863, celebrating the future King Edward VII's marriage to Alexandra, Princess of Denmark, is on the Birkhall estate. Their second son became George V. In 1889 their eldest daughter Louise married MacDuff, the 6th Earl of Fife (created Duke on his marriage) who was a great-grandson of William IV by his mistress Mrs Jordan and who owned over a quarter of a million acres of land in the vicinity of Balmoral and neighbouring counties. Somewhat typically of any ambitious mother of the time, Victoria wrote, 'It is a very brilliant marriage in a wordly point of view as he is immensely rich.'

PRINCESS ALICE *Princess Alice's Cairn* marks her marriage to Prince Louis of Hesse at

The Purchase Cairn, erected in 1852 to commemorate the purchase of the Balmoral Estate by Queen Victoria and Prince Albert

Osborne House in 1862 shortly after the death of her father, Prince Albert. Queen Victoria, in deep mourning, wrote to her eldest daughter that the ceremony had been 'more of a funeral than a wedding'. Of their seven children their daughter and sixth child, Alexandra, became the most famous when, as Tsarina of Russia, she was killed with her husband Tsar Nicholas II after the Russian Revolution.

PRINCE ALBERT   *Prince Albert's Cairn*, unlike the others a large pyramid of faced stone, was erected by Queen Victoria as one of his many memorials. An inset panel reads: 'To the Beloved Memory of Prince Albert, the Great and Good Prince Consort, Erected by his Broken-hearted Widow, VICTORIA. R. 21st August 1862' (Albert had died the previous December). The initials of the royal children are carved on individual stones on the north-east face.

PRINCESS LOUISE   *Princess Louise's Cairn* was built in 1871 to mark her marriage to the Marquess of Lorne, later the 9th Duke of Argyll. This was not a success as the Marquess, it was said, 'preferred guardsmen'. He was later Governor-General of Canada.

PRINCE ALFRED   Alone of all the children, Prince Alfred appears to have no cairn: no one quite knows why, although he married the Grand Duchess Marie Fedorovna of Russia in 1874 in St Petersburg. He served in the Royal Navy throughout his career, becoming Admiral of the Fleet in 1893, and succeeded his Uncle Ernest (Prince Albert's brother) as Duke of Saxe-Coburg-Gotha the same year.

PRINCESS HELENA   *Princess Helena's Cairn* was built to mark her marriage in 1874 to Prince Christian of Schleswig-Holstein in the Private Chapel at Windsor Castle.

BALLOCHBUIE   The *Ballochbuie Cairn* was erected in 1878 on Baderonach Hill towards the eastern border of the Ballochbuie forest to mark The Queen's purchase of about 2500 acres of this ancient forest of Scots pine – many over 400 years old – from the Farquharsons to prevent it being sold to an Aberdeen timber merchant. The inscription reads: 'Queen Victoria entered into possession of the Ballochbuie 15th May 1878. "The Bonniest Plaid in Scotland."' This somewhat enigmatic inscription is thought to be an allusion to a tradition that a Macgregor, perhaps under duress, had sold the forest to a Farquharson for a tartan plaid.

PRINCE ARTHUR   *Prince Arthur's Cairn* was erected in 1879 to mark his marriage to Louise of Prussia, the niece of his godfather, Kaiser Wilhelm I. Their eldest child Margaret married Gustaf Adolf, who became King of Sweden long after her death in 1920.

PRINCE LEOPOLD   *Prince Leopold's Cairn* celebrates his marriage to Princess Helena of Waldeck, a descendant of George II, in 1882. Prince Leopold was a haemophiliac and died after a fall aged 30. Their two children lived very different lives. Princess Alice, Countess of Athlone, devoted herself to charitable works in England. Her brother Charles, after Eton, became Duke of Saxe-Coburg-Gotha, fought as a German general in the First World War and subsequently became a member of the Nazi party.

PRINCESS BEATRICE   *Princess Beatrice's Cairn* was built to commemorate her marriage to Prince Henry of Battenburg in 1885 at Whippingham Church on the Isle of Wight. As the youngest child, Victoria expected Beatrice to be her constant companion. After she fell in love with Prince Henry, Victoria refused to speak to her for seven months before relenting on the condition that the couple lived with her. Their second child, Victoria, married Alfonso XIII and became Queen of Spain.

JOHN BROWN   *John Brown's Cairn* was erected by Victoria after the death of her personal servant, who had been born just a half a mile from Balmoral Castle. Brown's relationship with the monarch has been the subject of much conjecture and the cairn was later flattened on the orders of Edward VII, who loathed Brown.

THE QUEEN   In 2012 the present Queen's Diamond Jubilee was celebrated by the construction of a cairn of 60 stones – one for each year of her reign and collected from 30 different locations around Balmoral – in the neighbouring village of Ballater. The main stone from Inver quarry was carved by local stonemason Gregor Robertson and covered for the unveiling with the Balmoral tartan.

Right: Prince Albert's Cairn, erected in 1862 by his widow Queen Victoria

Albert's development of the royal residence

With the purchase of Balmoral, and a timely bequest, Albert determined that the old house should not just be extended piecemeal but be entirely replaced. The bequest was made by a wealthy miser, John Camden Neild, who had died in August 1852 and left almost the whole of his estate valued at half a million pounds (worth approx. £47 million today) to 'Her Most Gracious Majesty Queen Victoria, begging her majesty's most gracious acceptance of the same for her sole use and benefit'. Victoria commented in her diary: 'A very handsome fortune had inexplicably been bequeathed to me by a Mr John Camden Neild. He knew I would not squander it.'

John Smith had by now retired so Prince Albert worked with his son William Smith to design a vast, sprawling edifice with a central tower 24 metres (80 feet) high, two courtyards and a host of turrets and gables in the by then slightly old-fashioned Scottish Baronial style and 'skilfully arranged to command the finest views of the surrounding mountains and of the neighbouring river Dee'. Albert's preferred method was to make rough sketches from which he expected his architect to create working drawings. The stone, a whitish-grey granite, was quarried from the estate quarries at Glen Gelder. The main reception rooms and apartments were to be in the south-west block and the service functions in that to the north-west. Accommodation was planned for over 120 guests and courtiers plus attendant staff.

Demolition began of the old castle in 1853 (though parts of it continued to provide accommodation for staff until 1856) and on 28 September a formal ceremony marked the laying of the foundation stone of the new building. Even this small ceremony was meticulously planned by Albert. Lytton Strachey, in his biography of Victoria, wrote: 'With great ceremony, in accordance with a memorandum drawn up by the Prince for the occasion, the foundation-stone ... was laid.' The Prince's memorandum, which goes on for several pages, choreographs every second of the event:

'The workmen will be placed in a semicircle at a little distance from the stone, and the women and home servants in an inner semicircle. Her Majesty the Queen, and His Royal Highness the Prince, accompanied by the Royal Children, Her Royal Highness the Duchess of Kent, and attended by Her Majesty's guests and suite will proceed from the house. Her Majesty, the Prince, and the Royal Family, will stand on the south side of the stone ...'

It concludes: *'The workmen will then leave the dinner-room, and amuse themselves upon the green with Highland games till seven o'clock, when a dance will take place in the ball-room.'*

All the household, workmen and staff attended. In a cavity a time capsule – a bottle – was placed containing a parchment signed by the royal family and 'current coins of the present reign'. The stone was then laid on top and the festivities began – a staff dinner followed by Highland games and a dance for all – following to the letter the strict timetable set down.

It was to be two years before their apartments were ready, although the tower and much else of the new house was still half-finished (a covered wooden passageway connected the new to what remained of the old) and on 7 September 1855 the royal party first stepped into their new home. As they entered, in the Scots tradition, an old shoe was thrown after them for good luck. Victoria wrote in her diary that night: 'The house is charming; the rooms delightful; the furniture, papers, everything perfection.' Three days later, at about half-past ten at night, the stationmaster from Banchory, having ridden some 27 miles to do so, delivered two 'telegraphic despatches' that had arrived at his station, one for The Queen and one for the Minister in Attendance. They announced the end of the Siege of Sebastopol, the last act of the Crimean War and the final defeat of the Russian Army. Albert in celebration led the household, servants and people of the surrounding villages up to the top of a cairn where a bonfire had been built. This was lit, and a great deal of whisky drunk so that the people were in a 'great ecstasy'. The Queen was extraordinarily lenient, for one so puritanical in most things, of drunkenness amongst her Highland servants. She said she liked to see them merry.

The marriage of Frederick and Victoria at Balmoral, 1858

Within a week of moving in Prince Frederick of Prussia came to stay and almost immediately asked Victoria and Albert if he could marry Princess Victoria, who was then 14. Permission was granted and on 29 September, on an excursion up a nearby mountain, he presented a piece of white heather to Victoria whilst making 'an allusion to his hopes and wishes'. This 'led to a happy conclusion'. They married in 1858, when The Princess was 17. By all accounts, for the 30 years before his death from throat cancer, it was a happy marriage. They had planned to model their roles as Emperor and Empress on that of Victoria and Albert but they only reigned for three short months before his death. As a liberal he was determined to curb the powers of his chancellor, Otto von Bismarck. Had he lived the course of German history might have been very different.

In August 1856, The Queen wrote: 'on arrival at Balmoral ... we found the tower finished as well as the offices, and the poor old house gone!' Despite incessant horizontal rain, high winds and clouds of midges (a constant refrain in her diaries) Balmoral and its environs enchanted the royal couple, and Queen Victoria constantly waxed lyrical about it: 'Highlanders in their brilliant and picturesque dresses, the wild notes of the pipes ... the beautiful background of mountains, rendered the scene wild and striking in the extreme.' And also: 'such magnificent wild rocks, precipices and corries. It had a sublime and solemn effect; so wild, so solitary'. And again, in a fusillade of exclamation marks: 'Oh! What can equal the beauties of nature! What enjoyment there is in them! Albert enjoys it so much! He is in ecstasies here.'

The couple's enthusiasm for all things Scottish prompted the effusion of Scots themes in which Albert swathed the interiors of the new house. Tartans (including several new ones designed largely by Albert himself) were spread over carpets, linoleum, curtains, chintzes and upholstery. Wallpapers were decorated with motifs of thistles and heather – the thistles were in such profusion 'as would rejoice the heart of a donkey', according to Lord Clarendon, then Foreign Secretary. Stags' antlers were tortured into a variety of candelabra and other light fittings. Figures of highlanders covered in plaid were incorporated into a variety of furnishings. The walls were hung with drawings by Edwin Landseer and multiple prints of his paintings, largely of Highland scenes.

The Balmoral (Royal) tartan

'The deadening slime of Balmorality' was a term coined by disaffected Scots who sought to blame Victoria and Albert and their devotion to all things Scottish for the trivialization of such matters as the Scottish national dress. In fact, the mania for Scottish tartan had begun 20 years before Victoria and Albert's first visit to Scotland when, in 1822, Victoria's uncle George IV paid the first visit of a reigning monarch north of the border since Charles I in 1641 (in 1633 he had been crowned King of Scots). George IV's visit was also a chance event. Invited to attend a congress in Verona his government ministers, wishing to keep the control of foreign affairs in their own hands, proposed he visit Edinburgh instead. This led the civic authorities to search frantically through old documents to uncover the protocols, precedents and pageantry for such a visit.

Fortunately, that living repository of Scottish lore, real and invented, Sir Walter Scott, was at hand to advise and he headed a small committee to plan the festivities. Walter Scott was author of the hugely successful novel *Waverley*, published anonymously in 1814, in which an officer in the Hanoverian army changes sides and fights for the Jacobite cause in the 1745 rebellion. This popularized a romantic image of the Scottish Highlands. Intrigued, the following year George, then Prince Regent, invited Scott to dinner where he was reminded by Scott of his Stuart lineage and his entitlement to 'wear the garb of old Gaul'.

Sir Walter Scott posing in traditional Scottish national dress

Accordingly, in July 1822 The King placed an order with George Hunter and Co. for a complete Highland outfit in the bright red Royal Stuart tartan complete with all the necessary accessories and weaponry, which set him back about £100,000 in today's money – his considerable girth requiring more than the usual yardage of plaid. The following month he spent two weeks in Scotland, staying with The Duke of Buccleuch at Dalkeith Palace (Bonnie Prince Charlie had spent two nights there in 1754), just outside Edinburgh, as Holyrood Palace was in poor repair. His visit was a triumph, celebrated with scenes of magnificence and traditional pageantry, much of it including the 'revised ancient dresses' invented for the occasion by Scott's committee.

The committee had produced a prescriptive booklet advising on etiquette, general behaviour and style of clothing: 'HINTS addressed to the INHABITANTS OF EDINBURGH AND OTHERS in prospect of HIS MAJESTY'S VISIT'. Not all Scots were enthusiastic: One wrote: 'Sir Walter Scott has ridiculously made us appear to be a nation of Highlanders, and the bagpipe and the tartan are the order of the day.'

Clearly memories of the events of scarcely a generation before, when tartan had been outlawed, had faded. An ordinance issued by George II two years after the Jacobite rebellion of 1745 declared: 'no man ... will wear or put on the clothes commonly called Highland Clothes ... and that no tartan ... shall be used'. The penalty for a first offence was six months in prison, for a second, transportation for life. It was repealed in 1782 and since then seems to have been totally overlooked by the Scots.

The culmination of the royal visit was a Highland Ball in which the portly King was to be present in his Stuart tartan and the committee's manual demanded that, save those who were in uniform: 'no Gentleman is to be allowed to appear in any thing but the ancient Highland costume'. As Lytton Strachey observed, 'This can be seen as the pivotal event when what had been thought of as the primitive dress of mountain thieves became the national dress of the whole of Scotland.' And it sparked a fashionable frenzy – tartan became à la mode in Paris.

So the adoption of the tartan by Victoria and Albert at Balmoral some 20 years later was hardly a first. With his zeal for design, Albert created in 1853 a completely new tartan, the Balmoral, in three colourways. The Royal was in pale grey with overchecks in red and black to echo the rough-hewn granite of the castle, and is still used by The Queen today during her annual Balmoral holiday. The tartan can only be worn by the sovereign, the sovereign's personal piper and other members of the royal family with permission. The other two were Green and Lavender, each with the same background grey. Later a Victoria Stuart was created, Victoria's personal take on the Dress Stuart, with a red stripe added.

When Albert came to design the interiors of Balmoral, tartan was everywhere. Lytton Strachey again:

'the floors were ... covered with specially manufactured tartans. The Balmoral tartan, in red and grey, designed by the Prince, and the Victoria tartan, were to be

Above and below:
Queen Victoria in her private
rooms at Balmoral

seen in every room: there were tartan curtains, and tartan chair-covers, and even tartan linoleums. Occasionally the Royal Stuart tartan appeared, for Her Majesty always maintained that she was an ardent Jacobite. There were ... innumerable stags' antlers, and the head of a boar, which had been shot by Albert in Germany. In an alcove in the hall, stood a life-sized statue of Albert in Highland dress.'

Victoria declared that it was all perfection. 'Every year,' she wrote, 'my heart becomes more fixed in this dear paradise, and so much more so now, that ALL has become my dear Albert's own creation, own work, own building, own layout ... and his great taste, and the impress of his dear hand, have been stamped everywhere.' It is clear that Queen Victoria's feelings on anything were never less than intense.

The tartan kilt has since become embedded deep in the psyche of the royal family and successive generations have worn it as a matter of course when travelling north of the border. Bertie, later Edward VII, even sported a miniature kilt and sporran when, aged nine, he accompanied his parents to the opening of the Great Exhibition at the Crystal Palace in London in May 1851. As a young man ten years later, he again chose to wear the kilt as he walked behind his father's coffin in St George's Chapel, Windsor Castle.

Queen Victoria and her family at Balmoral. From left to right: Alexandra, Tsarina of Russia, her baby daughter Grand Duchess Tatiana, Tsar Nicholas II of Russia, Queen Victoria and Edward, Prince of Wales

From then on The Queen and The Prince travelled to Balmoral each year for their autumn Highland holiday. They much enjoyed the freedom they found there and went on daily expeditions, come rain or shine, into the mountains and forests, Victoria walking or riding her pony, sketching and painting as she went, whilst Albert darted off, rifle in hand, to shoot whatever moved.

Every year they would also make longer expeditions by carriage and train to stay with friends in grand houses and castles in other parts of the Highlands. Sometimes, under assumed names, they would stay in small hotels in picturesque locations, travelling a hundred miles or more by coach. Each landmark, loch, mountain, moor, battlefield, house (and its owner) was assiduously noted. Often, like a location scout for a television company, Victoria's private secretary would have gone ahead to discover people she might like to have 'presented' – that is, introduced to the royal presence, during the course of her journeys. The descriptions in her diaries and in the two books she published on her Highland excursions make constant reference to rain and cold and wind. Victoria seemed to positively relish the cold and even in winter windows were required to be left open. Her private secretary, Sir Henry Ponsonby, attempting to play billiards, once found frost on the cushion of the billiard table.

For her staff, the annual visits to Balmoral were not eagerly anticipated. The Castle was variously described as cheerless, dreary and, despite the reduced household that travelled to Balmoral, cramped.

Victoria also micro-managed all activities – which were compulsory. Apart from walks and excursions in the inevitable rain there was simply not enough to do to amuse and entertain her household or the Minister in Attendance. This was Victoria's one concession to affairs of state – apart from her red boxes. At Osborne on the Isle of Wight she and Albert had built state rooms to accommodate the rituals of government required of a monarch. At Balmoral, her private hideaway, there were no such rooms and a single government minister was in attendance at all times. In order to escape into even greater solitude Victoria and Albert refurbished and added onto a small cottage far up Glen Muick. Known as 'The Hut', they would retreat there for days at a time with the minimum of servants.

Victoria the Jacobite
The royal claim to the Stuart tartan

Victoria was right to declaim herself a Stuart, but perhaps not a Jacobite – if the Jacobite cause had won the day she would not have been Queen of England. Seven generations before, Elizabeth Stuart, daughter of James IV of Scotland (James I of England) and sister of Charles I, had married Frederick V, the Elector Palatinate. Their grandson became George I of England at the age of 54 in succession to his cousin Anne, youngest daughter of James II. So the first of the Hanoverian Kings of England was in fact one-quarter Stuart (but definitely not a Jacobite) and our present Queen is Elizabeth Stuart's ninth great-granddaughter.

The 'Jacobite succession', the descent from Charles II as opposed to the descent of Queen Elizabeth II from his sister Elizabeth Stuart, is in fact the most senior line of descent but it was nullified by the Act of Settlement of 1707, which required the next in line to the throne after Anne's death to be a Protestant.

When Charles II's brother James converted to Catholicism there was widespread disquiet and the fabricated 'Popish Plot', current in the late 1670s, which proposed that Charles should be killed and James would reign in his stead, produced anti-Catholic hysteria. When James succeeded his brother a succession of controversial measures stoked the fires and when he produced a Catholic heir in 1688, a group of noblemen invited James's nephew (and son-in-law), the Protestant William of Orange, to invade England. The 'Glorious Revolution' deposed James in favour of William and his wife Mary, James's eldest daughter, and the last Catholic sovereign of England was exiled and died in France in 1701, at the age of 77.

Victoria, the inconsolable widow

Prince Albert made his final visit to Balmoral in 1861, just months before his death of typhoid in December while at Windsor Castle. He was just 42. The Queen was in shock and deep mourning, for she had become to rely on Albert in every way – she had granted him the title Prince Consort in 1857 as he had become 'King to all intents and purposes' and a 'necessary and useful part of the mechanism of the State'. Victoria virtually abandoned Buckingham Palace and lived alternately at Windsor and, for increasing periods, in Scotland. From then on it was her custom to stay at Balmoral for nearly a month in early summer and for up to three months in the autumn. In the nearly 50 years of her occupation it has been calculated that she lived 12 complete years at Balmoral.

She wrote to her Uncle Leopold: 'My LIFE as a HAPPY one is ENDED! The world is gone for ME! ... Oh! to be cut off in the prime of life – to see our pure, happy, quiet, domestic life, which ALONE enabled me to bear my MUCH disliked position, CUT OFF at forty-two.' She added, 'it is my firm resolve ... his wishes, his plans about everything, his views about everything are to be my law'.

There were no changes to the fabric of Balmoral after this date: everything was kept as it had been ordered by the hand of Albert. Memorials were in due course erected, the pyramid, and also a copy in bronze of the marble statue of Prince Albert in highland dress, gun in hand and dog at his side, was placed on a rocky eminence near the Balmoral bridge. At the unveiling on 15 October 1876 (they had become engaged on that day 28 years before) all the servants, tenants, the household and a detachment of Highlanders attended. The pipes were played and the soldiers loosed off a '*feu de joie*'. The whole ceremony took place, of course, in pouring rain. Nearby there is a granite obelisk erected to his memory by the tenants and servants on the Balmoral estate.

'The Hut' being the repository of too

The unveiling of Prince Albert's statue, 1876

John Brown in tartan, 1870

many happy memories, and seeking further seclusion, Victoria built a cottage for herself on the opposite end of the Loch in 1868. This she called the 'Widow's House' and she would retreat there with only a few servants who knew her well, including John Brown. It was after Albert's death that she came to rely more and more on her abrasive Highland servant.

Brown, from a local family, had been a ghillie but had recommended himself to Victoria and Albert by his untiring devotion. Given to drinking (complications from which he eventually died), informal in manner to The Queen and others, and rude and divisive amongst the other servants, his general competence and the important role he played in The Queen's life were nonetheless recognized by her private secretary, Sir Henry Ponsonby. Sir Henry had shared the driver's 'box' with Brown on many of The Queen's arduous excursions and came to observe his qualities at first hand. When he died in March 1883 she was again distraught: 'Perhaps never in history was there so strong and true an attachment, so warm and loving a friendship between the sovereign and servant ... the Queen feels that life for the second time is becoming most trying and sad to bear deprived of all she so needs ... the blow has fallen too heavily not to be very heavily felt.'

During his lifetime, Victoria had built Brown a cottage in the grounds of Balmoral and after his death erected a cairn and statue to his memory. Every year on her birthday she would place flowers on Albert's statue and on the grave of John Brown. To perpetuate his memory she began to write the story of his life but her staff advised her against publication as the contents might be 'misunderstood'. Victoria was buried with mementoes of both men: Albert's dressing gown and a plaster cast of his hand; a lock of John Brown's hair, his photograph and also a ring he had given to her, which was put on a finger of her right hand. All the Brown memorabilia was hidden, covered discreetly by flowers. On his accession Edward VII destroyed most of Victoria's memorials to Brown and had his statue at Balmoral moved into the woods some distance from the castle.

A few years later, in 1887, she took an interest in two Indian servants selected in her Jubilee year to become her personal servants. She transferred the personal attachment she had felt for Brown to one of them, Mohammed Abdul Karim, known as 'the Munshi'. He was allocated Brown's room at Balmoral and in due course a cottage in the grounds. Surprisingly, he had none of Brown's qualities, was even more divisive, loathed by the other servants and regarded as taking advantage of his position for personal gain. Ponsonby also thought little of him, by comparison with his cautious approval of John Brown: the Munshi 'was a thoroughly stupid and uneducated man, and his one idea in life seems to be to do nothing and to eat as much as he can'. During her Balmoral visit in September 1889, she and Karim stayed for one night at the 'Widow's House', Glassalt Shiel at Loch Muick, which caused consternation in the household. On her death, however, he was allowed by Edward VII to be the last to view her body and then took part in her funeral procession. He was subsequently dismissed and returned to India.

During their lifetimes, Victoria and Albert had found solace at Balmoral from the formalities of court life at Buckingham Palace and Windsor. They revelled in the seclusion – The Queen could drop into the cottages of the local people without ceremony, Albert could disappear into the woods with his rifle in the mornings and they could explore together the surrounding forests and mountains on foot or by pony in the afternoons. After his death and her withdrawal from much of her role as head of state, the seclusion of Balmoral was even more precious and she spent much longer periods of time there. It became, for others, a considerable trial to serve her as she enforced her regime of 'seclusion, silence, 30-minute meals, non-smoking and open windows'.

Edward VII and Queen Alexandra

After Victoria's death, Balmoral continued to be used by succeeding generations for their autumn holidays. Bertie, the future Edward VII, had become an enthusiastic sportsman as he grew up – he was an exceptional shot, a keen and skilful fisherman, a successful yachtsman and his horses won many of the classic races. A convivial man, he delighted in large house parties, and for him the epitome of sport was to take groups of friends to the heather and forests of Balmoral in search of deer, grouse and ptarmigan and to the fields. His induction had started early. At the age of not quite seven he had been included in a deer-stalking party led by his father in the hills above the castle and witnessed his father claim his first

Edward VII poses with a deer shot on the Balmoral estate

Balmoral stag that day. Victoria wrote: 'a magnificent stag, a Royal [a stag with more than twelve branched antlers], which had dropped soon after Albert had hit him'. Two years later Bertie witnessed the Balmoral tenants fishing, or rather spearing and netting, salmon on the Dee, and in 1858, at the age of 16, he shot his first stag.

Birkhall had been purchased in Bertie's name when he was seven but with his large circle of friends he in due course found it too small, and from his marriage in 1863 he was lent Abergeldie, where he would entertain his large shooting parties, avoiding Balmoral as much as he could. The future Edward VII had an 'intense and commanding personality' and led a decidedly rackety life where he entertained lavishly, kept mistresses, was addicted to the theatre, smoked, drank, gambled at baccarat (then illegal) and became mired in scandal. Victoria had disapproved of him from a very early age, blaming him for Albert's early death. For all of her long reign she allowed him no formal role and excluded him from any responsibility with the almost inevitable result he lived a life of pleasure and excess.

With the reputation of the monarchy at a low ebb due to Victoria's seclusion at Balmoral or Osborne on the Isle of Wight, wrapped in a fog of grief and increasingly de-skilled as a monarch, it is no wonder that Bertie became the first modern 'gossip-column prince' whose every exploit was followed avidly by the society papers. At first the mood of the nation was against him – he had even been booed and hissed in public – but he was free of any racial or religious prejudice and had a rare ability to get on with people from all walks of life and put them at their ease. That trait, coupled with his near-death from typhoid fever, changed public perception. For two months, from mid-November 1871 to the middle of January of the following year, he was gravely ill and the nation read the daily bulletins with increasing anxiety and alarm. From then on he acquired affection from his subjects, which lasted for the rest of his life, and it is generally recognized that having been a somewhat dissolute Prince of Wales, as a monarch (1901–10) he acquitted himself admirably.

Victoria left most of her fortune to her younger children and Bertie was left with the considerable upkeep of the three privately owned royal houses, Balmoral, Sandringham and Osborne, which had been left to all the children. He calculated that the annual outgoings for the houses were £20,000, £40,000 and £17,000 respectively (approx. £1.9 million, £3.8 million and £1.6 million today). When negotiating the size of his civil list with the government of the day he undertook economies in the running of his establishments – 'I cannot live in and maintain five places!' – and despite protests from some of his siblings gave Osborne House, where Victoria had died, to the nation. In due course it became a school for naval officers and subsequently a convalescent home. It is now open to the public and administered by English Heritage.

At Balmoral Bertie enthusiastically continued and embellished the Scottish traditions of his parents. He wore a kilt every day, either Balmoral or Hunting Stuart, and at night changed into Royal Stuart. Bagpipers played round the dinner table – the noise must have been deafening. However, his hectic social life elsewhere necessitated a reduced stay and he rarely visited for more than a month.

He revived or reinvented all the old ceremonial attached to the monarchy, for the first time in 40 years driving to the state opening of Parliament in the old state coach. It was Edward VII who re-established the monarchy as spectacle, so important a role today, and made it glamorous again.

George V and Queen Mary

Edward VII's son George V – generally regarded as man less at ease in society – was much fonder of Balmoral Castle than his father and looked forward to his two months there each autumn. He had inherited his father's insistence on ritual and protocol but he was a very different man. Ordered, punctilious and punctual to a fault, he adhered to a clockwork, naval routine that required him to check the barometer on first rising and again before going to bed.

All his life a stickler for correct dress, George V was immaculately tailored. At Balmoral he swapped his frock coat and tall hat for a kilt, an Inverness cape and a feathered bonnet. At night he dined in a kilt with the Order of the Thistle on his breast. And yet, despite the insistence on correct protocol, he was a man who embraced the domestic virtues, not those of nightclubs, corridor creeping or gambling. He declared emphatically, 'I'm not interested in any wife except my own.'

Opposite page: Osborne House
Below: George V, his wife Mary, and their young family

A visitor to Balmoral in 1910, his first year as King, he described it as 'altogether different from former years ... the house is a home for children ... The Queen knits of an evening ... We go to bed early'. Prime Minister Lloyd George wrote: 'The King is a very jolly chap ... they are simple, very, very ordinary people.' Large shooting parties were replaced by much smaller gatherings. Not even bridge was played and so the evenings were torture for guests and the visiting Minister in Attendance – 'the evenings are rather tedious' – until relieved by the early, 11 o'clock bedtime curfew. It was all a far cry from the life of Edward VII who had required his guests to stay up until he went to bed, often well into the wee small hours. Anyone spotted as absent would have a page sent to rouse them out and return them to the festivities. George V's tenure of Balmoral was interrupted by the war, and it was six years before he resumed his annual Scottish holiday: 'I am glad to be in this dear place again', he wrote in August 1919.

The future King Edward VII with family and guests at a shooting party at Balmoral, 1900.

George V perpetuated the cult of the royal picnic that continues to this day. Even to brave the rain and the midges a strict dress code was observed. For men a heavy tweed suit with breeches, long, thick woollen socks, polished brogues and, of course, a hat were required. Women wore tweed suits with long skirts – and a hat. They were transported in large maroon Daimlers, complete with gold-plated radiators, which wound their way along the narrow tracks to the shores of Loch Muick. There the food would be unpacked and served by liveried footmen. On occasion a chef attired in whites would prepare freshly caught fish.

Like his father, George V was an excellent shot and the deer and grouse at Balmoral were an added attraction for him. The late Queen Mother, writing to her mother-in-law after a stay at Balmoral, was not quite so keen: 'even though I am the wife, daughter and sister of "guns", I fail to see what pleasure there can be in walking about all day in an icy wind and driving rain!' In another letter she was prescient about the future: 'You and Papa [George V] make such a <u>family</u> feeling by your great kindness and thought for everybody but David [later Edward VIII] does not seem to possess the faculty of making others feel <u>wanted</u> ... he had that extraordinary charm, and it all disappeared'

Edward VIII – and the abdication

Edward VIII inherited many of his grandfather's proclivities. He moved in a fast, metropolitan set, enjoyed parties and kept mistresses. In 1928 George V fell gravely ill. The Prince of Wales was on holiday in Kenya when he heard the news but did not choose to curtail his holiday, despite strong words from the courtier accompanying him who reported that:

Top: Edward VIII with his nieces Elizabeth and Margaret

Below: Princes playing in Loch Muick. From left to right: Prince George; Edward, Prince of Wales; Prince Albert and Prince Henry, 1912

looked at me, went out without a word, and spent the remainder of the evening in the successful seduction of a Mrs Barnes, wife of a local commissioner. He told me so himself the next morning.'

Edward VIII – 'David' to his family – had never liked Balmoral, and when he inherited he made sweeping and unpopular changes at both Balmoral and Sandringham, cutting staff and introducing swingeing economies. He spent his first summer holiday as King cruising with Wallis Simpson, returning to Balmoral in the autumn. Whilst at Balmoral he also demonstrated how his 'craving for private happiness' was becoming more important to him than his public duty. Scheduled to open a new hospital in Aberdeen he cancelled on the grounds that he was still in mourning for his father. The Duke (later George VI) and Duchess of York stood in for him. That same day he was photographed picking up Wallis Simpson and other members of his house party from the station in Aberdeen. In a telling juxtaposition the local paper printed photographs of both events side by side. It was at Balmoral that The Duchess of York so famously snubbed Wallis Simpson. Invited with her husband to dinner with Edward VIII's

house party she ignored Mrs Simpson's outstretched hand and declared loudly, 'I came to dine with the King!'

After the abdication of Edward VIII the interests of both Sandringham and Balmoral remained with him; George VI, in an acrimonious series of negotiations, had to buy them from him for £300,000, the equivalent of about £16 million today.

George VI and Queen Elizabeth

The Duke and Duchess of York had used Birkhall as their Scottish holiday house during the life of George V and during Edward VIII's short reign. Once Edward had abdicated, and the purchase price negotiated, King George VI and his consort, Elizabeth (the future Queen Mother), moved into Balmoral and their personalities, and the personalities of their children, transformed the gloomy castle. Now courtiers and servants enjoyed their annual visit and a certain informality was allowed – often, after dinner, a film was shown, which all the staff, household and estate workers came to watch (after no less than seven pipers had finished playing in the dining room).

The Princesses, Elizabeth and Margaret Rose, were at Birkhall when Hitler invaded Poland on 1 September 1939. The voice of the Nazi propagandist Lord Haw-Haw became a fixture on the radio and the little Princesses would throw cushions at it to try and shut him up. Sewing parties were arranged in the schoolroom to aid the war work and in due course evacuee children and their mothers from Glasgow were housed at Craigowan Lodge on the estate. Apparently this was not a success: it was reported the children were not used to the silence and were frightened by the forests. Elizabeth joined the ATS – the Auxiliary Territorial Service – and having learnt to drive taught her sister on the private roads of Balmoral, before she took her test in nearby Ballater.

After the surrender of the Japanese in August 1945, the royal family could at last take a holiday, and Balmoral was the perfect place to shed the anxieties of the war years. For the first time, the future Queen Elizabeth II went out deerstalking with the keepers, wearing her father's tweed plus-fours. During their next autumn holiday, in 1946, Prince Philip was invited to stay at Balmoral and it was during this stay that he and Elizabeth

Left: George VI, his mother Queen Mary, and the future Queen Elizabeth, c1924

Below: George VI and his family at Abergeldie, 1939

Above: Birkhall estate, 1947

Right: The young royal family on their way to Crathie Church in Balmoral

32

BALMORAL CASTLE

Balmoral Castle in the nineteenth century

became engaged. They were to return to Birkhall for the second phase of their honeymoon following their wedding on 20 November 1947, the seclusion of the estate very welcome after the public siege of Broadlands, the Mountbatten estate in Hampshire.

Elizabeth II and Prince Philip

Balmoral today is a hugely complex enterprise of nearly 50,000 acres made up of moorland, forests and 550 acres of arable farmland and pasture that supports Highland cattle. Also on the estate are five holiday cottages that are available for rent – including the Glen Muick bothy, 'Allt-na-giubhsaich', that Victoria and Albert created to be their rustic retreat.

The moors are managed to provide autumn shoots, as are the herds of deer in the surrounding forests. The red deer are still brought home on the back of a garron (a Haflinger or a Highland pony) after being shot, and when it comes to grouse shooting, a line of beaters one-mile wide drives the grouse toward the guns. The gundogs are transported to Balmoral from Sandringham.

Conservation is a high priority – with quality rather than quantity being a priority on the shoots. Sheep do not graze the landscape in the interests of bird numbers, and as a result of careful land management there is a healthy population of wild birds, from merlins, peregrines, ospreys and golden eagles, to red and black grouse, ptarmigan and a capercaillie population of around 200 birds.

The Queen Mother was a keen – and accomplished – salmon fisher in the waters of the Dee and current members of the royal family continue the tradition.

A staff of over 50 full-time workers keep the house, gardens and grounds immaculate and productive – a number that is doubled when The Queen and her family are in residence between late July and late September. The families of many of them have worked for the royal family for generations and, as many live on the estate, Balmoral is an intimate, interdependent community. That fact, and the relatively remote location far away and free from the ceremonial life, constantly on guard, that they live in London and Windsor, means that the two full months The Queen and Prince Philip spend there with their children and grandchildren coming and going, is of enormous importance to them. Of all their houses and palaces it is the only one not open to the public (apart from the ballroom and the castle grounds between April and the end of July, and occasional winter tours of the estate).

Outside the castle is a well-stocked walled kitchen garden, a rose garden and a small conservatory where flowering pot plants are banked up in an impressive display. The Duke of Edinburgh, aided by a team of seven gardeners, has redesigned the gardens to include a series of herbaceous borders. He has also enjoyed the creation of a water feature in the trees to the west of the castle, undertaking the work with a borrowed bulldozer. Of all the royal gardens, this is the one most challenged by climate and weather and it is, therefore, the least elaborate, though the views it commands add to its grandeur.

Significant events of both domestic and national importance have played their part on the Balmoral stage over the last 160 years. For The Queen and Prince Philip the ordered, domestic calm of their autumn break has been rudely shattered on several occasions. It was at Balmoral in 1992, while The Duke and Duchess of York and their children were staying, that photographs taken with a telephoto lens of Sarah, The Duchess, behaving inappropriately with her American 'financial adviser' in the South of France first appeared. The atmosphere at Balmoral was reported as frosty.

Above: The Duke of Edinburgh wearing his tartan at Balmoral, 2002

The couple divorced in 1995 but in 2013 were again at Balmoral for a holiday with their two children.

On 31 August 1997, Diana, Princess of Wales died from her injuries when the car in which she was being driven hit a concrete pillar in a Paris underpass. The royal family was at Balmoral when they heard the news from Sir Michael Jay, the British Ambassador in Paris. And so began The Queen's '*annus horribilis*'. The decision not to return immediately to London, issue a public statement or fly the Royal Standard at half-mast over Buckingham Palace produced a wave of popular criticism as the nation indulged in an extraordinary paroxysm of collective mourning. An estimated one million bouquets, together with teddy bears and associated messages, were stacked five-feet deep outside the gates of Kensington Palace. Prime Minister Tony Blair issued a carefully crafted public statement that caught the popular mood in which he described Diana as 'the People's Princess ... and that is how she will stay, how she will remain in our hearts and memories for ever'.

As the royal family remained, silent, in the seclusion of Balmoral, they appeared unaware of the mounting hysteria and anger, now reaching dangerous levels, directed towards them. The *Sun* on 4 September led with the banner headline: 'Where is the Queen When the Country Needs Her?' On Friday 5 September the royal family flew back from Balmoral to mingle with the crowds, for The Queen to make a well-received public broadcast and for the whole family to take a prominent part in Diana's funeral.

A greater understanding of The Queen's reasons for remaining at Balmoral – a desire to keep Princes William and Harry safe within the family and protected from both press intrusion and public scrutiny – is now acknowledged. This was a family tragedy as well as a public one.

Princess Anne and Commander Tim Laurence in their car after marrying at Crathie Church, Balmoral, 1992

But Balmoral harbours its share of happy memories too. Princess Anne wed the then Commander Timothy Laurence at the local Crathie parish church in 1992. The Earl and Countess of Wessex spent their honeymoon here in 1999. Former Prime Minister Tony Blair's wife Cherie revealed in her autobiography that their youngest son Leo was conceived during the Prime Minister's annual visit to Balmoral in 1999 (information that many would have been happy to forgo).

More recently Prince William and Kate Middleton, in breaks from St Andrew's University, escaped to the romantic seclusion of a cottage called Tam-na-Ghar on the Balmoral estate. In September 2013 the now Duke and Duchess of Cambridge took the brand-new Prince George with them to stay at Balmoral to meet his great-grandparents and to help play host to New Zealand Prime Minister John Key and his family. Prince William took the Keys' son Max grouse shooting and The Duchess took their daughter Stephanie on the traditional royal tramp through the surrounding woods. Prince Philip fired up the barbecue, a yearly tradition during the late summer Balmoral holiday. It was during this visit that Prime Minister Key flouted royal protocol by allowing a photograph of himself and The Queen in conversation at Balmoral to be published. The tartan-smothered interior, and The Queen in a Balmoral tartan kilt, surrounded by the kind of memorabilia and knick-knacks common in many a grandparent's household, caused much comment around the world with many newspapers attempting to decode, and even price, the decoration,

THE DUKE OF YORK AT BALMORAL CASTLE

furniture, paintings and family photographs. So much for privacy ...

Yet the estate does offer that in abundance, under the shadow of Lochnagar and its neighbouring mountains. For 60 years Balmoral has provided largely happy memories for seven generations of the royal family. No doubt the royal pipers will still be playing for the eighth – King George VII, if that is his chosen title – in the decades to come ...

Top: The Duke of York at Balmoral, wearing traditional dress

Below: The Queen and The Duke of Edinburgh with Prince Charles and Princess Anne (and corgis) in the grounds of Balmoral

Opposite page: The Queen attends a garden party at Balmoral, thrown to celebrate her Golden Jubilee, 2002

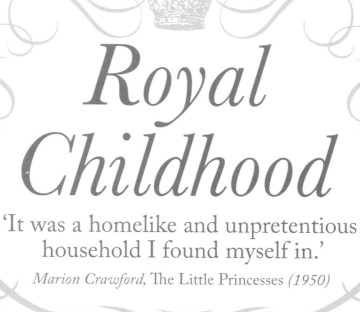

Royal Childhood

'It was a homelike and unpretentious household I found myself in.'

Marion Crawford, The Little Princesses *(1950)*

Above left: The young Princess Elizabeth with her pet dog, London, 1936

Above right: The young Princesses riding with their father George VI, 1938

For more than a century, in the upper echelons of society in Britain, the way families brought up their children remained more or less the same. As the present Queen's governess, Marion Crawford wrote, the nursery was 'a world in miniature, a state within a state'. And the 'Head of State was a nurse called nanny', who had the entire upbringing and training of her charges until, for the boys, at aged eight they were torn from her to be sent away to boarding school. Nanny was 'always there, a shoulder to weep on, a bosom to fall asleep on'. Most homesick little boys in their first weeks at boarding school, 'wept not for their mummys, but for their nanny … she was their childhood'. Until after The Queen's generation, girls were not usually given a formal education but tutored at home, with female accomplishments like dancing and music as important extra-curricular activities.

Until the public schools began to dominate the education of the aristocracy and minor royalty in the eighteenth and nineteenth centuries, most boys had also been taught at home, or had been sent as pages to other great houses or to the court, where they would be trained for knighthood. This strengthened bonds of kinship, if their training was with a family that formed part of a web of interrelated kin (the future Henry VIII was brought up in the household of his uncle, The Earl of Pembroke); it also helped secure upward mobility if with a family of higher status, or re-educate if children came from a dependent but rebellious kingdom, as happened with the children of Irish chieftains in the sixteenth century. By the fifteenth century, knighthood had become associated with a code of conduct bound up with the concept of chivalry. This required a fledgling knight to learn the arts of war, particularly on horseback, and to hone his behaviour so that it aligned with the current understanding of the virtues of honour (virtuous conduct combined with personal integrity) and courtesy (which meant a blend of refined good manners, decorum in all things and the art of conversation backed by intellectual refinement), gaining an 'effortless superiority' that survived as the goal of all aristocrats well into the twentieth century.

To acquire the necessary intellectual apparatus, the curriculum of a royal or aristocratic child was based on arithmetic, geometry, astronomy and music as well as French, the study of Greek and Latin texts, and contemporary poetry and prose. Physical development encompassed fencing, riding, hunting, hawking and dancing.

We know that the future Queen Elizabeth I was first tutored by Kate Champernowne who accustomed her to the 'elaborate code of politeness and subservience to her elders' then regarded as important attributes. Her education was rigorously supervised and she became a precocious child. In 1539 King Henry VIII's Secretary of State said after an encounter with her, 'though she was only six years old [she spoke] with as much assurance as a woman over forty'. She was taught by a stellar array of Cambridge scholars, including Roger Ascham, one of the best Greek scholars of his day, who would come to the royal palace at Hatfield. Ascham said of her intellectual attainments, 'Yea, I believe, that beside her perfect readiness in Latin, Italian, French and Spanish, she readeth here now at Windsor more Greek every day than some prebendary of this church doth read Latin in a whole week.' Elizabeth was also tutored in sewing, embroidery, music, archery, riding and hunting.

Queen Elizabeth I as a child

The surviving children of James VI of Scotland, who would succeed Elizabeth I as James I of England in 1603, were all farmed out to guardians to be brought up, as was the custom in Scotland. His eldest son Prince Henry was given to The Earl of Mar – The Earl's father and grandfather had served as Scottish royal guardians before him. Henry's schooling took place with a number of aristocratic youths of the same age who together formed a sort of royal academy before he died of typhoid in 1612 at the age of 18. In due course his younger brother would succeed as Charles I. Charles had initially been given to the Seton family in Scotland, only making the journey to England a year

Cliveden, childhood home of several British monarchs, c1750

after his father had succeeded, when he was four. He was then placed with Sir Robert Carey, a cousin of Elizabeth I who had first told James the news of Elizabeth's death and that he was now King of England. Carey's wife Elizabeth taught the weak, tiny (he grew eventually to be only 5 feet 4 inches), late-developing Charles to walk and talk at the age of three. Charles must have thought highly of his guardians – he made Carey 1st Earl of Monmouth on the day after his coronation in 1626. His son, Charles II, was also given over to a governess and then to a governor at the age of eight, when the Dean of Christ Church became his tutor.

With the coming of George I in 1714, the custom of the Hanoverian court, similar to the Scottish system, continued. A royal child was removed from his parents at birth and brought up in a separate establishment ruled by nurses and governesses. When it was time to begin formal schooling this role was entrusted to a tutor, almost always a cleric, under the supervision of a governor, a nobleman or distinguished soldier, who now took over The Prince's household. Prince Frederick, the eldest son of The Prince of Wales (later George II) was sent back to Hanover at the age of seven to be brought up as a German Prince. His two sons, including the future George III, were, in a break with tradition, brought up in England, at Cliveden House in Buckinghamshire and Norfolk House in London. At Cliveden they played early forms of cricket and baseball and were given their own plots in the garden to tend, but were also subjected to a rigorous timetable, six days a week, of academic work, which was leavened by classes in dancing, fencing, music and drama. Despite the best efforts of their tutors, one of their governors complained, 'they had but little weight and influence. The mother and the nursery always prevailed.' Nonetheless, despite a changing roster of governors and tutors, George III grew up to be the best schooled of the Hanoverians, leaving a considerable legacy to posterity. He helped found the Royal Academy, built the observatory at Kew and amassed a collection of over 1000 pieces of scientific apparatus now in the Science Museum in London and a vast collection of books, now the King's Library at the British Library.

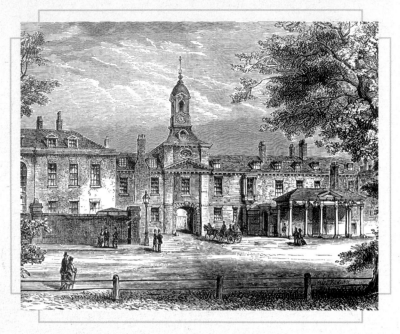

Kensington Palace in 1900

George IV, born in 1762, as a baby was put on display 'for the gratification of the public' for two hours every afternoon and gave his first, much rehearsed, speech aged three. He was placed in the care of the royal governess who was described as 'a woman of remarkable sense' and, as was the custom, established with a complement of staff, including both wet and dry nurses and two 'rockers of the cradle'. When it was time for his more formal education he and his closest brother were subjected to a tough academic timetable, based at the Dutch House at Kew, which sanctioned being beaten for infringements. One of his sisters reported having seen the two brothers 'held by the tutors to be flogged like dogs with a long whip'. Simplicity, punctuality, regularity, truthfulness and hard work were their precepts. Apart from a wide range of subjects George was also taught the cello, sang, drew, boxed and fenced, sowed and harvested from his own plot of land – to introduce him to the elements of agriculture, and baked his own bread.

George's brother William IV suffered from the strained relations between his father and his eldest brother – a Hanoverian trait – and he was sent to join the Royal Navy at the age of 13. Queen Victoria, born in 1819, was initially not considered to be William's probable heir but once it seemed there would be no other royal princeling to supplant her she and her mother (her father, The Duke of Kent, having died unexpectedly before she was a year old) were granted an apartment at Kensington Palace. There, she was brought up under strict supervision by her mother and by her mother's comptroller, Sir John Conroy.

Before she was four her formal education began, with her tutor coming daily to Kensington Palace – amongst many other services eradicating her German accent – and by the age of ten she was studying for five hours a day, six days a week. Alongside her academic curriculum she also studied music, learning the piano and singing, painting, drawing and dancing, all taught by highly accomplished practitioners.

After 1830, when Victoria was 11, Conroy instituted what became known as the 'Kensington System', which controlled the way she was brought up and which was intended to prepare her, as heir presumptive, for the throne, well away from the contamination and dubious morals of her Uncle William's court and totally dependent on her mother and Conroy.

Queen Victoria's pet dog Jeannie

She was even prevented from going to William's coronation. The plan was if William IV died before she was 18 her mother would be created regent and Conroy as her private secretary would be made a peer. Isolating her from other children – even her two cousins were kept away – she was constantly in adult company, whether walking in Kensington Palace or even in bed, which she shared with her mother until she was 18. She made do with a fantasy world of dolls and animals, being given her first pet, a King Charles spaniel called Dash, when she was 14 (it was this beloved pet she came back from her coronation to bathe before receiving her courtiers at a formal dinner later that evening). She was even taken on semi-royal 'progresses' around the country, so she could be exposed to her future subjects, much to the annoyance of William IV who eventually forbade them.

Her greatest influence was a strict Hanoverian lady, Baroness Louise Lehzen, who had been appointed her governess when she was five. A despiser of weakness, she instilled in the young Victoria a powerful streak of independence, a firm sense of her position and a strong work ethic, which was to stand her in good stead when she became Queen at the age of 18. The story goes that she had no idea she was the heir presumptive until a genealogical table of the royal succession was slipped into one of her history books: 'I see I am nearer the throne than I thought ... I cried much on learning it.'

Victoria's children with Prince Albert suffered from several disadvantages. The first was that, being fatherless herself, she saw Albert as a surrogate father to her, and so she was jealous of the attention he gave the children. She worshipped, even idolized, him and after his death her dependence had grown to such proportions she was quite simply devastated. She poured out her grief; she 'had leant on him for all and everything – without whom I did nothing, moved not a finger, arranged not a print or photograph, didn't put on a gown or bonnet if he didn't approve it'. When he was

Above: A childhood portrait of
Bertie, later Edward VII

Below: The Swiss Cottage at
Osborne House

away she felt 'quite paralysed'. During the years their children were growing up that dependence demanded his exclusive attention, and their children distracted him.

The second disadvantage was her dislike of pregnancy and the post-natal depression that seemed to be the inevitable consequence of giving birth. Finding herself pregnant again four months after the birth of her first child, Albert reported, 'she was not very happy about it'. In 1841, after the birth of her second child, Albert Edward, known as Bertie, she complained to her Uncle Leopold that she had been 'suffering so much from lowness that it made me quite miserable'. Her depression did not lift until a year after Bertie's birth.

The third disadvantage suffered by her children was simply that she didn't much like babies and found it hard to bond with them, a situation not helped by her post-natal depression. She described the infant Bertie as 'too frightful' and babies in general as 'mere little plants' with a 'terrible frog-like action'. She was also appalled by the notion of breast-feeding and all the children were given to wet-nurses. 'We princesses have other duties to perform,' she admonished her eldest daughter Victoria when she was breast-feeding the future Kaiser Wilhelm II. When she heard that Princess Alice was also breast-feeding, she delighted in telling her she had named one of her dairy cows 'Princess Alice'.

Despite these early disadvantages, her nine children had in many ways what would appear an idyllic childhood at Osborne House on the Isle of Wight where Victoria would spend up to five months a year. There a Swiss chalet was built for them (it has been recently restored) near their own private beach, with child-sized furniture, a working kitchen and wheelbarrows painted with their initials together with sets of gardening tools. They helped build it and were paid wages for doing so. The girls learnt to cook – serving biscuits and cake to their parents – and all the children cultivated their own plots, arranged in rows by age, and sold vegetables to their father at market prices. Nearby a miniature brick fort was built, sunk behind its own redoubt and defended by a working drawbridge and a number of cannon. However, for Albert, the Swiss cottage was meant to instil a certain competitiveness, an understanding of market forces and

Above: A postcard of the garden tools used by royal children at the Swiss Cottage at Osborne House

Below: Bertie (later Edward VII) as a schoolboy

an introduction to hard work. The cottage was built when Bertie was 12 and typically, always the rebel, he used it as a place to have an illicit smoke, safe from constant scrutiny.

The idyll was somewhat diluted, particularly for Bertie, when the children reached the age of seven and the female-dominated nursery gave way to the schoolroom, tutors and a strict academic timetable. Albert, with his strong work ethic and highly ordered ways, had been a model pupil at home, at the University of Bonn and on the Grand Tour. He absorbed information like a sponge and preferred work to socializing. Bertie, by contrast, had none of his father's traits and under the harsh regimen, alone with his tutor apart from 15 minutes with his parents at 9 a.m. and again before bed, he rebelled. He was rude and disobedient, and was whipped for his pains. His schooling continued during the annual round of house visits between Buckingham Palace, Osborne, Balmoral and Windsor, and he worked from 8 a.m. to 6 p.m. seven days a week. Tellingly, after accompanying his parents and elder sister on a state visit to Paris in 1855 aged 13, he asked if he could stay on. The Empress Eugenie replied, 'Your parents can't do without you.' Bertie's response was: 'Can't do without us! Don't fancy that, for there are six more of us at home, and they don't want us.' Later he was to say, 'I had no boyhood.'

It is no wonder Bertie eschewed the harsh, over-pressured educational methods of his youth when it came to his own children. Despite the efforts of his mother – 'Bertie should understand what a strong right I have to interfere in the management of the child or children' – the children of the future King Edward VII experienced a remarkable degree of freedom and informality. Bertie was 23 and Alexandra 20 when the first of their five surviving children was born. Albert Victor (known as Eddy) and George (or Georgy, later George V) were born a year apart in 1864–5 and grew up together. The three girls, Louise, Victoria and Maud (known as Toots, Gawks and Snipey), followed at yearly intervals after a short break. Bertie was a much more indulgent and affectionate father

than his own cold and distant father and fostered a close-knit and happy, high-spirited family circle, devoted to each other and with a penchant for practical jokes. Throughout Alexandra's life the children addressed her as 'Motherdear', even if her uncritical adoration could be at times suffocating.

The family's London base was at Marlborough House but a great deal of time was spent at Sandringham House in Norfolk and from those early years George V retained a life-long affection for Sandringham and the rhythms and ways of the countryside. From 1871, when George was six, a tutor was appointed to school the boys. He was to remain with them for the next 14 years. Three years later, when the boys were nine and ten, he wrote to their grandmother:

'They are living a very regular and quiet life in the country at Sandringham, and keeping early hours, both as to rising in the morning and retiring to rest at night; they ride on their ponies an hour each alternate morning, and take a walk the other three days in the week; in the afternoon they take exercise on foot; whilst as regards their studies, writing, reading and arithmetic are all progressing favourably ...'

Top: Edward VII, Princess Alexandra and young Prince Albert Victor

Above: Edward VII (far right) Queen Alexandra (third from left) and their five children in 1889. From left, Albert Victor, Duke of Clarence; Maud, future Queen of Norway; Louise, The Princess Royal, future Duchess of Fife. In front, George, Duke of York, the future King George V and Princess Victoria

The two boys were diametrically opposed. Eddy's mind, by contrast to the lively Georgy, was described as being in 'an abnormally dormant condition'. Georgy was always destined for the Royal Navy but after a brief flirtation with Wellington College it was decided that Eddy should accompany him as he found life without his brother's company difficult. Both boys began at Dartmouth when Eddy was 12 and Georgy 11. They slung their hammocks in HMS *Britannia*, an old wooden training ship moored in the River Dart. The idea was they should share the privations of the other cadets, except that they slept behind a bulkhead instead of in serried rows, had their own footman and were accompanied by their tutor who dined with the captain. Like most of the royal children through the recent generations, they were brought up without prejudice as to class, colour or race. Princess Alexandra wrote to their tutor that they should learn obedience, and be 'civil to everybody, high and low, and not get grand now they are by themselves, and please take particular care they are not toadied by ... any of those around them'. It was during his time in the navy that Prince George learnt his lifelong habits of regularity, punctuality and smartness of dress, as well as his brusque quarterdeck manner that became such a feature of his personality.

After the death in 1892 of his brother during a flu epidemic, Prince George proposed to Eddy's fiancée, Princess Mary of Teck, and they were married the next year. The Duke of York, as he had now become, settled into life as a country gentleman in York Cottage on the Sandringham estate where he could indulge his passion for shooting, becoming one of the best shots of his generation. He and Mary had six children and the two eldest, Prince Edward, known as David (later Edward VIII), and Prince Albert (later George VI), born 18 months apart, grew up together. After a gap of five years, four more children followed: a girl, Princess Mary, and three boys, Prince Henry, later Duke of Gloucester, Prince George, later Duke of Kent, and Prince John, who was to die aged 14.

The children made the traditional round of royal homes used by the heir to the throne: Frogmore when at Windsor, Abergeldie when at Balmoral, York Cottage at Sandringham and Marlborough House when at Buckingham Palace. York Cottage at Sandringham was nonetheless 'home' for most of their childhood, with the nursery and night nursery created on the first floor of the ever-expanding house, close to their parents' rooms. A nurse engaged to look after the two older boys proved a psychological nightmare: apparently jealous of their parents' affection, she would pinch the two babies to make them cry just as they were being taken down for their evening visit. Confronted by bawling babies The Duke and Duchess would tell the nurse to take them away again. It was three years before her secret was discovered when she was summarily dismissed. In slight mitigation it was also discovered she had not had a holiday during her years of employment. The under nurse took over and proved a more affectionate carer. The Duke of Windsor (as Edward VIII became after his abdication in 1936) recalled those early years: 'when there were only three of us children we all slept in this one room with a nurse. There we were bathed in round tin tubs filled from cans of water, brought upstairs by servants from a distant part of the house. Our windows looked out over the pond, and the quacking of wild duck that lived there'.

Top: Edward VII's sons Prince Albert Victor and George (later King George V)

Above: The young children of George V in 1907. Back row from left to right: Prince Henry, Prince Edward, Princess Mary. Front row, left to right: Prince Albert, Prince John and Prince George

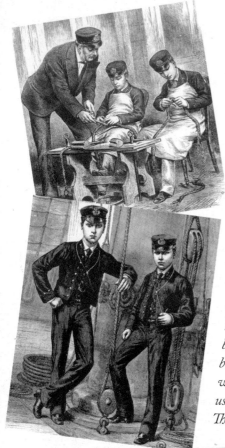

When he was seven a valet was appointed to look after the clothes – and the cleanliness – of the two eldest boys. Following tradition a tutor was engaged and he tried to recreate, as far as he could, the conditions of a typical classroom on the second floor. The Duke of Windsor in his autobiography remembered:

'He imported two standard school desks with hinged lids and attached chairs, with hard wooden seats and straight backs. A blackboard, a set of wall maps ... Next he drew up a daily timetable of work designed to make us follow the regime of ordinary school boys. Finch woke us at seven and saw to it that we were dressed and at our desks half an hour later for three-quarters of an hour's "preparation" ... before breakfast ... at 8.15 Mr Hansell would appear to take us downstairs for breakfast, and by nine we were back at our desks to study until lunch, with an hour's break in the forenoon for play. After lunch he would take us out, perhaps for a walk in the woods or to kick a football on the lawn. Then we would go back to our lessons for another hour, always stopping at tea-time for muffins, jam and milk, our last meal of the day.'

The future King Edward VIII was taken on his first shooting expedition aged 12 and, using the gun first used by his father and grandfather, he proudly recorded he shot three rabbits. In an effort to 'normalize' their lives, their tutor rounded up local boys to make up a football team and they were allowed to cycle into the local village to buy sweets. A local schoolmaster took them round the estate giving them lessons in nature studies.

Top and second from top: The naval training of the young Princes, Albert Victor and George

Above: George V, his wife Mary and their children Prince Henry, Prince Edward, Princess Mary, Prince Albert, Prince John and Prince George , c1905

Their father George V was much less tolerant than his own father, Edward VII. He expressed his feelings 'instantly and without reserve'. He had a loud voice, a gruff manner and indulged in chaffing, sometimes sarcastic banter, none of which was likely to endear him to his children or make them feel at ease. The Duke of Windsor recalled, 'My father had a most horrible temper,' and 'My father was a very repressive influence [on their mother] ... we used to have the most lovely time with her alone – always laughing and joking ... she was a different human being away from him.' All the children were subject to George V's broadsides. Prince Albert (George VI) grew up a very shy and sensitive boy and by the time his schooling started had

acquired a severe stammer that was to take many years of work by the speech therapist Lionel Logue to mask. Both Prince Henry and Prince George went to a preparatory school in Broadstairs, the first sons of a reigning monarch to do so. Prince Henry went on to Eton, another first, whilst Prince George took the usual route into the Royal Navy via Dartmouth Naval College.

When George V was in his last years, one of the tonics prescribed for his health was the presence of his granddaughter, Princess Elizabeth, the present Queen, to whom he was devoted – referring to her by the family name of 'Lilibet'.

The alternating hard and soft approach to bringing up children, which seemed to be the pattern characterizing each generation from Victoria and Albert onwards, continued with the children of George VI. He had a supremely happy life with his wife, Lady Elizabeth Bowes-Lyon, somewhat tempered by his unexpected call to the throne following the abdication of his brother, Edward VIII, in 1936. They had two children, Princess Elizabeth and Princess Margaret Rose. Based at 145 Piccadilly and Royal Lodge in Windsor Great Park, the children had a happy upbringing, at first looked after by their devoted nanny Mrs Knight, known as Alah, and latterly their equally devoted governess, Marion Crawford, dubbed Crawfie by the future Queen Elizabeth II.

Behind the house on Piccadilly was a communal garden which, for the two sisters, was their London playground – consorting with other children was discouraged – where they played hide and seek and sardines with Crawfie in the 'smutty bushes' (covered in soot from the pollution then so prevalent). On the top landing, under a glass dome through which a bomb would fall during the war, Princess Elizabeth kept her stable of toy horses and ponies, some 30 of them, all neatly marshalled, their reins and saddles immaculate. Their relationship with their parents was close and Princess Elizabeth was taught to read at the age of

five, not by a tutor, but by her mother. Neither princess went to school. They were schooled at home, the last generation of the royal family for which this was so.

The children of Queen Elizabeth II and The Duke of Edinburgh, Prince Charles and Princess Anne, followed after a gap by Prince Andrew and Prince Edward, had a more structured school upbringing. Prince Charles's nanny was Mabel Anderson, to whom he was greatly attached, calling her 'a haven of security'. She was recruited in 1949 and retired from royal service after 32 years in 1981 although she was lured out of retirement to help Princess Anne look after her son Peter. In 2006 Prince Charles hosted her eightieth birthday party at Clarence House. Charles acquired a governess just before his fifth birthday in 1953 and just before his eighth was sent for a year to Hill House pre-preparatory school, followed by his father's old preparatory school, Cheam, as a boarder. From there he went on aged 13 to Gordonstoun, where his father had been at school in the early 1930s. The Duke of Edinburgh, who is recorded as saying he wanted to make Charles 'a man's man', says he chose Gordonstoun because it was an institution that would 'free the sons of the rich and powerful from the enervating sense of privilege'. Prince Charles described his old school, which required cold showers at 6.45 a.m., with little affection as 'Colditz with Kilts'. To further strengthen his self-reliance he was despatched to Timbertop, a bush outpost of the Geelong Grammar School in Victoria, Australia. Charles was the first heir to the throne to gain a degree, a 2.2 from Cambridge, before proceeding, as tradition demanded, into the Royal Navy.

Prince Charles, as a child more sensitive than his no-nonsense sister Anne (who was sent to Benenden

Top: A smiling Princess Elizabeth, and an unhappy Princess Margaret pose in 1933

Above: The young Princesses and their beloved nanny 'Bobo' MacDonald, 1931

Right: Prince Charles plays with friends at prep school, 1957

School in Kent, another royal first), was less able to cope with his father's brusque manner, perhaps another hangover from a naval career. So his relationship with his own children, Princes William and Harry, has been warm and supportive. Their mother Diana, Princess of Wales, the first royal mother to give birth in hospital, gave them their baths and read to them, taking William on trips abroad before Harry was born, just as William has in his turn taken Prince George on his first overseas state visit. In another departure from tradition, The Duke and Duchess of Cambridge intend to share the rearing of their children between them. They have hired The Queen's housemaid, Antonella Fresolone, not as a nanny for Prince George, but as a 'general housekeeper'. Perhaps the alternating hard-soft royal approach to parenting has at last been broken.

Princess Anne as a schoolgirl at Benenden, 1964

Above: Prince Charles, Princess Diana and their two sons on Prince Harry's first day at nursery school, 1987

Right: Prince William on his first day at school, 1987

Sandringham

'Dear Old Sandringham, the place I love better than anywhere else in the world.'

King George V

The Queen and The Duke of Edinburgh arrive at King's Lynn station, 2013

Before he died of typhoid in 1861, Prince Albert had two things on his increasingly fevered mind that he thought might help settle his wayward eldest son Bertie, The Prince of Wales, then approaching his majority. The first was marriage to a suitable foreign princess and the second was a country house far away from the temptations to which Bertie seemed inexorably to gravitate. Accordingly he entrusted the search and negotiations to Sir Charles Phipps, Keeper of the Privy Purse, and Edward White, the Crown Solicitor, who investigated 18 estates in 13 different counties before Sandringham was settled on. Towards the end of November 1861 White wrote to Phipps that he had heard that Spencer Cowper's place, on the east coast near Lynn, was 'likely to be in the market'. He visited Sandringham on 28 January 1862, making a report on the house (which had 29 bedrooms) and the 7700 acres that comprised the estate, and on 3 February they took The Prince of Wales to see it. Ten days later the sale had been agreed for £220,000 (approx. £18 million today) and by October completed. Phipps reported that no one was quite sure why The Prince had settled on the Sandringham estate and wrote to The Queen, the day after The Prince's visit, that the house externally was 'very ugly – a white washed house with redbrick chimneys and a fanciful brown porch'.

The early Norfolk estate

The estate dated back many centuries and is recorded in the Domesday Book of 1086 as 'Sant Dersingham' – the sandy part of Dersingham. The earliest house on the site can be traced back to 1296, but a more detailed history begins in the sixteenth century by which time the name had been shortened to Sandringham. The Cobbe family had acquired it in 1517 and in due course a large Elizabethan house was built where the present house now stands. A mid-seventeenth century owner, Colonel William Cobbe,

Above: Charles Spencer Cowper, original owner of Sandringham

Opposite page: Sandringham House, 1880

was, appropriately, a Royalist through and through and fought against the Parliamentary Army. In due course he fell foul of the 'Ordinance for Sequestering Notorious Delinquents' Estates' announced by the Lords and Commons in March 1643. Sequestration (the forcible repossession) of 'papist' estates was used by Parliament as an easy source of revenue. Commonly two-thirds of the estates of those found guilty of 'recusancy' – the refusal to attend Church of England services – was sequestered. Cobbe was clearly regarded as a committed Royalist and the whole of his estate was sequestered.

Somehow, 'by humbly confessing his recusancy', by 1653 he had managed to retain his mansion house and one-third of his estate. He had to raise substantial mortgages on his properties to provide an income to live on and the estate became so heavily indebted that after his death in 1665 his son Geoffrey struggled to keep his inheritance and was forced to sell in 1686 to a James Hoste, a local landowner whose family had originated in Flanders (the family name had originally been Hoost). Three generations of Hostes and their descendants lived at Sandringham and in 1771 the Georgian house, much altered, that was bought for The Prince of Wales was erected by Henry Cornish Henley, whose wife Susan was a Hoste. The children of the last Hoste heir, Henry Hoste-Henley, all predeceased him, and the house and its estate of 5500 acres was again sold in 1836.

The new owner, John Motteaux, a wealthy bachelor and director of the East India Company, lived on a large estate at Beachamwell, some 17 miles from Sandringham. John Motteaux's grandfather had fled Rouen in 1698 after the Protestant persecution following the revocation of the Edict of Nantes and become a tea merchant in the City of London. Although John Motteaux enlarged the Sandringham estate to 7000 acres and set out the formal gardens there, strangely, he chose not to live in the house. A close friendship with the 5th Earl Cowper, his family and his wife, a sister of Prime Minister Lord Melbourne, induced him to leave Sandringham and Beachamwell in his will in 1843 to Charles Spencer Cowper, their third child and his particular favourite. And it was from him, nearly 20 years later, that Sandringham was bought for The Prince of Wales.

The circumstances of the estate being put up for sale are unusual, to say the least. Charles Spencer Cowper had become a diplomat but immediately resigned his post on hearing of his inheritance. It is said that at this time he was being pursued by lawyers and was in the habit of ignoring all communications from attorneys, so it was some considerable time before he learnt of the bequest. He sold the Beachamwell estate but retained Sandringham, which he used for sport. He also rented a townhouse in London and as a single man took up an increasingly hedonistic and extremely expensive lifestyle, entertaining lavishly in both London and Paris, mortgaging Sandringham to the tune of £89,000 (approx £7.7 million) to do so. But within ten years, in 1852, he had met and married Harriet d'Orsay who had been involved in a scandalous *ménage à trois*. Harriet was the daughter of the 1st Earl of Blessington, who had married the fashionable French artist and dandy Count d'Orsay at the age of 15 in 1827. There is some evidence that both her father and stepmother, the celebrated author and beauty, Marguerite, Countess of Blessington, were also in a sexual relationship with d'Orsay. The marriage understandably didn't last, and on their separation £100,000 (approx. £7.8 million) was paid to d'Orsay's creditors on condition he made no claim on the Blessington estate. On The Earl's death Lady Blessington set up a fashionable literary and artistic salon in London with d'Orsay and they are buried together in Chambourcy, in France.

BLACK & WHITE

THE ROYAL CHILDREN AT SANDRINGHAM

883

PRINCE EDWARD AND PRINCE ALBERT OUT FOR A RIDE

PRINCE HENRY AT SANDRINGHAM

THE HEIR-APPARENT AND HIS CHILDREN IN THE GROUNDS AT SANDRINGHAM

Photo by Lafayette

The royal children at Sandringham, 1907

Charles Spencer Cowper and Harriet moved to Sandringham after their marriage and had their only child, a daughter, Mary Harriette, in 1853, but she died of cholera as an infant. In 1857 Harriet decided to restore the church at Sandringham in her memory, engaging the aggressive exponent of high Victorian Gothic architecture, Samuel Sanders Teulon, for the restoration and to make alterations and improvements to the house, then known as Sandringham Hall. It was he who added the forest of tall chimneys, some with a mock-Tudor look, an extraordinary two-storey porch with heavy buttresses and sixteenth-century strapwork detailing bolted to the front of the plain Georgian house. To one side he added a very large, squat conservatory with complicated, arched detailing to the garden elevation. Both structures were built of red brick and different types of stone including a dark carrstone found in a nearby quarry. The result was colourful – and a startling contrast to the plain white stucco of the old house.

Lady Cowper, despite her rackety background, was pious and charitable, and established in 1858 an orphanage for children of soldiers who had fallen in the Crimean War. A schoolroom for them and the children of the estate workers was converted from one of the old farmhouses where she herself taught some of the lessons. Surprisingly, she also published, in Paris in 1851, a novel in three volumes which was translated into English as *Clouded Happiness: A Novel*, in 1855. Probably autobiographical, it has been described as 'a complex, almost Gothic tale of concealed identities, lurid coincidences, agonized death-beds, pronounced vice and virtue set mainly in Naples in 1830'. Clearly unputdownable.

Her husband did not care for the seclusion of Norfolk, preferring the delights of Paris where he repaired as often as he could, so the sale of Sandringham and all its contents to The Prince of Wales in 1862 – and the means to pay back his mortgages – was no doubt a blessed relief. After the sale both he and his wife went to live in Paris where Harriet died seven years later. In 1874 Cowper bought all the property – a considerable estate – belonging to his late wife's father, The Earl of Blessington, in Dublin.

The *Times* obituary of Charles Spencer Cowper in 1879 concluded, 'In many of the capitals of Europe, Mr Spencer Cowper was well known for his social charm and conversational talents.'

A sporting estate for Bertie

The Prince of Wales's father, Prince Albert, had been, with Germanic efficiency, closely involved in royal income and expenditure. Albert had managed to nearly quadruple the annual income of the Duchy of Cornwall from £16,000 to £60,000 (approx. £1.3 million to £5 million today) per annum, and the purchase price of Sandringham House, its approximately 7000 acres and five farms came from 'savings accumulated during the [his son's] minority from funds accruing to the Duchy of Cornwall'. A further £60,000 was released for immediate improvements to Sandringham.

The second of Albert's requirements for his eldest son was achieved when the prince married Alexandra of Denmark at St George's Chapel, Windsor, on 10 March 1862, in a glittering ceremony marred only by his mother's determination to cast a pall of gloom over the proceedings (she wrote later, 'what a sad and dismal ceremony it was!'). After the honeymoon at Osborne House on the Isle of Wight Bertie and Alexandra went to Sandringham to take up residence for ten days in their new house and observe the remedial work then underway. Over the next 50 years they were to transform both the house and the estate into the model of an immaculately run and comfortable Edwardian country house and a first-class agricultural and sporting estate. No expense was to be spared.

At first they updated the farms and buildings of the estate. A range of houses was built to house the rector of the church, the land agent and head gardener; Lady Cowper's school and the farms were rebuilt; a new stable range was created and new garden buildings added. New roads were driven through the estate and a carrstone wall was erected around the 300 acres of park and gardens that surrounded the house and culminated at the new Norwich Gates. These spectacular iron gates are surmounted by a plaque bearing The Prince of Wales's emblem, the

The famous Norwich Gates at Sandringham

Above: Keen country sportsman Edward VII out with his shooting parties

three feathers, on one side, and his coat of arms on the other. They had been designed by Thomas Jekyll and given as a wedding gift by the citizens of Norwich and Norfolk.

However, it was soon evident the house itself was too small. With the size of Bertie's household and the number of servants required to service his numerous guests, many more bedrooms than the 29 existing ones, and other facilities, were urgently needed. For a time his advisers attempted to stop his grandiose ideas – the prospect of the cost required to build an entirely new palace appalled them. And so the house was initially added to, piecemeal. In due course a cryptic note appears in The Prince's diary (he was never effusive) recording a meeting where the subject for discussion was whether to continue adding to the house or build an entirely new one. The laconic entry notes the latter course was decided on.

Albert Jenkins Humbert, an architect who specialized in building churches (ten years earlier, in 1854, he had begun Whippingham Church on the Isle of Wight, close to Osborne House, for Prince Albert), was retained to add the necessary space. His initial plans and elevations show a curious, truncated, Jacobean, Dutch-gabled redbrick house with twin towers linked to Teulon's conservatory; the new house was to be at a right angle to the conservatory and the main house. The plans evolved as the decision was taken to demolish the old house and completely rebuild it, although Teulon's conservatory was to be retained at The Prince's insistence. A plaque in Gothic script recording the completion of the house was erected above the front door, where it still hangs: 'This house was built by Albert Edward Prince of Wales and Alexandra his wife in the year of our Lord 1870.'

A year after taking possession of the old house, at Christmas 1864, The Prince began the tradition of the Christmas party at Sandringham, which has been adopted enthusiastically by the present royal family. Shooting played a prominent part and the fruits of The Prince's plans for stocking and breeding pheasants resulted in the kind of 'bag' which, in Edwardian times, was regarded as indicative of the health of the estate:

The Prince and Princess of Wales with their dogs, 1893

over 800 pheasants and hares. After Christmas The Earl of Leicester invited him to shoot at his neighbouring estate, Holkham Hall. Lord Leicester had taken a lead in the newly fashionable sport of driven-pheasant shooting and had created one of the great shooting estates in the country. Men and dogs in a long line beat the cover while walking slowly forwards, so that the birds took off over the guns stationed in front of them. 'Holkham Time' was kept 40 minutes ahead of London time to maximize the winter daylight for the guns, a practice The Prince adopted at Sandringham ('Sandringham Time', or 'ST', was 30 minutes ahead). On her first visit in 1871, Queen Victoria was not amused by this practice, declaring it 'a wicked lie'. On her second, all the clocks reverted to Greenwich Mean Time for the duration of her visit.

At Holkham a vast octagonal game larder lined in Derbyshire alabaster with slate shelves and with a cast iron octagonal game rack had been constructed earlier in the century to hold the huge number of birds and animals killed. It was then the largest game larder in the country. The Prince wanted to copy the idea at Sandringham and an even larger octagonal game larder to hold 'six thousand head' was in due course erected. A guest describes the game larder:

> 'The room presents a wonderful sight at the end of a shooting party, when it is well filled with pheasants, partridges, hares, rabbits and wild fowl, which are finally despatched to charitable institutions, to employees on the royal estate, to the different royal households, to the rich, and to the poor, neighbours of the King. No one is forgotten, but not a single head is allowed to be sold.'

The estate was extensively modified and cultivated to provide the right habitats for partridge, woodcock, pheasant and duck.

Shortly after it was purchased:

> 'the estate had comparatively little except the sandy soil to recommend it from a sporting point of view; the coverts were scanty, the cultivation poor – involving much necessary outlay for artificial feeding – the stock of game very limited, and the woods ill-adapted for that system of beating which has

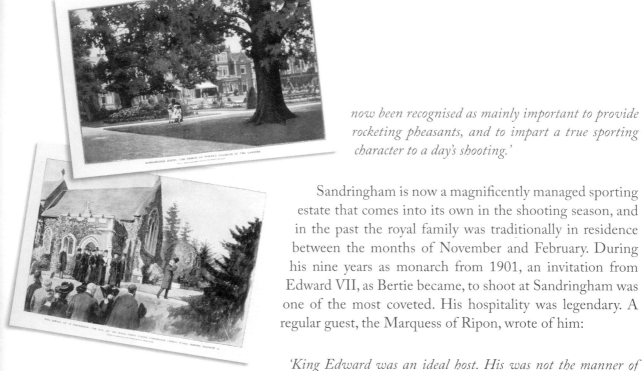

now been recognised as mainly important to provide rocketing pheasants, and to impart a true sporting character to a day's shooting.'

Sandringham is now a magnificently managed sporting estate that comes into its own in the shooting season, and in the past the royal family was traditionally in residence between the months of November and February. During his nine years as monarch from 1901, an invitation from Edward VII, as Bertie became, to shoot at Sandringham was one of the most coveted. His hospitality was legendary. A regular guest, the Marquess of Ripon, wrote of him:

'King Edward was an ideal host. His was not the manner of polished civility which is so often merely a cloak for indifference. His extreme courtesy was the outcome not only of good breeding and good taste, but of genuine kindness of heart ... When he took his guests round his places – gardens, stud, or farm – his delight lay not in the display of his wonderful possessions, but in the fact of being able to show each person the things which individually interested and pleased him most.'

Top: A photograph of The Prince of Wales's children at Sandringham, taken by The Queen.

Above: Edward VII arrives at Sandringham Church, 1901

He had two shooting parties each week, a Friday to Monday, and a Monday to Friday. The former would include a cleric for the Sunday service and some eminent politicians as well as a selection of celebrities who amused him, but never more than ten guns were allowed on any shoot. The other party would comprise perhaps a foreign dignitary and his suite, aristocrats and The King's personal cronies.

We have an anonymous guest to thank for a record of his time as an invited 'gun'. Arriving by Royal Train at Wolferton station on the branch line from King's Lynn, carriages and baggage wagons awaited the guests. 'Outer wraps' were removed by footmen on arrival and in the spacious hall, 'you are received with the distinguished grace and courtesy for which the royal host and hostess are so justly celebrated'. The shooting was eagerly awaited as for The King the 'preserves [parcels of land specifically given over to the raising of game for shooting] are his great hobby' and at Sandringham 'are among the finest and best stocked in the kingdom'. The statistics are impressive, if rather eye-watering by today's standards. Between 1878 and 1888 the bag ran between 6,831 to 8,640 head killed per annum. For the next roughly 20 years the bag ran from 10,000 to 20,000 head per annum of which never less than two-thirds were pheasants. The 'Sandringham Game Book' records it all with meticulous precision.

Breakfast was at 9.30 ST (Sandringham Time). The royal family breakfasted in their own rooms. Shooting commenced at ten (the breakfast must have been consumed at speed) and ended at four. The King, seated on his one-legged shooting stool, which gave him 'the appearance of being seated in the air', told 'good-natured jokes' during the waits. At about 11 o'clock some 40 beaters, 'looking picturesque in their blue blouses and low felt hats trimmed with royal scarlet, and armed with formidable looking quarterstaffs', assembled in front of the guns ready for the blast of a horn to signal the beginning of the beat.

The weekly shooting parties were varied from time to time with 'big' shooting days, which were important affairs, held on the birthdays of The King on 9 November and The Queen on 1 December (both happily falling at the height of the shooting season) and during the Christmas holidays. On these days guests might include the Kaiser or The King of Portugal, and a high proportion of expert shots. All work on the tenanted farms and estate had to cease, all machinery to be at a standstill, 'a complete silence having been secured for miles around', as shooting took preference and The King would not allow the birds to be disturbed by any noise except that of the beaters. Each member of the party had two loaders and worked with two to four guns so rapid fire was possible. When the Kaiser came to shoot, his loaders and beaters were dressed in gold-laced uniforms. He shot single-handed, as his withered left arm (due to a birth trauma) was about six inches shorter than his right. But he shot 'with a deadly certainty – as he is one of the surest shots in Europe', as was his first cousin, the then Prince of Wales, later George V. At a shoot during The King's birthday week The Prince killed two partridges in an outstanding display of shooting: 'two cocks, right and left – a feat, needless to say, opportunity for which can rarely arise, and then it is long odds against its accomplishment'.

On these big shooting days 'the Queen, the Princess of Wales, the Princesses, and any other lady visitors invariably grace the shooters' luncheon tent with their presence'. Lunch was always at one o'clock and was served hot (it would be interesting to know how the catering staff did that, if it was a tented lunch): an Irish stew, roast beef and Yorkshire

*Queen Victoria visits
Sandringham, 1889*

pudding or boiled beef and batter pudding. If the rabbit warrens were the shooting venue, the rooms added to Wolferton station would be the lunch venue or occasionally the party would take over one of the estate farmhouses – due notice having been served on the tenant – or a marquee erected. The beaters, maybe 100 in number on big shooting days, would wear blue blouses with lace fronts, each with a number on his chest and soft felt hats encircled by blue or red bands. The King and The Prince of Wales would always take outside places so the guests would have the best of the shooting. The King had, in his gunroom, one of the finest private collections of guns in the world.

Illness and Edward VII's return to favour

Back in 1871 at Sandringham for Easter, the future Queen Alexandra went into premature labour and gave birth to an infant son, six weeks early. He failed to thrive and was quickly baptized. Prince John died at just over a day old and was buried at Sandringham Church, Bertie weeping throughout the service. Alexandra had given birth to six children in eight years and Prince John was to be their last child. That same year, Queen Victoria's first visit to Sandringham – when she took such exception to Sandringham Time – was occasioned by the grave illness of The Prince of Wales. Soon after celebrating his thirtieth birthday at Sandringham on 9 November Bertie fell ill, and on 23 November The Queen was informed that he had contracted typhoid fever, the disease that had supposedly felled her beloved Albert almost exactly ten years before (a modern diagnosis points to Crohn's disease with pneumonia as a complication). On his way to Sandringham from Balmoral where he had been staying with The Queen, The Prince of Wales had visited his friend Lord Londesborough in Yorkshire and several of those visiting at the same time – and their servants – contracted the disease (The Earl of Chesterfield, also in the same party, died from it on 1 December). By 25 November, despite the favourable reports issued from Sandringham by his doctors, 'the course of the fever continues uncomplicated', Bertie became very ill.

When The Queen ordered a special train to take her to Wolferton station on the 29th, it was clear to the nation that the situation was grave. It took Victoria and her party from 11 in the morning, when they left Windsor, until three in the afternoon before the party arrived at Wolferton.

Victoria's entourage immediately swamped the guest accommodation at Sandringham, displacing many to houses nearby and forcing some of those remaining *in situ* to share beds. The Queen stayed a few days, until The Prince regained consciousness, before returning to Windsor. On 5 December, The Queen received a telegram which 'dreadfully alarmed' her, and she once more 'started our melancholy journey' to Sandringham. By 8 December The Prince's doctors acknowledged 'a considerable increase in febrile symptoms' and the next day the headlines read 'Dangerous Relapse'. The Prince in delirium shouted, sang and threw his pillows at his doctors, imagined he was back at the Curragh Camp – the site of his first sexual trysts with the actress Nellie Clifden – and became so indiscreet The Princess of Wales had to be removed from the room.

By Sunday 10 December the situation appeared desperate and Dr Jenner accordingly alerted The Queen who reported his message: 'that at any moment dear Bertie might go off, so that I had better come at once'. On the 11th the immediate family was told to assemble and expect the worst but the days passed with no change until the 13th (the day before the 'dreadful anniversary' of Prince Albert's death) when as a last resort the doctors massaged a mixture of old champagne and brandy into The Prince's body. Whether as a result, or given his liking for champagne and brandy – in moderation, he was not a heavy drinker and perhaps the heady smell gave him the strength to cling to life – by the next day the worst had passed and The Queen returned to Windsor. She was back again after a relapse on 17 December and again after Christmas on the 27th. It took until the beginning of February 1872 for The Prince to overcome his illness – a long and agonizing recovery both for him and his mother, and, as it transpired, for the country. His groom, however, had died on 1 December, the same day as Lord Chesterfield, and The Princess of Wales paid for his tombstone in Sandringham Churchyard, which bears the inscription: 'The one is taken, the other left.'

The length and severity of his illness had a beneficial effect on The Prince's popularity. His philandering, his love of pleasure and his name being linked to several of the high-profile scandals of the time had severely dented the estimation in which he had been held, with his carriage at Ascot being openly hissed at and booed. The fact that Queen Victoria had hidden herself away from the gaze of her public for so long had also allowed republican sentiments to gain ground. A remarkable reversal in public opinion now occurred: when The Queen and The Prince of Wales attended a Thanksgiving Service in St Paul's on 27 February 1872 they were besieged by a vast and enthusiastic crowd.

In April 1889 Queen Victoria paid another visit to Sandringham, on the betrothal of her granddaughter Louise to The Earl of Fife. She wrote of the match: 'It is a vy brilliant Marriage in a worldly point of view as he is immensely rich.' Bertie was determined to impress and had gone to great pains to honour the four-day royal visit and to make it a great success, including reverting from Sandringham Time to Greenwich Mean Time. A large crowd attended a decorated Wolferton station, where a triumphal arch had been erected. Driven in an open landau, Victoria was escorted by The Prince of Wales on horseback and 60 members of the hunt, 40 in red coats, and the route was lined with enthusiastic crowds. Two more triumphal arches and a row of 'Venetian masts' reaching from the final arch to the main gate had been constructed in her honour. Once at Sandringham she stood at the front door to review the hunt as its members passed by to pay their respects, and a Guard of Honour from the Norfolk Artillery marched past to the strains of the regimental band. The new ballroom had been converted into a theatre and a melodrama followed by a scene from Shakespeare's *The Merchant of Venice* were performed by some of the best-known actors of the era, including Sir Henry Irving in his celebrated and much-discussed role as Shylock and Ellen Terry as Portia. Victoria, who was never to visit Sandringham again, was impressed: '[we] spent a very pleasant time under dear Bertie and Alix's hospitable roof, and I was greatly touched by all their kindness and affection'.

At the end of October 1891 a fire broke out at Sandringham. In scenes repeated at Windsor over a hundred years later, teams of men repeatedly went into the burning house to rescue paintings, furniture and any other treasures that could be moved, as the pumps of the Sandringham Fire Brigade trained jets of water at the blaze. In due course ceilings fell, but the fire was contained within the top floor. The destruction had apparently been in some way connected with the number of fires that had been lit to air the house in preparation for The Prince of Wales's fiftieth birthday. The house was patched up, tarpaulined and dried out in time for the birthday celebrations. The Princess, however, did not attend – she had been away visiting her family in Denmark when news of her husband's involvement in yet another scandal, involving 'Daisy' Greville, reached her. She extended her trip abroad to visit her brother-in-law and sister, the Tzar and Tzarina. The day after the party, Prince George, known as

Prince Albert 'Eddy' Victor and his brother George, 1875

Georgy, The Prince of Wales's second son, afterwards George V, became seriously ill and was sent back to London where – in what must have seemed like history repeating itself yet again – typhoid fever was diagnosed. Fortunately Prince George recovered and returned to Sandringham in December with the rest of the family for the Christmas holidays, still very weak from the after effects.

1891 had not been a good year; it had been The Prince of Wales's '*annus horribilis*'. Earlier he had been the subject of a great deal of bad press about his involvement in the 'Tranby Croft' affair when he had been staying with friends and playing baccarat – a card game played for stakes, then illegal – when one of the party was found to be cheating. The Prince's continuing dissolute lifestyle and the virtual withdrawal of The Queen from public duties led, inevitably, to a period when the monarchy once again slumped in the nation's esteem. The Prince wrote to his sister: 'I cannot regret the year '91 is about to close as, during it, I have experienced many worries and annoyances which ought to last me for a long time. My only happiness has been Eddy's [The Prince of Wales's eldest son] engagement and Georgy's recovery.'

The following year Colonel Robert William Edis was contracted to design and construct a new range of rooms above Teulon's old conservatory. Edis had a mixed reputation; he had been proposed for fellowship of the Royal Institute of British Architects by the celebrated Gothic architect William Godwin, but the fashionable artist James Abbott McNeill Whistler said of Edis that he was not 'fit to have sharpened Godwin's pencils'. The ballroom was a huge, single-storey, barrel-vaulted room, over 18 metres (60 feet) long and 9 metres (30 feet) wide. Originally the walls had been covered with stamped leather, replaced later with wallpaper. Edis reused many elements from Teulon's distinctive porch, which had been added to the old Georgian house some 30 years before and demolished when the house was rebuilt, in the new visitors' entrance. Once these were completed the house had been enlarged to encompass a total of 365 rooms and from some aspects, with its many hipped roofs, now resembled a small village.

Prince Albert 'Eddy' Victor in uniform, 1890

The following year brought about a turning point in the line of succession. Back in January 1885 The Prince of Wales's eldest son, Prince Albert Victor of Wales, known as Eddy, had celebrated his twenty-first birthday at Sandringham. The majority of the events were held in Edis's new ballroom. Prince Eddy received addresses and deputations in the ballroom as well as reviewing a procession of retainers who gave him 'hearty cheers'. Circus acts performed for children from the estate and from other local schools. In the evening a great ball for 600 was held, 'the gentlemen in uniform, which looked extremely well', wrote The Princess of Wales.

Prince Eddy had been born two months prematurely, perhaps hastened by a skating party on Virginia Water attended by his mother. He was a lacklustre youth, mentally sluggish and with no great intellectual interests. One of his tutors, with singularly little restraint, described his mind as 'abominably dormant' though the tutor himself came in for some criticism for being an uninspiring teacher. As it happens, his father's character as a boy had been described in almost identical terms by his tutors. A school report for Edward VII as a schoolboy read:'His intellect – alas! is weak ... shocking laziness, which I fear has been far too much indulged ... Very bad manners and great insubordination, all most dangerous qualities' and 'no reflective or inductive powers – never asked questions or read books'. Eddy was sent on a gap year abroad with tutors, a chaplain and equerries 'of the highest character' to stir some intellectual interest but it was deemed a failure. He had no interest whatsoever in art or classical history but was interested only in 'gossip, dress and society'.

After schooling in the Royal Navy with his brother George, 17 months his junior, and a stint at Trinity College, Cambridge (where he was excused taking exams), Prince Eddy joined the 10th Hussars. His grandmother, Queen Victoria, described his life as 'dissipated' although she set the bar pretty high in such matters. He was implicated by rumour, though his participation was never proved, in the Cleveland Street scandal of 1889 when a male brothel was uncovered by the Metropolitan Police. The prostitutes revealed the names of their clients who included personalities of high rank in British society, including Lord Arthur Somerset, an Extra Equerry to Eddy's father, The Prince of Wales.

Prince George and his wife Princess Mary of Teck, 1909

A good wife was seen as an essential antidote to dissipation and Bertie, in an uncanny echo of his own circumstances three decades before, told The Queen: 'His education and future have been a matter of some considerable anxiety to us, and the difficulty of rousing him is very great. A good sensible wife with some considerable character is what he needs most, but where is she to be found?' After several dalliances, in December 1891 in what was virtually an arranged marriage in which his grandmother, The Queen, played a prominent part, Eddy proposed and was accepted by Princess Mary of Teck, the daughter of his grandmother's first cousin, and the wedding was immediately set for the following February. However, an influenza epidemic was in full spate and Eddy fell ill. The family gathered at Sandringham to prepare for the celebrations to mark his twenty-eighth birthday on 8 January. A shoot was held over three days when nearly 6000 head were accounted for. On 7 January Eddy returned from shooting feeling unwell. Within two days he had contracted pneumonia and, never physically very strong, he died on 14 January 1892.

In the tradition of her mother-in-law, Queen Victoria, Eddy's mother Alexandra kept the room at Sandringham where he died as a shrine throughout her lifetime. He was buried in the Albert Memorial Chapel at Windsor, his fiancée placing her bridal wreath of winter-flowering orange blossom on his coffin. He lies under a beautifully executed effigy in bronze by the celebrated sculptor Alfred Gilbert (also responsible for the statue of Eros in Piccadilly Circus), depicting him in his Hussar uniform. At Sandringham Church a brass plate is affixed to the royal pew which reads: 'This place was occupied for twenty-eight years by my darling Eddy next to his ever sorrowing and loving Motherdear, January 14th, 1892.'

His brother George, after a hesitant courtship, proposed to Princess Mary in May 1893 and married her in July at the Chapel Royal at St James's Palace. They were to become a devoted couple; it was to be a very successful and happy marriage. Although christened Victoria Mary Augusta Louise Olga Pauline Claudine Agnes, the future Queen Mary was always known within the family as May ever since her mother had first referred to her as 'my May-flower' on account of the month of her birth.

Sandringham winners

Besides shooting and the pursuit of women, the other great passion of Bertie, the future King Edward VII, was horse racing. He also had other interests, with the preface to *King Edward VII as a Sportsman*, published in 1911, describing him thus:

'Most country gentlemen hunt or shoot, perhaps visit Scotland and use the rifle as well as the gun; some keep racehorses or steeplechasers, others are yachtsmen, and a limited number have shot big game in other continents. Very few have ever gained distinction in all these sports alike: there is no record of any one who has approached the wide range and high degree of success achieved by King Edward VII'.

Above: George IV watches the horse racing at Ascot in the early nineteenth century

Below: Edward VII with his Derby winner, Minoru, 1909

However, it was the turf which was possibly his first love. Queen Victoria was ambivalent. 'Such success,' she remarked, 'only encourages gambling by others and the Prince Consort was so against it. But, if it makes the Prince of Wales happy, it is, perhaps, a better excitement than others!' A telling remark from a somewhat resigned mother. On the other hand, as he grew older, the nation loved him for his passion for racing, and his winning horses were greeted with adulation – a welcome relief, given the low esteem to which his reputation had sunk in earlier years when he had been enmeshed in so many public scandals. But then Edward VII's reputation as monarch far outstripped that which had been expected of him, and his brokering of the entente with France in the early twentieth century has only recently been fully recognized (having been unfairly credited solely to his prime ministers).

As King, Edward VII worked hard, but in the years preceding his accession he played hard too. In 1886, he established the Royal Stud at Sandringham with ten foundation mares. Purchasing wisely – he was a regular visitor to Tattersalls sales, accompanied by expert advice – he bought a mare that year which gave birth to a string of classic winners, and the Sandringham Stud became important in the development of thoroughbred bloodstock nationwide. The eight-year-old mare, Perdita II, produced two of racing's legends. The first, Persimmon, won the St Leger and the Derby in 1896, and the Ascot Gold Cup in 1897 (the horse's lifesize statue stands in front of the Sandringham Stud and his stuffed head is mounted in the National Horseracing Museum in Newmarket). The second, Persimmon's brother, Diamond Jubilee, won the 1900 Triple Crown – the 2000 Guineas, the St Leger and the Derby – as well as the Newmarket and Eclipse Stakes. The same year Bertie won the Grand National with Ambush II. A later horse, Minoru, won the 2000 Guineas and the Derby in 1909.

Edward VII with the winning horse at Epsom, 1896

Bertie invested much of his considerable prize money in the Sandringham estate, creating the vast walled kitchen gardens, now used as the stud paddocks. When Persimmon won the Derby in 1896 the race was filmed for the first time and the resulting film became a great attraction at the Alhambra music hall in London's West End and in due course was even being shown in Australia and New Zealand. A song, 'The Prince's Derby', also became popular in the music halls.

Bertie's wife Alexandra, a keen archivist, kept the Sandringham Stud Book from 1887 to 1917, now on display at the Sandringham Museum. She herself had been an avid horsewoman, frequently riding to hounds at Sandringham. As a record of the horses and mares associated with the stud, she compiled and wrote, in her own hand, a biography of each horse, its dams and sires and progeny – and successes where appropriate. On one of the pages she notes that as he lay dying, one of The King's horses had won, and he had gained solace from the result.

It is fitting perhaps that The King's last words should be about one of his horses, so dear to his heart. After a period of illness, on 6 May 1910 he suffered a number of heart attacks, but refused to be put to bed. In the afternoon the outsider Witch of the Air won at Kempton Park and George, The Prince of Wales relayed the news to his father. He replied, 'Yes, I have heard of it. I am very glad', the last words he ever spoke. He died later that evening.

Knowing The King lay stricken, the subdued crowd at Kempton Park,

Above: The Queen and Princess Anne with Anne's then husband Mark Phillips on the racecourse at Ascot, 1976

Below: The Queen with her Gold Cup winner, Estimate, 2013

noting that his purple and gold colours had been entered for the race, regarded the filly as 'a beacon of hope'. When she won after a tremendous tussle, the *New York Times* reporter described what happened next:

'then ensued a scene which no one present is ever likely to forget. It was no ordinary ovation to the royal winner simply because she was a royal winner. One recalled afterwards the scenes enacted at Epsom when the King won the Derby ... They were all very wonderful scenes, a noisy, frenzied acme of loyal enthusiasm, but they had little in common with today's outburst. It was now a subdued note of sympathy. Never before probably had a racecourse crowd been so stirred to the bottom of their hearts.'

Edward VII's son, George V was also involved in racing and breeding at Sandringham but major success eluded him until 1928 when he won the 1000 Guineas with Scuttle. In turn, George VI won the same race in 1946 with Hypericum, a Sandringham-bred horse. Queen Elizabeth II, from the time in 1942 when she attended her first Derby at Newmarket, the only classic race she has yet to win, has had a particular interest in bloodstock breeding – choosing all matings and the names of the resulting foals – and has had considerable success on the racecourse. Her first classic winner was in 1957 when she ended the season as Leading Owner. However, no horse bred at the Royal Stud has won a classic race since 1977 when Dunfermline won the Oaks and the St Leger. There are currently two stallions standing at Sandringham, happily spending their days in the paddocks in the old Walled Garden built with the proceeds of Persimmon's prize money, and a number of primarily flat-racing mares.

Above: An early image of York Cottage

Below: York Cottage today

George V and York Cottage

On the announcement of the engagement of Prince George, now Duke of York, and Princess May of Teck in 1893, they were granted a London base in part of St James's Palace, which was renamed York House, and at Sandringham they were given the old Bachelor's Cottage. Renamed York Cottage and situated to the south of Sandringham, the cottage and Park House to the west had originally been built by Bertie as overflow accommodation when the original Sandringham House was found to be too small to accommodate all his guests and their many servants.

In due course it was to York Cottage that the couple came on honeymoon after their wedding on 6 July 1893 at the Chapel Royal, St James's Palace. The Duke wrote: 'I am intensely happy ... we are spending our honeymoon here in this charming little cottage which my father has given me & it is most comfortable & the peace and rest after all we went through in London is indeed heavenly.'

Princess May had lived abroad for a while in the 1880s, including some time in Florence, where she became an habitué of the art galleries and museums. She was consequently knowledgeable about the decorative

YORK COTTAGE. SANDRINGHAM.

arts, of painting and the arrangement of furniture in particular, and it was a particular passion for her in later life to rearrange the interiors of the royal houses and palaces. Her husband's official biographer, Harold Nicolson, described her as 'well read and interested in the arts ... She was full of initiative, of intellectual curiosity, of energy, which needed outlets and wider horizons'. It apparently came as a bit of a shock therefore to find her new home had been completely redecorated and furnished by Heal's, the famous furniture supplier on the Tottenham Court Road on the instructions of The Duke.

When Bertie and Alexandra, The Prince and Princess of Wales, and their two daughters came to stay at Sandringham House a fortnight later, by all accounts May found herself at odds with her new relations. None of them shared her intellectual interests and her desire to know more about the world outside the immediate family circle and as a result they found her 'dreadfully dull'.

Each of George and May's six children (the *Dictionary of National Biography* described George V as 'scrupulously and contentedly monogamous') was born at York Cottage between 1895 and 1905, except their eldest Edward, known to the family as David (the future Edward VIII), who was born at May's parents' house, White Lodge in Richmond Park, in 1894. As a result, continual extensions were required to be built to York Cottage. The first was a three-storeyed wing designed by a local firm, Beck's of Norwich. A tussle ensued between Alexandra and May about the internal arrangements and decoration of the new wing. 'Motherdear', as The Princess of Wales was known within the family, kept up a proprietorial, even cloying, relationship with all her children during her lifetime.

The Bachelor's Cottage at Sandringham

The Duke of York's formal naval career came to an end a year before his marriage in 1893, although he continued in honorary rank until 1898 when for a short few weeks he was captain of the first-class cruiser HMS *Crescent* of the British Channel fleet. In 1892 George had been created Duke of York and after his retirement from the navy he became in effect a moneyed country gentleman, despite being 'in the shadow of the shadow of the throne', as an obituarist of his brother Eddy had written of the role of the eldest son of The Prince of Wales. He worked closely with his father on the management of the Sandringham estate – with one of the estate farms under his direct responsibility – and, as one of the most admired shots of his generation, he took a particular interest in the management of the autumn shoots. His job was ensure that the 'preserves' for raising game were in first-class condition.

For The Duke, Norfolk, particularly Sandringham and for many years York Cottage, was his emotional home. In these leisured years before his father succeeded to the throne as Edward VII in 1901 and he took on the role of Prince of Wales and heir, his other major pastime became stamp-collecting and he devoted three afternoons a week to building up his collection of stamps of Britain and the Empire – a collection which has become, arguably, the finest in the world. He was a serious player in the philatelic field, often paying well over the odds for a rare specimen and paying a record price for a stamp in 1904. He declared to his philatelic adviser, 'I wish to have *the* best collection & not one of the best collections in England.' His collection today is housed in a strongroom at St James's Palace in 328 albums of 60 pages each.

On Victoria's death in 1901, in preparation for the negotiations with the government over the new King's parliamentary grant, Edward VII's expenditure was itemized with the help of his friend, the financier Ernest Cassel. Sandringham was by far the most expensive of his private houses to maintain.

When Edward VII came to the throne he attempted to persuade his son to vacate York Cottage and rent a larger house in the vicinity of Sandringham as befitted the status of the heir to the throne. Lord Esher made an expedition with The King to nearby Houghton and wrote afterwards: 'I have been driving with the King most of the day.

A souvenir from the coronation of George V and Queen Mary, 1910

We went to Houghton, Cholmondeley's place, a splendid house built by Walpole but frightfully neglected owing to poverty. A sleepy hollow of a park. Possibly the Duke of York may rent it'. Houghton had been offered to The Duke of Wellington after Waterloo but he had refused it, and it had failed to make its reserve price when it was put up for sale in 1884.

It was to no avail, The Duke positively *loved* York Cottage and its warren of tiny rooms. Having learned to live a spartan life in small spaces during his naval schooling and service he detested lavish living. Twentieth-century writers were decidedly unkind about the 'pseudo-Gothic house with joke-oak additions'. In 1947, Harold Nicolson visited York Cottage and wrote disparagingly, 'It was and remains a glum little villa ... indistinguishable from those of any Surbiton or Upper Norwood home' and a 'horrid little house'. In 1956 James Pope-Hennessy, the art historian commissioned to write the official biography of Queen Mary, was even more dismissive: 'Tremendously vulgar and emphatically, almost defiantly hideous and gloomy. To sum up this is a hideous house, with a horrible atmosphere in parts and in others no atmosphere at all.' But, in fact, the royal couple, who hated their role in the unrelenting public gaze (so much so that when George was required to read the speech outlining the government's plans for the coming session on the opening of Parliament, George's hands shook with nervousness), found the seclusion to their taste. The fact that the relative smallness of the house precluded entertaining on any scale was, from their point of view, an advantage. It was all a far cry from the hectic social round so enjoyed by George's father.

Park House, another significant residence on the Sandringham estate, was later to be, in 1961, the birthplace of Lady Diana Spencer, later Princess of Wales, and had also been the birthplace of her mother, Frances Fermoy, in 1936. In 1983 The Queen offered the house to the trustees of the Leonard Cheshire Disability charity, which converted it into a country house hotel for disabled people, which, as Park House Hotel, was opened by Her Majesty in 1987.

Edward VII, on his death in May 1910, bequeathed Sandringham, as a personal possession of the monarch, to his wife Alexandra for her lifetime, together with a legacy of £200,000 (approx. £18 million today). For the

'FULL OF INITIATIVE,
OF INTELLECTUAL
CURIOSITY, OF ENERGY,
WHICH NEEDED
OUTLETS AND
WIDER HORIZONS'

Harold Nicolson

next 15 years, until her death in 1925, her son and daughter-in-law, now King George V and Queen Mary, their six children and entourage of courtiers and staff, continued to make do with York Cottage on the estate as the dowager Queen rattled around in the 'Big House' with its 365 rooms. But it was their choice.

In due course a schoolroom with desks and a blackboard was set up at York Cottage and tutors employed. It was not all a grind – although their regimen was strict – and the royal children benefitted too from being brought up on a large estate. They all, especially Albert, who was in time to succeed his brother as King George VI, imbibed the sights, sounds and smells of the countryside from a local schoolmaster. They learned to shoot, unsurprising given the dominant part it played in day-to-day life at Sandringham. Prince Albert wrote his first entry in the Sandringham Game Book at the age of 12 in 1907.

The elder children, Edward and Albert, escaped the schoolroom at Sandringham and their martinet of a father who treated his children as if they were a bunch of recalcitrant midshipmen on the quarterdeck, when they followed him into the navy as cadets. George V's severity towards his children was all the more surprising, given his ideal relationship with his own father, Edward VII. The junior officer training college had, since 1903, been located at Osborne, Prince Albert and Queen Victoria's hideaway on the Isle of Wight, which Edward and Albert's grandfather had given to the nation.

The First World War made its presence felt at Sandringham in 1915 in many different ways. In January two German Imperial Navy Zeppelins, intending to drop their bombs and incendiary devices on industrial Humberside, were caught up in bad weather and attacked the coastal towns of Norfolk instead. One bomb was dropped on the estate and its crater was later enlarged to make a haven for wildfowl. In Great Yarmouth a bomb killed a civilian – the first ever to be killed by aerial bombardment. The Zeppelins returned in greater numbers the following year, some flying directly over the house. Towards the end of that year King George V was thrown from his horse while inspecting troops in France, breaking his pelvis. He came to Sandringham to recuperate and throughout the Christmas festivities that year was in considerable pain.

The most devastating blow to befall the estate happened in August. 'E' Company of the 5th Territorial Battalion the Royal Norfolk Regiment

A recruitment poster for the Royal Norfolks, which included 'The Sandringhams'

was comprised of estate workers from Sandringham. The company had been formed in 1908 at the suggestion of Edward VII under the command of the Sandringham land agent, Frank Beck, whose father Edmund had been agent before him. Beck recruited over a hundred men to join the colours. Known as the 'Sandringhams', the company was shipped out from Liverpool to the Dardanelles to take part in the ill-fated Gallipoli campaign. They landed at Suvla Bay and on the afternoon of 12 August, led by 54-year-old Captain Beck, they went into battle against the Turks. In the ensuing brutal, hand-to-hand fight all but two of the Sandringhams were killed, many of them bayoneted or shot after surrendering. A war memorial outside the church on the estate commemorates their sacrifice. Only a 14-year-old boy and William Prentice, who had been a gardener on the estate, survived. Over 150 men from local families were lost that day. In 1919 Captain Beck's gold fob watch was located in Turkey, presumably looted from his body. It was presented to his daughter on her wedding day.

In 1919, Prince John, the youngest of George V's children, died at Sandringham after a severe epileptic seizure and was buried at Sandringham Church. He had been born in 1904 and suffered from epilepsy and some other condition, possibly autism, which required specialist support. From 1917 he had been brought up separately from the other children with his own establishment on the Sandringham estate, forging an especially close bond with his nanny, 'Lalla' Bill.

In all other respects life at Sandringham carried on with naval precision – George V maintaining the house and grounds in immaculate condition, at considerable cost – and with punctilious regard for dress and protocol. In 1921 a letter from the wife of The King's assistant private secretary describes a dinner after which, 'We at last wandered back to the billiard room where the King and Prince of Wales [then 26] were having a match. They both looked delightful types of English Gentlemen, each wearing white carnation buttonholes.'

By all accounts guests found the royal family friendly and approachable. The same correspondent describes George V's extreme devotion to routine. Having already completed a session of paperwork:

'immediately after breakfast he would walk out of the front door, with a cigarette (in holder) in his mouth and Charlotte, his grey-pink parrot, on his

left wrist, his dog following him, to examine the sky and judge of the weather. Wet or fine, winter or summer, he never varied this procedure at Balmoral, Sandringham or Windsor, and indeed, he usually followed it at Buckingham Palace.'

In November 1925 Alexandra, The Queen Mother, 'Motherdear', died at Sandringham. It had been ten years since she had retired there, increasingly deaf and isolated, and over 60 years since she had first become its chatelaine. Always an inveterate collector of bibelots and souvenirs of all kinds, in that time she had amassed a vast collection, which ranged from the utterly priceless to total junk. The following year Queen Mary set to work to go through it all – the late Queen's sitting room had 'not an inch of space' it was so overcrowded. During this process The Prince of Wales (the future Edward VIII, known as David) came to Sandringham to stay with her. His mother wrote to The King:

> *'It was a good thing for me that David came down for two nights & he was simply enchanted with Sandringham in the summer, and with the lovely flower beds in front of the house and with the garden. I don't think he had ever been here in the summer since he was a child ... really this place is too lovely just now and I am so glad to see it once in all its beauty.'*

By August of 1926 all was ready and The King and Queen finally moved, after 33 years at York Cottage, to the 'Big House'. It was from Sandringham on Christmas Day 1932 that The King made his first broadcast via the Empire Service of the BBC, the precursor of the World Service. Two years before it had been calculated that every second home in the country had access to a radio.

In the years until his death in 1936, King George V, punctilious in his duties as in everything, felt the responsibilities of his role as industrial unrest at home, the international financial crisis, the growing threat from Irish militants and the waywardness of his eldest son took their toll.

King of the fast set

In many ways, like his grandfather Edward VII, The Prince of Wales was a paid-up member of the fast set, delighting in women, cocktails,

Top: *Queen Victoria and a very young Prince Edward, the future Edward VIII, 1894*

Above: *Edward VIII, now Duke of Windsor, and Wallis Simpson, 1942*

nightclubs and dancing. He was not much interested in the rural delights of Sandringham (despite having written in later life, 'Sandringham possessed most of the ingredients of a boyhood idyll') and from 1930 lived at Fort Belvedere in Windsor Great Park, close enough to the fleshpots of London and discreet enough to pursue a series of relationships with married women. His private secretary, Sir Alan Lascelles, after seven years in his service, wrote of him presciently in 1927: 'the Heir Apparent ... in his unbridled pursuit of wine and women, and of whatever selfish whim occupied him at the moment, was going rapidly to the devil and would soon become no fit wearer of the British Crown'. When Lascelles resigned the next year, The Prince told him, 'I suppose the fact of the matter is that I am quite the wrong sort of person to be Prince of Wales.' Lascelles reflected later: 'He had, in my opinion and experience, no comprehension of the ordinary axioms of rational, or ethical, behaviour; fundamental ideas of duty, dignity and self-sacrifice had no meaning for him.'

On 15 January 1936 George V went to bed at Sandringham, complaining of a cold, and by the evening of 20 January he was dead, his end hastened by the administration of a lethal injection of cocaine and morphine, it was said, to preserve The King's dignity, to prevent further strain to the immediate family and to ensure the announcement was carried in the morning papers and not by the 'less appropriate ... evening journals'. His body lay in state in Westminster Hall, encased in a coffin made of oak from the Sandringham estate, before burial at St George's Chapel, Windsor Castle.

The late King's will was read to the family in the hall at Sandringham to the consternation of the new King. Each of David's (Edward VIII's) brothers was left about three-quarters of a million pounds in cash (equivalent to over £45 million today). He was left nothing except the accumulated revenues of the Duchy of Cornwall and whatever grant Parliament would vote. More than that, he was prevented, under the terms of the will, from converting into cash The King's personal assets, the racehorses, stamp collection and so on – 'the Kingship without the cash' as Lascelles (by then private secretary to the late King) described it. Edward was reported to have said to the lawyer 'Where do I come in?' before storming out and spending a great deal of time on the telephone,

The young Duke of York (later George VI) and his wife, formerly Elizabeth Bowes-Lyon, 1923

it was assumed to Wallis Simpson, his current mistress.

One of Edward VIII's first acts was to abolish Sandringham Time, instituted by his grandfather. Another was to ask his brother, The Duke of York (later George VI), to look at the expenses of running Sandringham and the estate, which to him had become a 'voracious white elephant', and to see how costs might be reduced. The Duke recruited his friend Lord Radnor, whose well-run estate he admired, and the two of them spent some time looking closely at the number of people employed – over 400 – what they did and the cost of doing it, as well as the maintenance costs of buildings and plant. The wage bill alone in 1936 was in the region of £34,000 (approx. £2 million today) with further costs of £38,000 (approx. £2.3 million today), making total outgoings of £72,000 (approx. £4.4 million today) a year. Set against that was an income of half that amount. Model estate as it might have been, it was being subsidized to the tune of £36,000 (approx. £2.2 million today) every year, money which had to be found from the Privy Purse. The final report, largely written up by The Duke, proposed economies that might be implemented over the coming years. These were put in train, reducing the staff employed by some 25 per cent, including the land agent, the Head Gamekeeper (no pheasants were bred that year) and the Head Gardener, though the youngest of them was 67. The stud, the stables and kennels were all closed and various items sold off.

King Edward VIII was not cut from the same cloth as his forebears. For all his womanizing and his high-octane social life, his grandfather Edward VII was a diligent monarch and worked hard at his job, particularly in the field of foreign affairs where his charm, his fluent French and his companionability yielded beneficial results. His grandson was indifferent to the responsibilities of his role, so much so that the government doubted his discretion, fearing that state papers might easily be read by any of the social set that tumbled through Fort Belvedere at all hours of the day and night.

In August and September 1936 he cruised the Mediterranean with Mrs Simpson and in mid-October brought a shooting party to Sandringham. He spent one night there – the only night he stayed there as King – before an urgent message from the Prime Minister brought him back to London. For the next six weeks the government and The King were locked in

Wartime at Sandringham

negotiation over his intention to marry a divorced woman (in fact at that point Mrs Simpson was still married; she had yet to divorce her second husband) until finally, after consultation with the Heads of the Dominion Governments, an ultimatum was put to him. The King chose to abdicate rather than give up Mrs Simpson, and by mid-December 1936 he was gone.

War and the modern era

The Duke of York now, reluctantly, inherited the throne as George VI. He did not inherit Sandringham and Balmoral, which as personal property had descended to Edward VIII, now Duke of Windsor, via his father's will. A great deal of money, perhaps a million pounds (approx. £62 million today) lump sum, and a further annual sum, was paid to The Duke to annul his life tenancies in favour of his brother, the new King.

But Sandringham was shortly to feel the effects of another world war. On Sunday 3 September 1939 Queen Mary was at morning service in Sandringham church when the rector set up a wireless in the nave and at 11 a.m. the Prime Minister broadcast the fateful words: 'this country is at war with Germany'. Sandringham was closed up, in the event of it becoming a target for bombing raids and in response to the 'Dig for Victory!' campaign (Britain was a net importer of food and in order to prevent starvation the need to boost home production was vital, as was rationing of food, a measure also brought in soon after the war began). The nine-hole golf course was ploughed up and rye and potatoes planted.

The young daughters of George VI, Elizabeth and Margaret Rose, were sent to Windsor Castle for the duration and The King and Queen divided their time between Buckingham Palace and Windsor at the weekends. Occasional visits were made to Sandringham, when the royal family stayed in one of the farmhouses on the estate. The government, fearful for their safety given the possibility of imminent invasion, set up a bodyguard drawn from the Coldstream Guards, known as the 'Coats Mission' after its commander, Major James Coats, which The King

Above and below: The Illustrated War News reports on the increasing use of female farm workers to replace men fighting in the war, 1916

referred to as his 'private army'. One detachment was stationed at Wellington Barracks, beside Buckingham Palace, and another at Windsor. When The King spent a fortnight at Sandringham in September 1941 shooting partridges, a team from the Coats Mission accompanied him and were quartered in York Cottage. In the event of invasion the guard was to spirit away the royal family in two armoured Daimlers to one of three 'safe houses' known only to them at the time: Madresfield Court in Worcestershire, Pitchford Hall in Shropshire or Newby Hall in Yorkshire, where arrangements were made to keep the royals in secret, and in safety. By 1942 the threat of invasion had receded and the bodyguard was disbanded.

In December 1945 the royal family were able to celebrate Christmas at Sandringham for the first time in six years. A lady-in-waiting observed how the atmosphere had changed: 'The radio, worked by Princess Elizabeth, blared incessantly ... the new atmosphere was very much more friendly than in the old days, more like that of any home.' She also noted how hard The King was driving himself and how 'tired and strained' he looked. She felt fearful 'of another short reign'. Within a few years he was diagnosed with arteriosclerosis and in 1951 cancer of the lung. He was at Sandringham for Christmas as usual that year and in early February enjoyed some successful duck shooting. On the morning of 6 February 1951 his valet found him dead in his bed; he had died in his sleep, aged 56. Like his Great Uncle Prince Eddy in 1892, his grandmother Queen Alexandra in 1925 and his father George V in 1936, he, too, was borne across Sandringham Park to the little church of St Mary Magdalene before being taken by gun carriage to the station at Wolferton. There an immaculate train was ready to take the coffin to Westminster Hall for the traditional lying-in-state and on for burial at St George's Chapel, Windsor, on 15 February.

It is over 60 years since the death of George VI, years which have seen many changes at Sandringham under the ownership of Queen Elizabeth II. After inheriting it from her father she asked her consort Prince Philip to assume the task of overseeing the running of all the

Above: The Duke of Edinburgh arrives at Sandringham church with Prince Andrew, Prince Edward, Sophie, Countess of Wessex, their daughter Lady Louise and Sir Timothy Laurence, 2012

Below: Prince William and Prince Harry play football on Christman Eve, 2013

private estates. Once a year in January he and Prince Charles meet with those in charge of each establishment together with the Keeper of the Privy Purse and his deputy to review progress and plan strategy. At Sandringham Prince Philip has continued the economies put in hand by his father-in-law, but also established a wider income stream, not least from visitors who are now allowed to view both house (opened to the public in 1977) and gardens at certain times of year. The biggest change by far to the house was the 1975 demolition of the old 120-metre (400-feet) long, three-storey service block of around 100 rooms to the south of the house, which contained staff accommodation on the upper floors and a range of food preparation and storage areas below. The estate, too, has been rationalized. Larger farms have been created by amalgamating smaller, uneconomic units so the number of tenant farmers has dropped from 30 to about a dozen, and the percentage of the estate directly farmed has risen to around one-half of the whole acreage but with far fewer workers – less than 10 per cent of the number employed before the war. Wood products from forestry, produce from the farm, rents from the many houses on the estate and those used as holiday cottages, and entrance fees and merchandise sales to visitors became the major sources of income as the estate clawed its way towards the goal of self-sufficiency.

The Queen and The Duke of Edinburgh and many other members of the royal family – in 2013, 30 of them, including for the first time four generations – traditionally spend Christmas at Sandringham and stay on until the anniversary of the death of The Queen's father, George VI, on 6 February when they return to Buckingham Palace during the week and Windsor at the weekends. Family members arrive the day before Christmas Eve in time for tea at 5 p.m. – each is given a timed slot so that they don't all arrive at once. In recent years Princes William and Harry have taken part in the annual Christmas Eve football match between Sandringham estate workers and the neighbouring village of Castle Rising. In 2013

Children present The Queen with flowers for Christmas, 2013

Prince Harry scored a goal in the 2–2 draw. Presents (following the Danish tradition of Queen Alexandra) are exchanged that evening.

After presents it's time for a glass of champagne or a cocktail in the hall (gin and Dubonnet for The Queen) before changing into evening dress for dinner. The women retire after dinner, and port and brandy are circulated among the men who remain at the table. The next day, after stockings and breakfast, it's the Christmas Service at the Church of St Mary Magdalene, a brisk walk across the park or a short trip in the maroon state Bentley for The Queen. Christmas lunches are then served in relays through the late morning and afternoon for all the different grades of staff – it is said that 24 of the largest Norfolk turkeys are required to feed everyone. The royal family eats at 1.15 p.m., the head chef carving for the table.

All must be over by 3 p.m. when The Queen's Speech is relayed to the nation and Commonwealth via television, radio, the internet and even the headsets on long-haul flights. The Christmas message has been a tradition since 1932, when the first speech was written by Rudyard Kipling for George V and delivered live from his study at Sandringham. In 1992, the year of her '*annus horribilis*' speech, The Queen reflected on what Sandringham meant to her: 'I first came here for Christmas as a grandchild. Nowadays my children come here for the same family festival. To me this continuity is a great source of comfort in a world of tension and violence.' Traditionally the speech is filmed in the week before Christmas and The Queen prefers to watch the actual broadcast on her own. Afterwards there are walks, board games, charades and then a huge Christmas cake for tea. The family reconvenes again at 8.15 for dinner. Non-family guests are invited for Boxing Day lunch and the traditional pheasant shoot.

At Sandringham, steps are now being taken to provide accommodation for future heirs to the throne. In 2013 planning permission was granted to make changes to the internal arrangements and security of the ten-bedroom Anmer Hall on the Sandringham estate, about two miles from the 'Big House', as the country home for The Duke and Duchess of Cambridge and baby George. Prince William has known the house since he was a child when it was leased to the van Cutsem family. Before that The Duke and Duchess of Kent rented it for nearly 30 years until 1990.

The gardens at Sandringham

The gardens at Sandringham are particularly welcoming. The park has existed in roughly its present form for over 200 years – in 1797 it was depicted on Faden's map of the county which also shows The Avenue running for over a kilometre through Dersingham Wood, as it still does today. In 1862 a lady-in-waiting to Alexandra, The Princess of Wales reported on her first visit that Sandringham had 'no fine trees, no water, no hills, in fact no attraction of any sort'. The extensive and beautifully maintained gardens and pleasure grounds covering an area of over 49 acres (20 hectares) that exist today are a testament to the taste and enthusiasm of four generations of the royal family, and in particular to the prize money and stud fees of Persimmon, Bertie's spectacularly successful racehorse which won over £2 million in today's money in the 1890s.

The gardens date from the 1860s onwards, after the estate was purchased by The Prince of Wales (although some mature trees both in the

gardens and the park survive from earlier owners) and were initially laid out to the designs of William Broderick Thomas with later help from Baron Ferdinand de Rothschild, a friend of The Prince's who owned Waddesdon Manor, a vast house built in the 1870s and 1880s in the style of a Loire chateau. It was around this time that over 100 gardeners were employed at Sandringham. The layout is largely informal, mainly grass and trees punctuated by walks or 'rides' with more formal terraces to the north and west.

The main entrance is on the east front of the house and has a forecourt extending to a gravelled sweep, bordered by clipped yew hedges and lawns planted with commemorative oaks. There is a pleasing continuity to the oaks at Sandringham – in 2006 The Queen planted an oak tree to mark her eightieth birthday, which in turn was grown from the acorn of an oak tree planted in 1947 by Queen Mary to mark her own eightieth birthday. The most dominant feature of the garden extends for some distance to the north of the house.

Above: The Pulhamite rock garden, seen from across the lake

George VI was an enthusiastic and knowledgeable gardener and in 1947 he commissioned Sir Geoffrey Jellicoe to create a garden that he could look out over from his own rooms. He and Sir Geoffrey had a close working relationship, with The King writing to him with suggestions throughout the design and construction stage. The resulting garden is a calm and peaceful series of hedged enclosures in a garden otherwise characterized by wide vistas. Extending from the north of the house, Jellicoe laid down a central path that divides a long rectangular garden laid out as formal 'rooms' of box-edged beds filled with herbaceous plants and flanked by pleached limes. The path is closed by a stone statue of Father Time brooding over the transience of life, bought by The Queen in 1951. Not far from Father Time an ancient Buddha squats, closing another pleached lime avenue. Dated to the end of the seventeenth century it was brought from Peking in 1870 aboard the battleship HMS *Rodney* as a gift from one of The Prince of Wales's friends, Admiral Sir Henry Keppel. From King's Lynn it was placed on a carriage and hauled by sailors the nine miles to Sandringham. Originally it sat beneath a pagoda, but this has rotted away.

Around the north and north-west boundary wall just beyond this formal garden, mixed woodland shrubberies include rhododendrons, azaleas and camellias – the sandy, acid soil suits them well. In the 1960s Sir Eric Savill was asked by The Queen and The Duke of Edinburgh to redesign this area of the garden. Savill had earlier been commissioned by George V to create the famous woodland garden in Windsor Great Park, completed in the 1930s, which now bears his name. At Sandringham, he used many of the rhododendron and azalea species he had been breeding at Windsor where he was deputy ranger, and in the spring this part of the garden is ablaze with colour.

The west front terrace originally faced a complex, formal parterre of bedding, fashionable at the time, which had replaced the old lake. These were dug up during the Second World War and never replaced. Now the terrace looks onto a simple expanse of lawn, cross-cut like the weave of a tartan in spring and summer and dotted with specimen trees (there had been many more, which interrupted the views from the house, but they were removed by George VI). Directly south of the lawn lies the irregular Upper Lake. When The Prince of Wales purchased the house in the 1860s there was an L-shaped expanse of water almost directly in front of the old house which The Prince filled in, creating the ornamental Upper Lake in the 1870s with a nineteenth-century Pulhamite rock garden (named after James Pulham who had invented a convincing artificial stone) and a boathouse on the house side. On the opposite side is a summerhouse known as 'The Nest', erected in two months in 1913 by the Comptroller of the Household, Sir Dighton Probyn, as a surprise for Queen Alexandra, to whom he was devoted.

Below: Part of the garden designed by Sir Geoffrey Jellicoe

From the Upper Lake a meandering waterway leads into the larger Lower Lake with its tree-covered island. Grassland borders the lakes, kept long to encourage wild flowers and planted with a variety of trees and shrubs. A small stream running from the north-east feeds into the eastern end of Lower Lake. This, now known as the Stream Walk, is edged with rocks and in 1996 was planted with moisture-loving plants by the then head gardener, Fred Waite. Various other walks meander through the woodland: the Dell Walk leads west from the lake and north up through the woodland to join the Church Walk, which leads to the church of St Mary Magdalene, replete with so many royal associations.

The highly ornamental walled kitchen garden, over six acres in extent, once had seven enormous glasshouses – extending to 213 metres (700 feet) – one of the great attractions of the garden and a must on every guest's compulsory perambulation through the grounds on a Sunday. The glasshouses were filled mainly with exotic fruits and flowers, and one was devoted solely to pink carnations. The entrance doors to this great range of vanished glasshouses still exist. Set in a glazed, pedimented wooden frame inset into a brick wall they now frame a vista of the sky and garden beyond.

Lying about 300 metres (1000 feet) from the house the kitchen garden was begun at the same time but was very much enlarged in the twentieth century when the gates, piers, pergola and dairy were added and the paths enlarged to allow the passage of carriages for guests. At the west end, curved entrance gates and piers lead directly onto a rose pergola built of brick piers that once carried oak cross beams and that leads onto the main

Left: Looking back towards the house from the garden designed by Sr Geoffrey Jellicoe

Above: The house viewed from the Lower Lake

east-west path within the walled garden. This area, which once provided the fruit, vegetables and cut flowers for the house in an ornamental arrangement of beds, is now laid to grass divided into quarters, which provide pasture for the stallions in the stud nearby. Fenced gravel paths converge on a central circular pool with a fountain, and old pear trees are still trained on the south wall.

The Duke of Edinburgh confesses that when it came to making alterations to the garden at Sandringham he 'left well alone'. However, he did plant an avenue of copper beeches leading up to the Norwich Gates to the north of the house and created a vista to the woods to the west of the Visitor Centre.

At the end of July the traditional Flower Show, first inaugurated in the mid-nineteenth century, is held at Sandringham, complete with show gardens and floral displays. The Queen Mother was a regular attendee and it is now under the patronage of The Queen and The Prince of Wales.

I have been lucky enough to be a house guest of The Prince of Wales at Sandringham during Flower Show week, and can only say that the hospitality and company are second to none. The Prince of Wales is an attentive host who works harder at his despatch boxes than most people realize, and the Flower Show itself has a charm equalled by few others. I love Sandringham for its friendliness and its country-house atmosphere – probably as much as King George V.

The Palace of Holyroodhouse

Above: The Palace of Holyroodhouse, 1845

Below: Mary, Queen of Scots

It is somehow fitting that the Palace of Holyroodhouse lies at the end of the steep slope known as the 'Royal Mile', which climbs up to Edinburgh Castle. To the Scots it is The Queen's official house, and its regal roots go back to the twelfth century, since within its grounds are the substantial remains of an abbey originally founded by King David I of Scotland in 1128. The Augustinian community of Canons Regular – priests living together in an open community – flourished and in due course guest lodgings were built for the use of the sovereign as its location in parkland, secluded from the public gaze unlike the exposed castle, made it a favourite lodging for successive Kings.

The lodgings gradually grew in importance and size, and were rebuilt as a new Gothic palace by James IV, who ruled Scotland for 25 years from 1488, for his new bride, Margaret Tudor, daughter of Henry VII, King of England. They were married in the abbey church in 1503. In 1512 he added a building to contain his new menagerie of exotic animals – most royal gardens, it seems, began their lives as the precursors of zoos.

The earliest buildings to survive date from the late 1520s, when the palace was again remodelled, this time for James V, who had become King of Scots in 1513. Some 20 years later the palace was ransacked – the lead stripped from the roof, bells removed and the treasures plundered – along with much of the town by The Earl of Hertford when Henry VIII attempted to coerce the Scots into agreeing a marriage between his son Edward and the infant Mary, Queen of Scots. The period of conflict is known now as the Rough Wooing, a rather colourful description coined by Sir Walter Scott.

James V's daughter, Mary, Queen of Scots, married not Edward VI

of England but Francis, the Dauphin of France, as her first husband. Not long after he had succeeded as King Francis II he died, in December 1560, and Mary moved to Holyrood Palace (as the Palace of Holyroodhouse is still often called) eight months later. Her marriages to her second and third husbands – her first cousin Henry Stuart, Lord Darnley, in 1565 and The Earl of Bothwell in 1567 – took place at the palace, the first in the chapel and the second in the Great Hall.

It is thought that her close relationship with her Italian private secretary and 'decipherer', David Rizzio, and rumours of an affair with him, caused Darnley to be consumed with jealousy. In March 1566, he and Lord Ruthven and a posse of supporters found Mary and Rizzio with a group of five others at dinner in a private room off her bedchamber at the palace. Seven months pregnant with the future James VI of Scotland and James I of England, Mary attempted to shield Rizzio, but he was dragged screaming to the stairway outside. In a frenzied attack he was stabbed 56 times before his lifeless body was thrown down the staircase. A brass plaque now marks the spot where the body was left after the murder.

Darnley himself died in an explosion in February 1567 and Mary married Bothwell, who was thought to have been responsible for Darnley's death. The story is a salutary reminder that the lives of previous monarchs put those of our present-day Kings and Queens into a rather conservative perspective.

Mary's subsequent imprisonment and long exile in England meant that she never saw her son James again after he was ten months old. James became King of Scotland at the age of 13 months, after Mary was forced to abdicate in his favour. He was crowned not at Holyrood but at Stirling in 1567. In 1570 the choir and transepts of the old abbey at Holyrood, neglected since the looting and destruction of the Reformation and now ruinous, were demolished, leaving only the nave standing as the local parish church.

Top: Holyroodhouse, 1860
Above: Holyroodhouse Palace Chapel
Right: David Rizzio and Mary, Queen of Scots, 1754

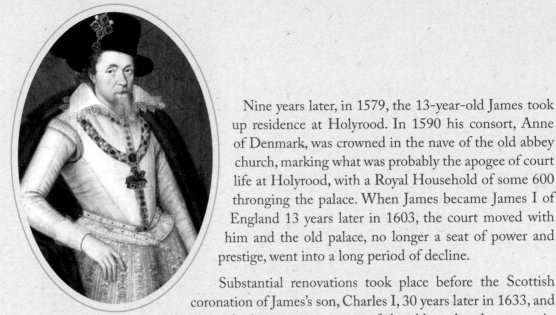

Nine years later, in 1579, the 13-year-old James took up residence at Holyrood. In 1590 his consort, Anne of Denmark, was crowned in the nave of the old abbey church, marking what was probably the apogee of court life at Holyrood, with a Royal Household of some 600 thronging the palace. When James became James I of England 13 years later in 1603, the court moved with him and the old palace, no longer a seat of power and prestige, went into a long period of decline.

Substantial renovations took place before the Scottish coronation of James's son, Charles I, 30 years later in 1633, and the nave, the last remaining part of the abbey church, was again restored. Charles journeyed north with a large entourage that included 150 English nobles; 1000 horses pulled 200 carts loaded with the royal baggage including Henry VIII's fabled silver-gilt 280-piece dinner service. But tragedy struck. All was lost when a boat, carrying the royal baggage on The King's progress round Scotland following his coronation, overturned in a squall. It was blamed on witchcraft so several known witches were rounded up and subsequently died in prison.

Above: James I of England and VI of Scotland
Right: Holyroodhouse in 1753

For the occasion of the coronation, Edinburgh was *en fête*. Fountains flowed with red wine and portraits of The King hung in the Royal Mile as he made his way from the castle to the Palace of Holyroodhouse for his coronation. In 1646 Charles made James, 1st Duke of Hamilton, Hereditary Keeper of Holyroodhouse. The position remains in the family, for today the Keeper is Alexander, 16th Duke of Hamilton.

After Charles I's execution, Commonwealth soldiers in 1650 caused a fire in the eastern range of the palace. What had not been burnt, as so often with royal buildings, was used as a barracks, but in the 1670s, after the Restoration of the monarchy, the gentleman-architect Sir William Bruce

rebuilt the palace for Charles II. One of the first to introduce the new

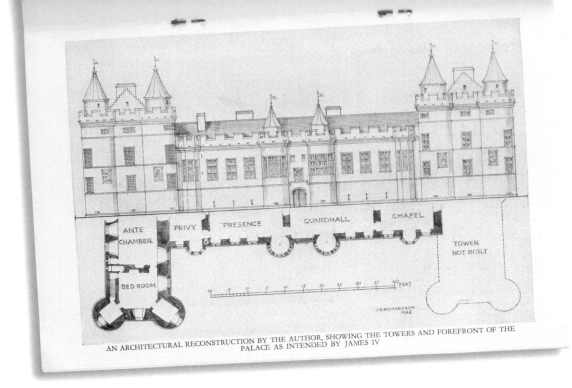

AN ARCHITECTURAL RECONSTRUCTION BY THE AUTHOR, SHOWING THE TOWERS AND FOREFRONT OF THE
PALACE AS INTENDED BY JAMES IV

Palladian style of architecture to Scotland, Bruce skilfully married the old parts of the building with new additions to create a symmetrical facade. The old sixteenth-century tower built by James IV of Scotland almost 200 years earlier was balanced with a matching tower. All was complete by 1679, in the form we see today, in time for the arrival of The Duke of Albany – the Scottish title given to The King's younger brother. He was Duke of York in England, and became James VII of Scotland and James II of England in 1685. He remained in Scotland for several years, returning to England once the political climate had swung once more in his favour.

Bonnie Prince Charlie, the Young Pretender and grandson of James II, held court at Holyrood in September and October 1745, before the bloody Battle of Culloden the following April saw an end to the Jacobite Rising. The victor that day, The Duke of Cumberland, a younger son of George II, also stayed at Holyrood on his way to Culloden.

In 1822, George IV became the first reigning monarch since Charles I to visit the palace. It was, by then, in too run down a state for him to stay but he held a reception there, stage-managed by Sir Walter Scott, where the corpulent King George presided over a sea of 'revived ancient dresses' and plaid pageantry in a swirl of red Royal Stuart tartan. Victoria, with her love of all things Scottish, acquired an apartment in the palace and Albert,

HOLYROOD PALACE

with his indefatigable industry, laid out the gardens much as we see them today.

During the reign of George V modern conveniences, electric lighting and central heating were installed and by the 1920s Holyroodhouse was comfortable enough to be designated the official residence of the monarch in Scotland and the focus for regular royal ceremonies.

Today The Queen spends one week a year at the Palace of Holyroodhouse where she holds investitures, audiences and garden parties. Prince Charles also spends a week there and performs duties under his title as Duke of Rothesay. At other times parts of the palace, managed by the Royal Collection Trust, are open to the public.

HOLYROOD PALACE: ARTHUR'S SEAT IN THE BACKGROUND

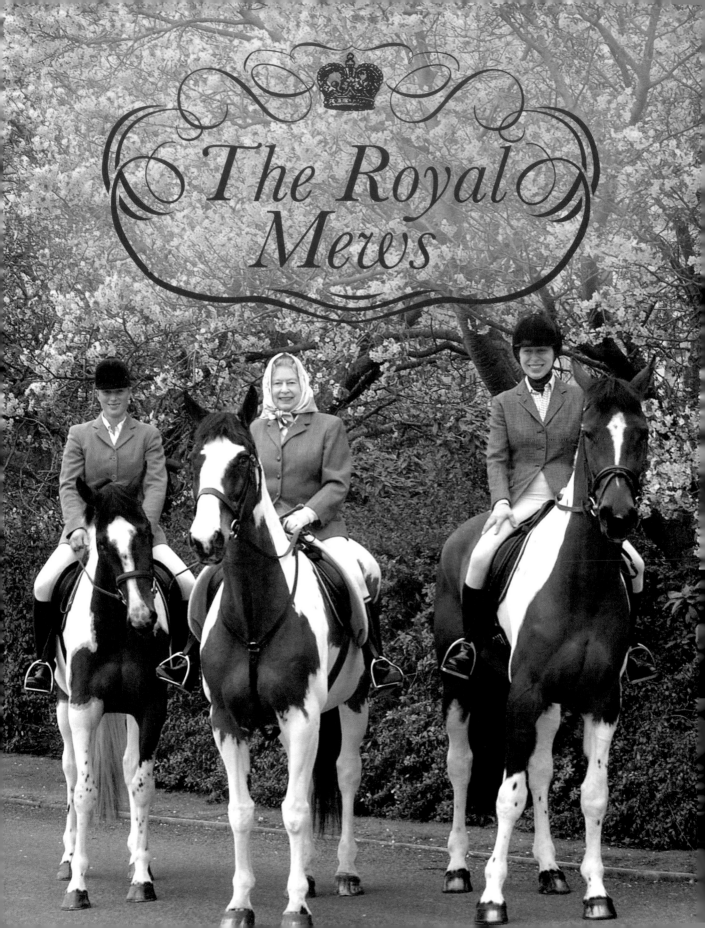

'Few more brilliant or more beautiful sights are to be seen
than the royal cortege as it wheels into line. With all the
trappings and circumstance of State, the glitter and pomp of
uniforms and action, it recalls in some measure the brilliant
pageants that were the pride and glory of our forefathers.'

Royal Ascot: Its History & Its Associations, Cawthorne & Herod, 1901

Grand houses can usually boast a handsome garage block; a few can
even offer accommodation for horses and carriages as well as limousines,
though none of them is as regularly used – or in such fine working order
– as that at Buckingham Palace.

The Royal Mews, its entrance facing onto Buckingham Palace Road,
was first built in the garden of the old Buckingham House by the
architect John Nash in the 1820s as part of George IV's great scheme to
transform Buckingham House, his parents' country house in London, into
a metropolitan palace. It was built next to the Riding School designed by
Sir William Chambers for George III 60 years earlier and sited over the
old kitchen garden. Generations of royal children have been schooled in
this sandy-floored enclosure, including the present generation of royals.

The great Nash quadrangle at Buckingham Palace Mews, its entrance

Above: The Royal Mews in 1888

Below: A postcard showing the ceremonial hats of The Queen's coachmen

gates flanked by the grand house for the Crown Equerry and the matching office and superintendent's residence facing it, replaced the former Royal Mews in the area now occupied by Trafalgar Square. This was a rambling complex of buildings comprising the Great Mews and the smaller Green Mews divided by the Crown Stables, a long building designed by the celebrated architect William Kent in the early 1730s during the reign of George II. Old engravings from the 1790s show the Crown Stables had a handsome arcaded facade in the balanced, symmetrical, Palladian manner sporting a central pedimented carriage entrance and twin cupolas sprouting from the roofs to either side. It faced an exercise yard – an open area rare in the crowded, narrow streets of the city in those days. In 1826 John Nash was asked to draw up plans for a large public space, clearing the area south of the Crown Stables, which was subsequently laid out as Trafalgar Square. The Crown Stables themselves remained as a menagerie, an exhibition space and a storage depository for public records until they too were demolished in 1835.

The earliest records of the Charing Cross Mews, at the western end of the modern Strand, date to 1377 as a building where the royal hawks, usually falcons, were kept during their annual moulting or 'mewing' time

between late April and October, when they were removed from court (Mews comes from the French *muer* meaning 'to change'). These building were destroyed by fire in 1534 and rebuilt as stables in 1537, keeping the name 'Mews', which is now synonymous with a building used for stabling horses, during the reign of Henry VIII.

There were also other mews serving the

The Royal Mews, 1750

Crown attached to different palaces at different times. St James's Palace, built in the 1530s by Henry VIII, had extensive stables that stood on the site of Lancaster House, designed in the 1820s. A ground plan of the palace drawn up in 1792 (before the great fire of 1809 destroyed much of the Tudor palace) shows a Stable Yard and 'a way to sundry stables'. The postal address for Lancaster House today is still 'Stable Yard'.

When St James's Palace was granted by James I to his eldest son Prince Henry (who died of typhoid aged 18 in 1612), the first documented purpose-built riding house was added in 1607–9 for his education – a Renaissance Prince was required to be an expert and elegant rider – and for his amusement. The riding house, some 39 metres (128 feet) long, was reputed to have been the biggest in the country. The Royal Stables, meanwhile, were at Hampton Court Palace, having been built in 1536 by Henry VIII soon after he took over the palace from Cardinal Wolsey. George II was the last monarch to reside at Hampton Court and when he moved out the stables were much depleted and the east side converted to become the Chequers Inn. In 2009 it was mooted that the stables should be sold to help pay for repairs to other royal palaces. Located on Hampton Court Road they are still used as accommodation for staff and as the headquarters of the Horse Rangers Association. The new stables at Windsor Castle were built in 1839, where previously houses of 'ill repute' had stood. The carriages used for the procession at the royal meeting at Ascot are housed there, as are horses for the use of the royal family riding in Windsor Great Park. The carriage horses are also trained there.

The liveries of the staff of the Royal Mews

George III acquired Buckingham House in 1761. Moving out of St James's Palace, he transferred almost immediately those horses and carriages required for his day-to-day needs from the Royal Mews at Charing Cross, leaving behind those required for state occasions. His son George IV died before the conversion of Buckingham House into his new palace was complete and his brother William IV chose not to live there. It was only when the young Queen Victoria in 1837 made Buckingham Palace her home, as well as the centre of state affairs, that the Royal Mews at Buckingham Palace really came into its own, a busting village full of activity from morning to dusk.

The functions required of the Royal Mews have evolved over the centuries. Initially all matters to do with the sovereign and transport were under the control of the Master of the Horse, an important office in the household, third in seniority behind the Lord Steward and the Lord Chamberlain. These titles and the organization of the Royal Household and functions of the office holders originally came to England with the Norman invasion of 1066. For centuries the Master of the Horse provided the sovereign with horses in times of war, for travel and for sport, at first for hunting and later for horse racing. The post continues to this day, though its duties are now a little less onerous.

Constant travel was a feature of court life in the summer months, particularly in the Tudor period. The sovereign travelled around the country during 'progresses', literally taking the throne to the people in an age when most lived out their lives without a glimpse of their ruler. The progress demonstrated the power and magnificence of the sovereign, a necessary activity in an era devoid of any media to spread the message, and was an enormous undertaking, particularly in the reign of Elizabeth I.

Elizabeth I insisted that her household serve her on the road as if she was in one of her palaces, so each department was required to pack up and transport all the necessary equipment. Each

PROCESSION OF QUEEN ELIZABETH TO HUNSDON HOUSE

Elizabeth I on royal progress, 1603

department was assigned carts by the Lord Steward according to function, status and position at court: 13 for the jewel coffers, 10 for the wardrobe of the bedchamber, 10 for the kitchen, 8 for the robes and so on down a very long line. The resulting baggage for the court, retainers and household might require 300 or more carts – and more than a thousand horses to pull them. Elizabeth I went on 23 progresses in her reign, during which she and her nobility travelled in carriages pulled by teams of six horses.

Elizabeth I had a stable of between 100 and 150 horses for her own use and double that for pulling carts and carriages, which swelled dramatically at times of progress. It was the job of the Master of the Horse, to feed, water, house, saddle, shoe and stable them all (he would be today described as in charge of 'transportation and logistics'). As one writer put it, 'the sight of hundreds of carts, horses, and bedecked nobility stretched along dusty English roads offered no small dose of pageantry and spectacle'. On the other hand, Thomas Smith, Elizabeth's Secretary of State, writing while on the progress of 1575, wrote, 'men are weary, the way and the wether fowl, the countery sore vexed with carriage'. The total number of personnel on such journeys amounted to around 2000 souls, all of whom had to be accommodated by her hosts. No wonder a visit bankrupted more than a handful of them.

The old offices of state have in many instances become hereditary and ceremonial. Today, the Master of the Horse – Lord Vestey since 1999 – is still the senior officer responsible for the Royal Mews, and the carriages and horses (and formerly the hounds) of the sovereign, together with the royal studs. However, in practice the day-to-day management of the Royal Mews and any travel by horse, carriage or car has devolved to the Crown Equerry, first appointed in 1854. Since 2011 the Crown Equerry has been Colonel Toby Browne, who retired as Commander of the Household Cavalry the previous year.

When the sovereign rides on horseback or travels by horse-drawn carriage on state occasions – the sovereign's Birthday Parade and the State Opening of the Houses of Parliament – then the Master of the Horse is in attendance. A nineteenth-century description puts it nicely: 'at any solemn cavalcade he has the honour to ride next behind the King, and leads the Horse of State'.

Today the activities of the Royal Mews are consolidated at Buckingham Palace. The carriages and coaches used on state occasions and for schooling the carriage horses are housed there together with their horses, as well as cars used by the royal family for state business. John Nash's stables, completed in 1825, were built to accommodate 100 horses. More recently some stables have been converted to garages and others into exhibition spaces but there is still plenty of stabling and, today, there are roughly 30 horses in residence at any one time. There are usually around ten Windsor Greys, renowned for their steady temperament (named after Windsor Castle where the breed was kept in Victorian times), which pull the state carriages. Eight of them are required to pull the hugely heavy Gold State Coach. There are usually some 20 other bay horses, mostly Cleveland Bays,

A silk Hermes scarf depicts the various coaches of the Royal Mews

the others cross-bred. The Cleveland Bays originated in the north-east of England and are one of the oldest breeds in Britain. Today they are bred at Hampton Court Royal Paddocks, a Royal Stud founded in the sixteenth century.

The horses are largely used to pull, roughly 50 times a year, the carriages that take newly appointed high commissioners and ambassadors from one of the 172 foreign missions based in London to Buckingham Palace to present their credentials to The Queen. The Marshal of the Diplomatic Corps leads in a state landau whilst the ambassador's suite follows in another. There is also a daily messenger service by brougham (a four-wheeled carriage with an open driver's seat) delivering post between

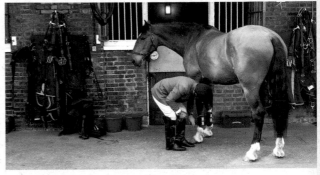

Above left and right: Coachmen prepare the horses for the Diamond Jubilee procession, 2012

Below: The Gold State Coach, built in 1762 for George III

Buckingham Palace and St James's Palace. The working life of a horse in the Royal Mews lasts around 15 years, from the age of 4 when they are broken in to saddle and then to the harness, to retirement around 19 or 20.

And what of the manure? For a start, it is not called 'manure'. The waste products from the horses are known as 'arisings' and they are composted at Buckingham Palace and used there and at other royal sites as soil enrichment – just a part of the self-sufficient approach to household management.

The jewel in the crown of the carriage collection at the Royal Mews is the enormous gilded Gold State Coach designed by Sir William Chambers for George III in 1762 and used at every coronation since that of George IV in 1821. Until 1946 it was used also for the State Opening of Parliament.

The carriages are an important part of royal ceremony – allowing the monarch and the royal family to be seen by their subjects. Colonel Toby Browne, who organized The Queen's Diamond Jubilee carriage procession in 2012, stresses the importance of this: 'For The Queen ... to be seen by the people in a procession like this is incredibly important and is the crowning moment of the Jubilee celebration weekend ... we have this great panoply of state on show: troops, carriages, horses, military bands. To see the whole thing come through in one moment is spectacular.' The Queen, The Prince of Wales and The Duchess of Cornwall rode in the 1902 State Landau (built for Edward VII by Hooper & Co.), most recently used by The Duke and Duchess of

Edward VII prepares for a drive in his Daimler, 1905

Cambridge on their wedding day in April 2011. Other members of the royal family rode in a Semi-State Landau.

Of the closed coaches, the Irish State Coach, originally built for the Lord Mayor of Dublin in 1851, has been used since 1946 to take the monarch to the State Opening of Parliament. The Glass Coach was built in 1881 as a sheriff's coach but purchased for the coronation in 1911. It is most often associated with royal weddings – it took the newly married Princess Elizabeth and The Duke of Edinburgh from Westminster Abbey to Buckingham Palace in 1947 and Lady Diana Spencer to St Paul's for her wedding to Prince Charles in 1981. Other coaches on display at the Royal Mews, and also regularly used, include the Australian State Coach given in 1988 by the People of Australia to mark the Australian Bicentenary, and Queen Alexandra's State Coach of 1865, converted in 1893 into a 'glass state coach'.

When a carriage and horses are needed on any of The Queen's estates – for the opening of the Sandringham Flower Show, for instance – they will travel in a specially equipped horse box and arrive at the function shining and immaculately turned out, with groom and postilion in fine livery.

It was Edward VII who introduced the motor car to the Mews at the turn of the twentieth century. He was given a demonstration in a Daimler by John Douglas-Scott-Montagu, later Lord Montagu of Beaulieu, in 1898 and was so impressed he bought a mail phaeton (a light car without weather protection now on display at Sandringham Museum) in 1900. Two years later he bought a second Daimler, at the same time giving Daimler cars a

A poster from 1910 illustrates The Petrol Era, which powered the reign of George V. The images include a farm wagon, aeroplane, dirigible balloon, motorboat and George V about to enter his Daimler car.

Royal Warrant. Edward VII was photographed leaving Windsor Castle in his new car in July 1902 and this was reproduced on the front cover of the *Car Illustrated*. Queen Alexandra wrote to her children that she was confident in their father as a driver. She would sit in the back seat, with The King in the chauffeur's seat: 'I poke him violently in the back at every corner to go gently and whenever a dog, child or anything else comes in our way!' Edward was so addicted to cars he was dubbed the 'motoring monarch' and became the first patron of the Royal Automobile Club in 1907.

His son George V continued to support Daimlers, then built under licence in Coventry, and purchased two 1910 Daimlers with Landaulette bodies. Later purchases included a 1924 Daimler shooting brake (The King was a crack shot) and a 1935 Daimler limousine for Queen Mary. In 1934 the then Crown Equerry wrote to the chauffeur-mechanic Ernest Capel, who had been with the Royal Household Motor Staff since 1906, informing him that The King 'wants to be driven slowly in his car, as HMs nerves are not what they were'.

Daimlers continued to be the car of choice for many years until a persistent problem in 1950 with the transmission of a royal Daimler led to Rolls-Royce being given the contract to supply state cars. The car pool at the Royal Mews today consists of, for official duties, five State Limousines (three Rolls-Royces and two Bentleys, now the most-often used); there are

also two Semi-State stretched XJ Jaguars and three Daimler limousines, all painted in royal claret livery. The private cars are painted in 'Edinburgh Green', a colour adopted in 1948 for The Duke of Edinburgh's livery.

The Duke has owned a black cab – a Metrocab converted to run on liquefied petroleum gas – for many years and uses it for incognito trips around London. The latest car, a 2002 Bentley, was presented to The Queen to mark her Golden Jubilee. It was specially made a metre longer than normal and with a clear Perspex roof that gives an uninterrupted view of royal passengers. The oldest car is a 1950 Rolls-Royce Phantom IV originally purchased by Princess Elizabeth but still in use today. It is particularly favoured by The Prince of Wales. There are several other features unique to The Queen's state cars: a solid silver radiator mascot depicting St George slaying the dragon can be swapped between cars; they fly a small Royal Standard and display a shield bearing the royal coat of arms; and they carry no number plates. For her personal use The Queen uses a dark green Bentley Mulsanne, an armoured Jaguar XJ and a number of other cars. There are eight chauffeurs in attendance, all part of the Crown Equerry's staff.

Over 40 members of staff are employed at the Royal Mews. Not only is it a working mews, with horses being groomed, fed, schooled and exercised daily, carriages and harnesses being cleaned and repaired, and cars being

Above: One of the Phantom V Rolls Royce state cars, c.late 1950s

Below: The Queen drives a Daimler with Prince Charles and Princess Anne as passengers, 1957

Opposite page: Three of the Rolls-Royce state cars, c1960

kept in immaculate condition, it is also an enormously popular visitor attraction open on most days throughout the year. Few come away unimpressed by the high standard of workmanship and maintenance of the finest collection of carriages in the world. The horses, the limousines and the immaculate turnout of the staff all contribute to the impressive style that is so much a part of monarchy. The length of service of many of the employees in the Mews demonstrates a great pride in their work and a degree of job satisfaction hard to find elsewhere.

Visiting the Queen's Houses

Sandringham

The Sandringham Estate
Estate Office
Sandringham
Norfolk
PE35 6EN

Tel: 01485 545400

www.sandringhamestate.co.uk

House: open daily until early November

Gardens and museum: open daily until early November

Balmoral

The Estates Office
Balmoral Estates
BALLATER
Aberdeenshire, AB35 5TB

013397 42534

www.balmoralcastle.com

Grounds, gardens and exhibitions: open daily between 1st April and 31st July between 10am and 5pm.

Buckingham Palace

Ticket Sales and Information Office
The Official Residences of The Queen
London SW1A 1AA
Buckingham Palace

020 7766 7300

www.royalcollection.org.uk/visit/
the-queens-gallery-buckingham-palace

www.royalcollection.org.uk/visit/royalmews

The Queen's Gallery: Open daily between 10:00-17.30

The Royal Mews

3 February - 31 March
Monday to Saturday 10:00-16:00

1 April – 31 October
Open daily 10:00-17:00

1-30 November
Monday to Saturday 10:00-16:00

Windsor Castle

Windsor Castle,
Windsor,
Berkshire
SL4 1NJ

020 7766 7304

www.royalcollection.org.uk/visit/windsorcastle

Opening times: open daily March to October, 09:45-17:15

November to February, 09:45-16:15

Palace of Holyroodhouse

Palace of Holyroodhouse,
Canongate,
The Royal Mile,
EH8 8DX

0131 556 5100

www.royalcollection.org.uk/visit/
palaceofholyroodhouse

Opening times: open daily

November – March, 09:30-16:30

April – October, 09:30-18:00

Bibliography

Bellamy, David, *The Queen's Hidden Garden: Buckingham Palace's Treasury of Wild Plants*, David & Charles, 1984

Benson, A C and, Viscount Esher (eds)., The Letters of Queen Victoria (in three volumes) John Murray, 1908

Bickersteth, John and Dunning, Robert W, *Clerks of the Closet in the Royal Household: Five Hundred Years of Service to the Crown*, Alan Sutton, 1991

Bradford, Sarah, *Elizabeth: A Biography of Her Majesty the Queen*, Heinemann, 1996

Bradford, Sarah, *The Reluctant King: The Life and Reign of George VI, 1895-1952*, Penguin, 2011

Brandreth, Gyles, *Philip and Elizabeth: Portrait of a Marriage*, Century, 2004

Brewer, John, *The Pleasures of the Imagination: English Culture in the Eighteenth Century*, Harper Collins, 1997

Brown, Ivor, *Balmoral: the History of a Home*, Collins, 1966

Brown, Jane, *The Garden at Buckingham Palace: an Illustrated History*, Royal Collection, 2004

Brown, Raymond, *John Brown: Queen Victoria's Highland Servant*, The History Press, 2011

Bruce, Graeme, *The Story of Buckingham Palace*, Hutchinson, 1928

Camp, Anthony J, *Royal Mistresses and Bastards: Fact and Fiction 1714-1936*, privately printed, 2007

Cheape, Hugh, *Tartan: the Highland Habit*, National Museums of Scotland, 1995

Clark, Ronald, *Queen Victoria's Highland Home*, Thames & Hudson, 1981

Coats, Peter, *The Gardens of Buckingham Palace*, Michael Joseph, 1978

Churchill, Randolph S, *They Serve the Queen: a New and Authoritative Account of the Royal Household Prepared for Coronation Year*, Hutchinson, 1953

Cornforth, John, *Pyne's Royal Residences*, Michael Joseph, 1976

Coutts, James, *Dictionary of Deeside*, Aberdeen University Press, 1899

Cox, Montagu and, Norman, Philip (eds)., *Survey of London: Volume 13, part II: Whitehall*, 1930

Crawford, Marion and, Bond, Jennie (Intro)., *The Little Princesses: The Story of The Queen's Childhood By Her Nanny, Marion Crawford*, Orion, 2003

Ditchfield, P H and, Page, William (eds)., *A History of the County of Berkshire: Volume 3*, 1923

Duff, David (ed)., *Victoria in the Highlands*, Muller, 1968

Franklin, Jill, *The Gentleman's Country House and its Plan 1835-1914*, Routledge, 1981

Glasheen, Joan, *The Secret People of the Palaces: the Royal Household from the Plantagenets to Queen Victoria*,

Batsford, 1998

Girouard, Mark, *Windsor: the most Romantic Castle*, Hodder & Stoughton, 1993

Groom, Susanne and, Prosser, Lee, *Kew Palace: the Official Illustrated History*, Historic Royal Palaces in association with Merrell Publishers, 2006

Hardman, Robert, *Monarchy: the Royal Family at Work*, Ebury Press, 2007

Hardman, Robert, *Our Queen*, Hutchinson, 2011

Harris, John, de Bellaigue, Geoffrey and, Millar, Oliver, *Buckingham Palace*, Nelson, 1968

Harris, John, *Sir William Chambers*, Zwemmer, 1970

Harris, John and, Snodin, Michael, *Sir William Chambers, Architect to George III*, Yale University Press in association with the Courtauld Institute of Art, 1997

Harris, John, *William Talman, Maverick Architect*, Allen & Unwin, 1982

Healey, Edna, *The Queen's House: a Social History of Buckingham Palace*, Michael Joseph in association with the Royal Collection, 1997

Hibbert, Christopher, *Edward VII*, Allen Lane, 1976

Hibbert, Christopher, *Queen Victoria: A Personal History*

Hope, W H St John, *Windsor Castle: An Architectural History*, Country Life, 1913

Hubbard, Kate, *Serving Victoria: Life in the Royal Household*, Vintage, 2013

Innes-Smith, Robert, *Windsor Castle*, English Life Publications, 1981

James, Paul, *At Her Majesty's Service*, Collins, 1986

Knight, Charles, *The Journey-Book of England: Berkshire: Including a Full Description of Windsor Castle*, Charles Knight, 1840

Johnson, Paul, *Castles of England, Scotland and Wales*, Weidenfeld & Nicolson, 2000

Lindsay, William A, *The Royal Household*, Paul, Trench, Trubner, 1898

Longford, Elizabeth, *Victoria R I*, Weidenfeld & Nicolson, 1964

Mackenzie, Compton, *The Queen's House: a History of Buckingham Palace*, Hutchinson, 1953

Nash, Roy, *Buckingham Palace, the Place and the People*, Macdonald, 1980

Mansbridge, Michael, *John Nash: a Complete Catalogue*, Phaidon, 1991

Matson, John, *Sandringham Days: the Domestic Life of the Royal Family in Norfolk 1862-1952*, The History Press, 2012

Morshead, O F, *Windsor Castle*, Phaidon, 1951

Munby, Julian, Barber, Richard and, Brown, Richard, *Edward III's Round Table at Windsor*, Boydell Press, 2007

Murphy, Paul Thomas, *Shooting Victoria: Madness, Mayhem and the Modernisation of the Monarchy*,

Pegasus Books, 2012

Nares, Gordon, *Royal Homes*, Country Life, 1953

Nicolson, Adam, *Restoration: the Rebuilding of Windsor Castle*, Michael Joseph in association with the Royal Collection, 1997

Olwen, Headley, *Windsor Castle*, Hale, 1967

Pope-Hennessy, James (ed), *Queen Victoria at Windsor and Balmoral*, Allen and Unwin, 1959

Pote, Joseph and, Leake, S. Martin, *The History and Antiquities of Windsor Castle, the Royal College, and Chapel of St George*. Joseph Pote, 1749

Powe, Joan, Royal Chef: Recollections of Life in Royal Households from Queen Victoria to Queen Mary, William Kimber, 1954.

Raite, Robert S and, Hollings, Marjory (ed)., *Royal Palaces of England*, J Pott, 1911

Rhodes, Margaret, *The Final Curtsey: a Royal Memoir by the Queen's Cousin*, Birlinn Ltd and Umbria Press (jointly), 2012

Roberts, Jane (ed)., *Royal Treasures: a Golden Jubilee Celebration*, Royal Collection, 2002

Robinson, John Martin, *Buckingham Palace: the Official Illustrated History*, Royal Collection Trust, 2013

Robinson, John Martin, *Royal Palaces: Windsor Castle: A Short History*, Michael Joseph in association with Royal Collection Enterprises, 1996

Rose, Kenneth, *King George V*, Macmillan, 1984

Rose, Kenneth, *Kings, Queens and Courtiers*, Weidenfeld & Nicolson, 1985

Rowse, A L, *Windsor Castle in the History of the Nation*, Weidenfeld & Nicolson, 1974

Ridley, Jane, *Bertie: A Life of Edward VII*, Chatto & Windus, 2012

Sainty, J C and, Bucholz, R O, *Office-Holders in Modern Britain: Volume 11 (revised): Officials of the Royal Household 1660-1837, part 1; The Lord Chamberlain and Associated Offices*, Institute of Historical Research, 1997

Sainty, J C and, Bucholz, R O, *Office-Holders in Modern Britain: Volume 12 (revised): Officials of the Royal Household 1660-1837, Part 2: Departments of the Lord Steward and the Master of the Horse*, Institute of Historical Research, 1998

Shawcross, William, *Counting One's Blessings: The Selected Letters of Queen Elizabeth the Queen Mother*, Pan Macmillan, 2012

Shawcross, William, *Queen Elizabeth, The Queen Mother*, Macmillan, 2009

Simon, Robin, *Buckingham Palace: a Complete Guide*, Apollo Magazine in association with the Royal Collection Trust, 1993

Sloane, Barney, *The Black Death in London*, The History Press, 2011

Souden, David with, Worsley, Lucy and, Dolman, Brett, *The Royal Palaces of London*, Merrell in association with Historic Royal Palaces, 2008

Smith, Clifford, *Buckingham Palace: its Furniture, Decoration and History*, Country Life, 1931

Stoughton, John, *Windsor: A History and Description of the Castle and the Town*, Ward, 1862

Strachey, Lytton, *Queen Victoria*, Harcourt, Brace, 1921

Summerson, John, *The Life and Work of John Nash, Architect*, MIT Press, 1980

Thomas, Edward, *Windsor Castle*: Blackie, 1946

Titchmarsh, Alan, *Elizabeth: Her Life, Our Times*, BBC Books, 2012

Tooley, Sarah A, *Royal Palaces and Their Memories*, Hutchinson, 1902

Various, *Holbein and the Court of Henry VIII*, The Queen's Gallery, 1978

Various, *The Queen: a Penguin Special*, Penguin Books, 1977

Vickers, Hugo, *The Royal Mews at Buckingham Palace: Official Souvenir Guide*, Royal Collection Trust, 2013

Walch, Helen, *Sandringham: an Estate for 150 Years*, Sandringham Estate, 2012

Weintraub, Stanley, *Albert: Uncrowned King*, John Murray, 1997

Williams, Robert Folkestone, *Domestic Memoirs of the Royal Family and the Court of England*, Hurst and Blackett, 1860

Wright, Patricia, *The Strange History of Buckingham Palace*, The History Press, 2012

Worsley, Lucy, *Courtiers: The Secret History of the Georgian Court*, Faber & Faber, 2010

Zeigler, Philip, *King Edward VIII*, Harper Press, 2011

Websites

archive.spectator.co.uk

http://darkestlondon.com/2011/11/10/giro-londons-favourite-dead-nazi-dog/

www.gatehouse-gazetteer.info

www.parliament.uk

Calendar of the Fine Rolls of the Reign of Henry III [henceforth *CFR*] 1223–24 (available both on the Henry III Fine Rolls Project's website (http://www.finerollshenry3.org.uk) and within *Calendar of the Fine Rolls of the Reign of Henry III 1216–1234*, ed. P. Dryburgh and B. Hartland, technical ed. A. Ciula and J.M. Vieira, 2 vols. (Woodbridge, 2007), no. 1) Accessed 2013.

www.queen-victorias-scrapbook.org

www.royal.gov.uk

www.thetimes.co.uk

www.unofficialroyalty.com/

www.wallingwonderland.info/Pages/Balmoral_Cairns.html

www.westendatwar.org.uk

http://en.wikipedia.org/wiki/Burial_places_of_British_royalty

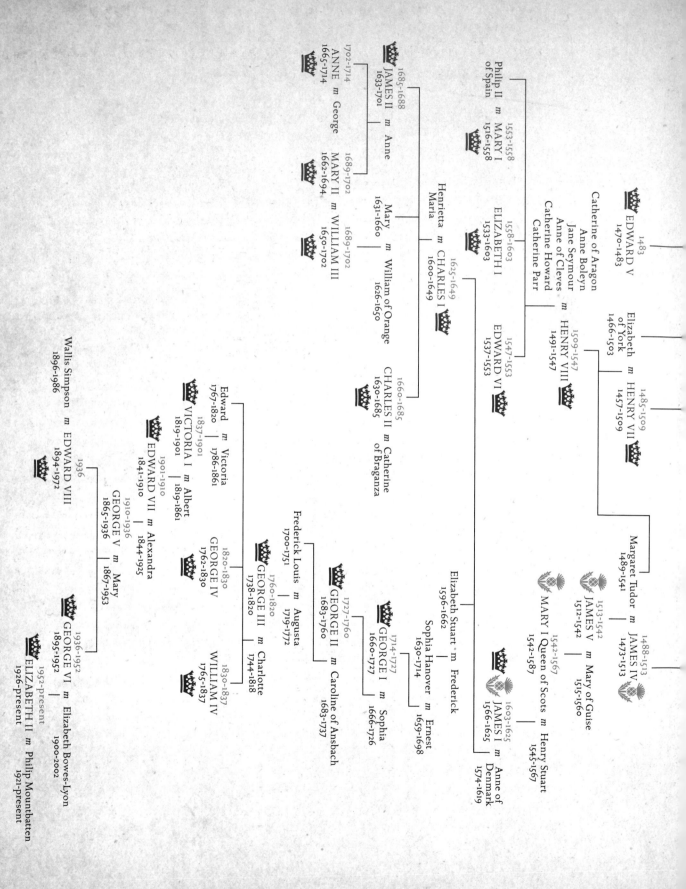

THE BRITISH ROYAL FAMILY FROM THE TIME OF WILLIAM THE CONQUEROR

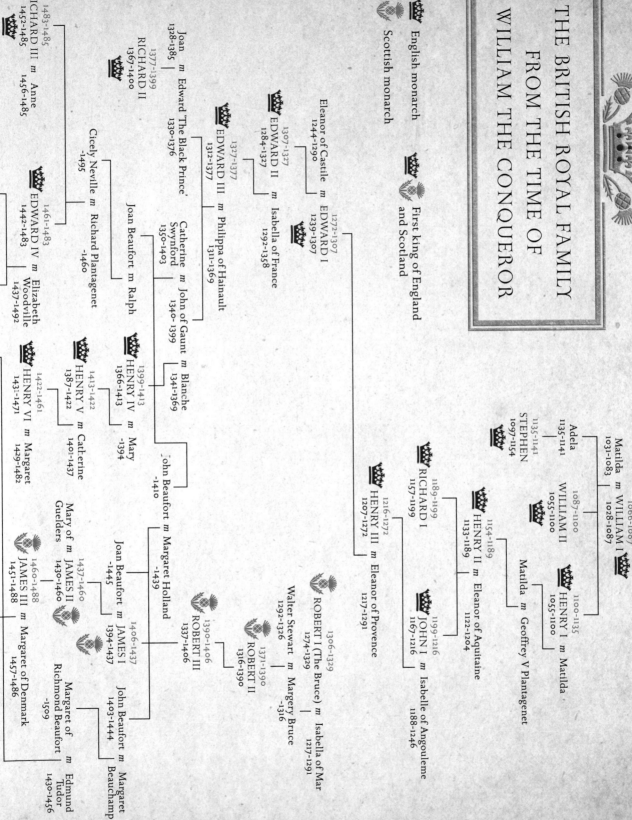

Index

Index

ACKNOWLEDGEMENTS

This is not an official history of The Queen's Houses, rather a personal delving into the stories behind The Queen's residences, both official and private, but I am grateful to many people associated with them who have helped me in the production of this book. My especial thanks go to Michael Dover for his extensive research, to Lorna Russell and Charlotte Macdonald for editorial input, to Toby Browne, The Crown Equerry, for advice on the chapter about The Royal Mews and to other members of The Royal Household who have, from time to time, furnished me with answers to my assorted questions. Any errors or mistakes that have slipped through the net are my own.

Alan Titchmarsh, Hampshire, 2014

IMAGE CREDITS

The author and publisher gratefully acknowledge the permission granted to reproduce the copyright material in this book. Every effort has been made to trace copyright holders and to obtain permission for the use of copyright material. The publisher apologises for any errors or omissions in the below list and would be grateful if notified of any corrections that should be incorporated in future reprints or editions of this book.

All of the photographs used in this book were provided by Getty Images apart from those listed below:

p.10 Rex Features, p. 14 Alamy, p. 15 Alamy, p. 18 t Corbis, p. 19 Corbis, p. 27 Alamy, 28b Alamy, 30 Topfoto, 31 Corbis, 35 Corbis, p. 37 Alamy, p. 40b Corbis, 41 Alamy, p. 42 Alamy, p. 46t Alamy, p. 50 Corbis, p. 51 Bridgeman Images - Pyne, James Baker (1800-70)/Private Collection/The Stapleton Collection., p. 52 Corbis, p. 55 Corbis, p. 57 Corbis, p. 69t Alamy, p. 70 Corbis, p. 72t Mary Evans Picture Library, p. 72b Topfoto, p. 73 Mary Evans Picture Library, p. 74t Alamy, p. 84b Corbis, p. 85 Press Association Images, p. 88 Mary Evans Picture Library/Illustrated London News Ltd., p. 93 Mary Evans Picture Library, p. 95 Alamy, p. 108 Alamy, p. 110 Alamy, p. 117b Corbis, p. 118 Alamy, p. 119 Alamy, p. 121t Corbis, p. 123t Alamy, p. 125 Press Association Images, p. 141 Press Association Images, p. 142 Alamy, p. 143 Mary Evans Picture Library, p. 148 & 149 Courtesy of Walkhighlands, p. 151 Alamy, p. 153 Alamy, p. 167t Topfoto, p. 169 t l&r Press Association Images, p. 169c Mary Evans Picture Library/Illustrated London News Ltd., p. 169b Corbis, p. 172 Corbis, p. 175 Corbis, p. 177tl Corbis, p. 178 Corbis, p. 179 Mary Evans Picture Library, p. 181 Corbis, p. 182b Corbis, p. 187b Mary Evans Picture Library/Illustrated London News Ltd., p. 189t Corbis, p. 192 ©National Portrait Gallery, London, p. 193 Corbis, p. 195 Akg-images, p. 203 Mary Evan Picture Library, p. 206t Corbis, p. 209t Mary Evan Picture Library/Francis Frith Collection, p. 209b Alamy, p. 210 Alamy, p. 214 Mary Evan Picture Library/Robert Hunt Library, p. 218b Corbis, p. 220b Corbis, p. 222b Alamy, p. 241b Alamy, p. 245 Alamy

Memorabilia photographed by Karl Adamson. Map on page 8 by ML Design.

5 7 9 10 8 6

Published in 2014 by BBC Books, an imprint of Ebury Publishing. A Random House Group Company.

The Random House Group Limited Reg. No. 954009. Addresses for companies within the Random House Group can be found at www.randomhouse.co.uk

A CIP catalogue record for this book is available from the British Library.

ISBN: 9781849902175

The Random House Group Limited supports the Forest Stewardship Council® (FSC®), the leading international forest-certification organisation. Our books carrying the FSC label are printed on FSC®-certified paper. FSC is the only forest-certification scheme supported by the leading environmental organisations, including Greenpeace. Our paper procurement policy can be found at www.randomhouse.co.uk/environment

Commissioning editor: Lorna Russell / Project editor: Charlotte Macdonald / Copy-editor: Howard Watson
Designer: Lucy Stephens / Picture researcher: Claire Gouldstone

Colour origination by Altaimage Printed and bound in China by Toppan Leefung

To buy books by your favourite authors and register for offers visit www.randomhouse.co.uk